WHERE MADNESS LIES

WHERE MADNESS LIES

The Double Life of
VIVIEN LEIGH

LYNDSY SPENCE

PEGASUS BOOKS

NEW YORK LONDON

WHERE MADNESS LIES

Pegasus Books, Ltd.
148 West 37th Street, 13th Floor
New York, NY 10018

Copyright © 2025 by Lyndsy Spence

First Pegasus Books cloth edition January 2025

ISBN: 978-1-63936-805-1

10 9 8 7 6 5 4 3 2 1

Printed in the United States of America
Distributed by Simon & Schuster
www.pegasusbooks.com

For Louis, with love

'Yes, there is something uncanny, demonic and fascinating in her'

– *Anna Karenina*, Leo Tolstoy

Contents

Author's Note

Ever since I was a young girl, I have been fascinated by Vivien Leigh (born Vivian Mary Hartley) and was delighted to discover her on the Irish side of my family tree, albeit a very distant connection through an Irish great-grandfather whose family, the Robinsons, came from western Ireland. I am positive the fascination sprang from something familiar, or perhaps I was like every other mortal and spellbound from that first glimpse of her as Scarlett O'Hara in *Gone with the Wind*.

Given the themes in *Where Madness Lies* and the sensitive subject matter of mental illness, it would be easy to cast Vivien as a tragedienne. I do not see her as a victim; however, I think it is important to look at her life within the period she lived, particularly when it came to women's health and understanding the complexities of the female mind. Attitudes to mental health were draconian, to say the least, and the medical treatment she received left a lasting impact on her. From my own perspective, I see Vivien as a complex woman and the ongoing narrative surrounding her is filled with grey areas, which, to me, makes her all the more interesting. She was a headstrong woman who trusted her instincts, for better or worse, and stood by her convictions. I find that admirable: where there is truth, there is integrity, even if her behaviour was far from noble.

As with all my subjects, I am always intrigued by the woman behind the myth, as opposed to the mythical image which has been cultivated, thanks, mostly, to her film legacy. Everyone knows Vivien as Scarlett O'Hara and Blanche DuBois, and numerous books and articles have been written about her famous stage and screen personas. With that being said, Vivien only made a handful of feature films and managed to win two Academy Awards: the first for *Gone with the Wind* (1939) and the second for *A Streetcar Named Desire* (1951) – an astonishing achievement, even by today's standards. In terms of her career, her first love was the theatre but, to a larger extent, she was celebrated for her marriage to Sir Laurence Olivier, known as 'Larry' to Vivien and those close to him. Again, her singular identity was split in half but she was proud to be his wife and then, later, to use the courtesy title of Lady Olivier, even after their divorce in 1960.

Vivien Leigh's professional life changed in 1939, after she played Scarlett O'Hara, but her private life (and her latter career) was completely altered after her nervous breakdown and the diagnosis of 'manic depression' (now known as bipolar disorder). Therefore, I open my book in Ceylon (now Sri Lanka) in 1953, the scene of Vivien's affair with Peter Finch during the filming of *Elephant Walk* and her mental breakdown, which has allowed me to manipulate the time frame of this book while adhering to facts. It moves forward from 1953 until her untimely death in 1967 more or less in chrono-logical order with triggers to her past. In scenes where Vivien is losing her grip on herself, I took inspiration from photographs and details from her letters to convey those times when her reality was skewed and she felt genuinely afraid of being suspended in a dream world.

The aforementioned has also been done to emphasise Vivien's strug-gles after her first course of electroconvulsive therapy (ECT), which Larry felt had erased the best parts of her. The contemporary scenes, which go back in time, allow Vivien, our protagonist, to discover her-self and what led her to mental collapse and the subsequent breakdown of her celebrated marriage to Larry. Also, in Chapter 12, the penulti-mate chapter, there is a sense of displacement after she suffers another breakdown and attempts to, once more, rebuild her life. I wanted the narrative to reflect her ongoing strength in the face of adversity.

The Afterword, 'A Reimagining', was inspired by real sessions with a psychic medium. I was surprised to learn of Vivien's friendship with Sybil Leek, a famous trance medium and a self-confessed witch whose occupations consisted of an antique dealer, astrologer, herbalist, author, and, of course, communicating with the dead. Sybil is an intriguing subject and someone whose life I am interested in exploring further. For the time being, in the Afterword, Sybil's channelled messages from Vivien's spirit allowed me to also write of Vivien's unrealised dream of buying the abandoned villa of St John of the Pigeons, south of Benitses in Corfu, and retiring there to paint when she was 60. It was an ambition cut short by her untimely death in 1967.

I have purposely avoided writing about Vivien's and Larry's respective descendants who are still alive and living as private people. I have, where possible, avoided speculating about Larry's private life with Dame Joan Plowright, who has remained incredibly sympathetic towards Vivien even when she did not necessarily warrant such kindness.

Likewise, in the past, many disparaging things have been written about Vivien's mental illness and the effects it had on her personality and judgement. I have not censored the uglier side of her illness and how it altered her personality and destroyed most of the things she held dear. But, at the same time, I wanted to give Vivien her power back. The common theme throughout the book is Vivien's quest to find her way back home, even if 'home' is a place of peace and acceptance within herself.

It has been a great privilege to write about Vivien Leigh, who is one of my heroines, and I hope my admiration for her talent and courage is conveyed in this book. As a nod to Vivien herself, her life is told in thirteen (large) chapters, as thirteen is a powerful symbol of femininity and I felt the mysticism fitted her perfectly. As she was a woman of the theatre, I wanted to give my book a theatrical air with symbolism and subtext.

A note on the title, *Where Madness Lies*: I was drawn to the ambiguity of the title, especially the term 'madness' and its play on 'O, that way madness lies' from William Shakespeare's *King Lear*. It is in no way meant to be a damaging term for Vivien's mental illness. The subtitle, *The Double Life of Vivien Leigh*, referring to her double life, was drawn from a magazine headline, circa 1953, which exposed her breakdown in Hollywood. For me, the 'double life', as such, was a reflection of her two selves: Vivien, whom everyone loved, and the mental illness which warped her perception of herself and how others saw her. It was the fiercest battle she ever fought and for which I have nothing but admiration.

Lyndsy Spence
County Antrim

Acknowledgements

During my research and the writing of this book, I was aware of the biographies of Vivien Leigh which have come before mine, each one a unique telling of her life through different variations. As a biographer, my goal is to offer a new perspective on whomever I write about and with Vivien, I wanted to tell her story in a way that I felt was authentic to her. I hope it adds to the ongoing narrative about her life.

A note on sources: Vivien Leigh's letters have been published in past biographies, most significantly in books by Anne Edwards (1973), Alexander Walker (1987) and Hugo Vickers (1988) – I consider those first biographies as groundbreaking regarding the information they disclosed. Laurence Olivier's personal papers were published in 2005 in an authorised biography by Terry Coleman and in Philip Ziegler's book, published in 2013.

Vivien Leigh's personal papers are held at the Victoria and Albert Museum (V&A Theatre and Performance Collections) and Laurence Olivier's papers are with the British Library Manuscript Collections. Vivien's letters to Olivier are also in his archives at the British Library. There are further substantial archives relating to Vivien Leigh held at the New York Public Library and the Charles E. Young Research Library UCLA. Please see *Notes* for detailed information on sources.

I am eternally grateful to several people: firstly, my family for supporting my work; the Vivien Leigh fanbase who encouraged my work; and the collectors who have kindly shared their collections online. I am thankful to Kendra Bean, author of *Vivien Leigh: An Intimate Portrait* and founder of vivandlarry.com; Andy Batt; the Vivien Leigh

Circle; David Barry, author of *The Final Curtain*; Rachel Nicholson; Michelle Beck; Ana Claudia Paixao; Dean Rhys Jones; Nuri Lidar; Andrew Budgell; Eric Sanniez; the late Julia Lockwood; Molly Haigh at Charles E. Young Research Library UCLA; Alexander Turnbull Library/National Library of New Zealand; the State Library of Queensland; Dale Stinchcomb, Associate Curator of the Harvard Theatre Collection; and Greta Ritchie for her kind permission to use photographs from her collection. Thank you to Mark Beynon for encouraging me to write this book and to everyone at The History Press whose support is incomparable.

Lastly, I wanted to reserve my final token of thanks for Shiroma Perera-Nathan, author of *God and the Angel: Vivien Leigh and Laurence Olivier's Tour de Force of Australia and New Zealand* for our discussions on Vivien Leigh, her permission to use photographs from her collection and believing in my hare-brained ideas before they came to fruition.

Chapter One

'O, that way madness lies'

King Lear, William Shakespeare

1953

'Oh, the bliss of not having to go mad, commit suicide, or contemplate murder,'[1] Vivien Leigh told the waiting reporters as she stepped off the aeroplane and on to the airfield in Colombo, Ceylon. They came to interview her about *Elephant Walk*, her new picture for Paramount, to be shot on location there. She was exhausted after the long flight by way of London, Rome, Beirut, Bahrain and Bombay. Her leading man, Peter Finch, took her by the arm and escorted her through the sea of reporters and curious faces who hoped to catch a glimpse of the star. The humidity was suffocating and the heat swept over her like a furnace. She stopped to catch her breath, before adding, 'My character is … a normal healthy girl.'[2]

On the journey to the bungalows – where the cast and crew were to live for a month – the scenery, familiar from her childhood in the east, filtered through the taxi window. The palm trees, colonial buildings and British cars filled the streets, but an air of unrest stirred beneath the surface during those final days of the empire. Perhaps she thought of her mother, Gertrude Hartley, unhappy in her marriage and heavily pregnant, gazing at the Kanchenjunga – the Five Treasures of the Great Snows – from her window at Shannon Lodge, praying to the saints for her child to be beautiful. Born in Darjeeling on Guy Fawkes Day in 1913, little Vivian – it was spelt with an 'a' and not an 'e' back then – always thought the fireworks were for her. In those days, her mother's lies were harmless: 'Remember, remember, the fifth of November', Gertrude might have said, as a kaleidoscope of colours exploded above her.

In the back of the taxi, Vivien crossed herself and said a prayer to St Thérèse of Lisieux,[3] the patron saint of missions. Although her fellow Catholics considered her a sinner – she left her first husband, Leigh Holman, to run away with Laurence Olivier – she liked the saints and was drawn to mystical things and religious iconography. A trio of crystals – carnelian, citrine and clear quartz – were kept on her dressing table and she carried a carnelian agate in her handbag. The combination of those crystals was, and is, generally believed to attract abundance. But an abundance of what? As for spirituality, she called herself a 'Zen–Buddhist–Catholic'[4] and favoured churches with beautiful architecture and stained-glass windows.[5] Her first real experience of the theatre was attending Mass at the Convent of the Sacred Heart in Roehampton in London, which was later bombed by the Luftwaffe during the Blitz.

'All that Catholic mumbo jumbo,'[6] Peter said of organised religion. His voice sounded exactly like her husband, Sir Laurence Olivier's. Larry was his idol – he had been knighted in 1947 for his contributions to the stage and screen – and for Peter, there was no greater actor.

'No problem, then. Opt out and be a good Protestant,'[7] she said.

The Comet carrying them to Colombo would crash two flights later. So, to her mind, the prayer to St Thérèse had worked.

The seclusion of the set unnerved Vivien and everything felt static as she took in her surroundings: the flower-scented air, the sprawling tea fields and the hills in the distance, and the scrutinising glares from the locals, some of whom did not want the production there.

'The Devil Dancers,' Vivien's stand-in, an Australian woman named Carrol Hayward said, as she crept up behind her. 'The wild folk of Ceylon.'[8]

'Sinhalese rituals,' Peter corrected Hayward. As a boy, he had followed his mother to a theosophical community near Madras. Despite his drinking and womanising in adulthood, and the pain it caused others, he identified as a Buddhist. He detested Christianity and the symbol of the crucifix, saying, 'I think a man dying on a cross is a ghastly symbol for a religion.'[9]

It had taken a mere few days for Vivien to lose interest in the picture and she had trouble memorising her lines. It belonged to the adventure genre but felt like a horror story when she analysed the undertones of the script. Her fictional home, a mansion in the jungle called Elephant Walk, was named after the trek of the elephants who marched past it and was haunted by the Governor, her character's late father-in-law. She was cast as Ruth, the unhappy wife of a tea planter, John Wiley, an unsympathetic character who preferred to drink with his cronies than tend to her. Close-ups were shot of Vivien looming on the staircase, serpent-eyed and commanding him to come to bed. As the plot unfolds, she ends up falling for a fellow planter, Dick Carver – played by Dana Andrews, who was often drunk in real life, but was harmless – and contemplates eloping with him. After typhoid fever breaks out, she remains at the house, which is ransacked by elephants, thus concluding the story.

The truth was, Vivien knew the script was beneath her and not very good, despite being a Hollywood production with a big studio budget. Larry had declined the part of Wiley and dismissed the script as a pale imitation of *Rebecca*. A little dig, for she had wanted to appear with him in the film adaptation of *Rebecca* in 1940 but David O. Selznick, the producer, considered her too beautiful for the mousy Mrs de Winter and the part went to Joan Fontaine. In a way, Larry's rejection of *Elephant Walk* was serendipitous, or so he thought at the time, and it allowed Peter an opportunity to star opposite Vivien. She had planned the entire thing.

Peter was the first to crack and, after a long day of filming, he hated to be alone at night. Vivien, an insomniac all her life, was glad of the company. They spent their nights in her bungalow, sitting at the sugarcane table, playing Canasta, chain-smoking and drinking too much gin. All Peter wanted to do was talk about Larry, and Vivien was tired of him fishing for compliments and looking to be reassured of his talent. At almost 40 and yet to have his big break, he said he was grateful for anything he could get.

'But you don't take what you can get. You let people persuade you as to what they think is best for you and throw dust in your eyes,' she said, exasperated. 'You're a good enough actor to stand alone as someone quite different and still do what you really want as an actor, but you have no follow-through. You play at life, play with women, and you dissipate your God-given talents because you don't believe in your own wonderful star.'[10] There was sincerity in her words: she had believed in Peter's talent from the first moment she saw him in *The Imaginary Invalid* at O'Brien's Glass Factory in Sydney in 1948. Both she and Larry felt he was unstoppable.

As a child, Peter had been sent to Australia to live with his great-uncle, as his mother, Alicia Fisher, known as Betty, was incapable of looking after him. Betty was too busy with her love affairs, which had disastrous consequences for Peter, both in his childhood and adulthood. The man whom he thought was his father, George Finch, was not, and his mother's second husband, Jock Campbell, an Indian Army officer, was, in fact, his biological father.

Vivien did not try to console him, they were both too intoxicated. She had abandoned her only child to run away with Larry, who, in turn, left his child, a boy named Tarquin. Vivien's mother had abandoned her, too – sort of. She had been sent from India to Roehampton at the age of 6 and put into a convent school: she was pupil no. 90, Vivian Mary Hartley.

After Peter returned to his bungalow, Vivien stayed up drinking. She had the odd feeling of being fixated on something. On what? She could not decide; everything inside her brain was that of white noise, desperately searching for a connection and failing.

The following morning, she sent Larry several telegrams, begging him to come to Ceylon for a week. As her mental stability declined, her writing became worse and she dashed off erratic postcards to people.[11] Only later would it become known as a symptom of her condition, manic depression, then undiagnosed. There was no answer and she suspected the crew were intercepting her mail in order to manipulate her into doing their bidding. Larry's picture, *The Beggar's*

Opera, was in post-production and he went to Ischia to stay with friends. Those details escaped Vivien. In her diary, she wrote his name several times, underlining it each time, as though she were performing a ritual to summon him.

Outside in the fields, she imagined Larry was coming towards her, his shirt sleeves rolled up and his body bronzed from the sun. 'Larry,' she called to Peter, who tried to correct her. She ignored Peter as she walked into the water. His instincts told him to follow her. She swam out as far as she could go, weighed down by her flimsy dress, and floated on her back, staring at the blistering sun creating prisms. Or was it a dream? She heard bells, the way Blanche DuBois also heard bells at the end of *A Streetcar Named Desire*. The bells from the temple purified the air, reminiscent of the Sacred Heart's daily toll for Mass: *The precious blood of our Jesus Christ, wash away our sins.*

Later that day, Vivien returned to her bungalow and opened her diary, scribbling, 'Please come!!!' under Larry's name, and then she started to sob. There was a knock on the door and she opened it, without concealing her tears. Her makeup was streaked down her cheeks. It was Peter and Dana Andrews, the latter puzzled by her sadness. They invited her on an excursion into a nearby village and she agreed to go without saying a word. She closed the door and hooked on to Peter's arm.

In the village, the locals gave the trio quizzical looks and Vivien's spirits were lifted by the bazaar and its stalls of colourful saris, sweets, silver and gold paper, and imitation antique knives and swords covered in rust to look more valuable to gullible tourists. The aroma of spices coming from the *dekshis* filled the air, suffocating the senses in the heat and humidity. A snake charmer caught her eye. 'Oh look, isn't he a pet,'[12] she said as a baby cobra slithered out of its basket and swayed to the music of the flute.

The charmer invited her to sit on his stool and he coiled the snake around her neck while she roared with childish laughter and a cigarette burnt between her fingers. She stared into his black eyes, her laughter stopping. The lilting music drew larger cobras from the baskets and they danced in unison. Astrologically speaking – as she did believe – it was the year of the water snake. They, the snakes, were not to be trusted; they only cared about their own agenda.

Once, she had read a book called *The Martyrdom of Man* and under-lined a passage that resonated with her: 'And the artists shall inherit the earth and the world will be as a garden.'[13]

The Garden of Eden.
The Garden of Evil.

～～～

The production moved to Kandy, a city situated at the foot of a circle of mountains, for three days to shoot among the ruins of the old kingdom. Vivien became impossible to work with and made a scene when the dresser tried to put her in shorts. 'My legs are not designed for shorts!'[14] she said and refused to film unless they were discarded. Her hands, legs and feet were her biggest insecurities and she felt they were too large for her petite frame.

As a star, Vivien had autonomy over her body, something that was not the case in 1939 when she filmed *Gone with the Wind*. Its producer, David O. Selznick, was fixated with, what he called, the 'chest exper-iment'[15] and he ordered Walter Plunkett, the costume designer, to use adhesive tape and padding to create the illusion of cleavage from her (Selznick's description) flat chest. So, Vivien suffered the indignity of standing naked from the waist up, while Plunkett and his assistant applied the tape, all the while she complained it cut off her circulation and she could not breathe. High on Benzedrine, which Selznick ate like popcorn,[16] he admired the results of her period costumes which no longer caved in at the bust.

On the set of *Elephant Walk*, all her fears came to light. One day, a young Sinhalese man came to the makeup department to ask if she was ready to go to the set. She began trembling and remained shaken, even after he left.

'What's the matter?' the makeup man asked her.

'I'm sorry. I'm … I'm so frightened of black eyes. I've always been frightened of black eyes,' she replied.

'But my eyes are black and you're not frightened of me,' the makeup man said.

'No. Your eyes are not black. They're dark brown. I mean black – Indian black.'[17]

The producer, Irving Asher, came and tried to reason with Vivien but to no avail. Asher escorted her to her chair, where she continued to tremble. The stand-in, Carrol Hayward, and her husband, who was standing in for Peter, hovered close by, watching and whispering. Vivien hated them, especially Hayward, whom she rightly sensed was conspiring against her, even if everyone else thought it was paranoia.

'Lady Olivier,' Hayward slipped up behind her.

'Honey,' Vivien said, in a Mississippi drawl reminiscent of Blanche DuBois, 'in the profession, I am just Vivien Leigh.'[18]

The long day of filming in the blazing sun was pointless, as they only managed to capture long shots of Vivien while the rest of the cast had to interact with her stand-in. Having felt listless all day, at two o'clock in the morning, she decided she wanted to throw a party, and banged on the doors of the cast and crew. The ones who answered her call declined.

'Oh stick-in-the-mud,'[19] Vivien said, uncaring of their hostility towards her.

The night was spent writing more letters to Larry, sending bizarre orders for him to pack her evening dresses and bring them to her in Ceylon. In her diary, she noted her lobster dish, the absence of elephants, and the dancing cobras on the set. She could not sleep: she thought she heard voices and it kept her up all night.

In the morning, she reported to hair and makeup and was told there would be no close-ups taken of her that day. Demanding to know why, Asher told her she looked like hell; her face was bloated from a combination of heavy drinking and sleep deprivation. They took more long shots and managed a few with dialogue, but she stumbled over her lines. 'She'd spend hours meeting natives,' Carrol Hayward observed. 'The strain's too much for her.'[20]

'Natives' was how Hayward referred to the locals and to the Sinhalese extras, who kept to their segregated area between filming ... 'The wild folk'. She did not hide her disapproval of Vivien associating with them.

Vivien's mother, Gertrude, was rumoured to have been mixed race, but the terminology in those days was far more blatant: she was called a 'half-caste'. Then and now, the caste system in India dictated a person's social rank and the respect they could command; however, nobody in the immediate family delved too much into their ancestry. Vivien knew the truth: Gertrude, with her porcelain skin and grey-blue eyes, favoured her maternal Irish side – the Robinsons from western Ireland; but her paternal side, Yackjee, was Armenian and often mistaken as Parsi. Gertrude's family was intertwined in the complicated tapestry of British India: her maternal grandparents were killed in the Indian Rebellion of 1857 and her father, Michael Yackjee, who died when she was 5, had worked as a station master for the East Indian Railway Company. One day, Gertrude would marry an English gentleman, but not quite: she married a Yorkshireman born in Scotland whose forebears ran a pub in Pontefract.[21]

That's when Gertrude played the part of denying her true self and negotiated the unforgiving caste system. Gertrude pretended to be white and so did Vivien, and they drew on their Celtic heritage at the mere mention of India. As an adult, Vivien would have what she described as her crinkly hair straightened before being set in rollers – a tedious routine but the smooth results were to her liking. 'I'm not really English,'[22] Vivien said as she grew older and embraced the cultural differences around her. She did not identify as English or British or anything in particular, viewing herself as a citizen of the world with no prejudices towards colour, creed, religion, gender or sexuality. People were people, she did not adhere to social rules.

On the day Carrol Hayward had to film the stampede scenes, a dozen real elephants were brought to the set. It took five takes, as Hayward was terrified of the elephants and outran them each time. Vivien watched from afar, as if in a trance. She had touched the elephants, once, and recoiled from their hot flesh.[23] Or had she dreamt it?

Hours later, Peter found Vivien sitting in a tea field on the hillside watching the faraway fires from Sinhalese rituals. The locals warned against sitting out in the night air: its dampness would purge any hidden fever or sickness from the body.[24]

'You're an old soul. Larry's a brand-new soul with a plastic karma and a marital deficit balance,'[25] she said, perhaps adopting the supernatural beliefs she was privy to in Ceylon.

'That crow …' Peter's voice was distant, 'is saying you're lonely. Are you?'[26]

She fell into his arms sobbing and calling him Larry,[27] pleading with him to sleep with her. In the moment, and in the guise of Larry, he consented to her wishes.

Wracked with guilt, Peter continued the charade of becoming Larry when she needed him most. He recalled the first time he saw Vivien, at O'Brien's Glass Factory in Sydney, after his performance in *The Imaginary Invalid*. She intrigued him; there was something so helpless in how she clung to Larry, afraid that, if she let him go, she would be set adrift.

And then, as if by magic, Vivien was told Larry would be coming to Ceylon the following day. The logistics of his journey escaped her and she stayed up all night, anticipating their reunion. She went to Ratmalana airport to greet him and stood on her tiptoes, looking above the travellers' heads, with nervous anticipation. There she waited, dressed in a thin cotton dress, her hair curling from the humidity, and her nose and cheeks bronzed from the sun. This image of vulnerability did nothing for him and he stunned her by asking why she was not before the camera acting. In front of the travellers passing through the small baggage area, she flew into a blind rage and accused him of plotting against her.

In the car, she suggested stopping at a rest house for a 'little drink and a little relaxation'.[28]

His mouth moved but she heard nothing of what he said. To her, he was a mirage. He was beginning to resent the time and money he had spent travelling to Ceylon.

They went to Helga's Folly, a hotel in Kandy overlooking the jungle and rumoured to be haunted by the ghosts of star-crossed lovers. Peter was waiting in the foyer and he muttered a polite greeting to Larry and vice versa. Vivien slid next to Peter and wrapped her arms around him, all the while she stared at Larry. It became clear to Larry that Peter had replaced him, though he felt no resentment and was relieved someone else was shouldering the burden. If she wanted a violent brawl, she did not get it.

Instead, Vivien and Larry climbed the hill to Karunaratne House, the building designed by Minnette de Silva. They were silent for the first part of their ascent: he was harbouring his own little secret. During the filming of *The Beggar's Opera*, in which he played

Macheath, he had had an affair with Dorothy Tutin, who was cast as Polly Peachum in the picture. Tutin was 23 and a graduate of the Royal Academy of Dramatic Art (RADA), having completed the course in 1949. If coincidences in timing were anything to go by, he knew, in 1949, that his marriage to Vivien was over but continued to cling to their image instead of the real thing. As they climbed higher, they began to improvise a one-act play of two cockney naval ratings talking crudely. Vivien was gruff and spat over the rails of an imaginary destroyer and was scolded by Larry, her boss.[29] Acting was the only way they could communicate, or as Larry said, 'It's a great relief to be in someone else's shoes.'[30]

When they came back down to earth, they had nothing more to say. Larry spent a full day talking to Irving Asher and observing Vivien. On set, she seemed unaware of his presence and, a day later, he disappeared.

The production left Ceylon for the soundstages of Hollywood. As the aeroplane began its ascent over the Indian Ocean, Vivien unfastened her seatbelt and stood up, screaming that the wing was on fire. She became hysterical and made for the exit, threatening to throw herself out. Then, she tore at her clothes, ripping her dress down the middle, and fought with Peter, who tried to reason with her. The stunned passengers watched, in horror, as she was restrained and forcibly sedated with sleeping pills, which periodically wore off on their journey. Coming to, she began her outbursts all over again and, once more, would be sedated for the next eight hours or so.

Seventy-two hours later, the plane finally touched down in California. On the way to the Beverly Hills Hotel, Vivien decided she wanted to stay with Peter in the house he rented for himself, his wife and their daughter. So, the car was detoured to the Finches' house in Hanover Drive. At the house, she began to divide her living quarters from Peter's family.

Peter's wife, Tamara, and their 3-year-old daughter, Anita, had sailed to New York on the *Queen Elizabeth* and then flew to Los Angeles. After the long journey, Tamara was faced with Vivien, on a high, dressed in a red and gold sari and looking like Scarlett O'Hara. She demanded that Tamara change into a sari for a party given in her honour and seethed with jealousy when Peter showed his wife affection and praised her appearance – her dark, Romanian looks were compared to that of an Arab stallion.[31]

Within moments, close to seventy guests descended on the small property and Vivien was nowhere to be found. She was locked in her bedroom, lying across the bed, sobbing and trying to reach Larry on the telephone. Knocking on the door gently, Tamara tried but failed to coax her out. Still, the wretched sobs continued and were heard by the guests downstairs.

Although Tamara never found Vivien easy to be around, she had always admired her. When she met her in Sydney in 1948, she considered her beautiful and vulnerable, and was astounded by her ability to remember everyone's names and little titbits about their daily lives. It charmed everyone. Tamara, thinking she had made a friend in Vivien, confided that when she first met Peter, at the beach, she was reading *Gone with the Wind*. It was a sweet story but Vivien remained unmoved; she had first read *Gone with the Wind* after snapping her ankle on the ski slopes of Kitzbühel. In a way, it would change both of their lives.

In England, when Tamara began socialising with Vivien and Larry, she felt out of place and knew they had wanted Peter's company and not hers. There was a certain tone that Vivien used when she wished to be imperious – an efficiency which one acquired when ordering servants to do their bidding. In turn, Vivien expected others to show her the slavish devotion that her Ayah (nursemaid) had in India. Tamara, who was also cultured, realised that Vivien's beauty was not her greatest weapon but her brain. Vivien was a magpie who collected knowledge from others, memorising wine lists, plays, poems, witty anecdotes and foreign languages – French, German, Italian and Spanish – anything to cut others down to size. Nevertheless, Tamara did not recognise the woman, behind the door, who was falling to pieces.

Suddenly, for Tamara, everything fell into place and she realised Vivien had set her sights on Peter. Back in 1948, the first thing Vivien said to Tamara was, 'You bring that clever husband of yours to England. You must promise.'[32]

Tamara had delivered on her promise, and then some. But she was not the fool Vivien thought her to be and had known, for some time, that her marriage to Peter was coming to an end. Concerned individuals asked how she could stand such things. 'Ballet is a cruel business. Very cruel,'[33] Tamara said of her art and, perhaps, similarly justified her life with Peter.

Tamara set off to find Peter, when Vivien suddenly appeared at the top of the stairs. She glared in Tamara and Peter's direction before walking towards them. Something about Tamara's elegance – she had danced with the Ballets Russes de Monte Carlo – rattled her. The women had become a threat to each other and Peter was unsure who would be the victor. Both had honed their survival skills in infancy: Vivien, alone in the convents of Europe, and Tamara, a nomadic life after her grandparents were slain by Soviet bayonets.

Vivien, for now, succeeded in wounding Tamara and lost an expensive ring Peter had bought her in Ceylon by discarding it in the airport bathroom.[34] It was no accident and she reminded him that Tamara was unaccustomed to displays of wealth, having married him when he was poor. Vivien understood the symbolism: her father was a womaniser and her mother always knew when he had had an affair – mostly with her friends – for he would buy her a trinket.

Later that night, Tamara exerted her superiority and shared Peter's bed. At two o'clock in the morning, Vivien pushed the door open and tore off the bedclothes, screaming obscenities at both of them. 'You haven't told her, you haven't told her!' Vivien railed at Peter. 'How could you be sleeping with her, you monster? You're my lover!'[35]

The following morning, Vivien wrung her hands and sobbed like a child, searching for sympathy from Tamara, explaining that her behaviour was not her fault and it was the result of Larry's coldness towards her. There was sincerity in her voice and Tamara believed her, as she seemed more balanced than before, and they spent the day sunbathing by the pool and eating avocado salad.

Vivien told Tamara they could only converse in French and the two women discussed trivial matters and it was apparent that Tamara, who had lived and worked in Paris, was far more fluent in the language. Distressed, Vivien jumped into the swimming pool and swam laps, which exhausted her and she struggled to stay afloat and breathe.

She screamed that she wanted to drown, she wanted to die, as Tamara dragged her to safety.[36]

In that state, Vivien was unpredictable and violent: she flew at Tamara with a knife and, soon after, cut up all her clothing. She told Anita to shut up and asked for her to be removed from her sight. To appease Vivien and give the child a sense of normality, Anita was placed in a Hollywood preschool.

Things weren't much better on the set when Vivien recited her dialogue from *A Streetcar Named Desire* to Dana Andrews, as though he were the character of Mitch. Dana was too drunk to respond and fluffed his own lines to her. When corrected, she broke down sobbing, 'You're all telling me what to do. I know what I've got to do. I've got to get back to work.'[37]

The studio dismissed Vivien that day and sent her home. Arriving at Peter and Tamara's house, she found her bags packed and waiting in the hallway. Peter delivered the news: she would have to go. In his own words, he wanted to 'blot out the bloody business once and for all'.[38]

Chapter Two

'We know what we are, but not what we may be'

Hamlet, William Shakespeare

1953

The house in Hanover Drive had its curtains drawn. Vivien hated sunlight and loathed to be seen in full glare; it was her latest fixation and, like all of her phases, it would pass. Just as the character of Blanche DuBois did, she avoided strong light. It was not method acting but, rather, the parts she played revealed layers of her psyche; each character awakening the pieces she had suppressed.

The door was on the latch and Larry pushed it open without much effort. He was jet-lagged, owing to his journey from Ischia to London to board a flight to New York and then a connection to Los Angeles. How many hours had he been travelling? How many days and time zones had he crossed? It was now 11 March, so three, almost four days, in total. Funny, how things worked out: it was on 11 March 1937, some sixteen years earlier, she had begged him to leave his first wife and run away with her. Months later, they had executed their plan and eloped. It was a date not to be forgotten.

Then and now, Larry was an emotional wreck, torn apart by his duty to his wife and passion for his mistress – the latter description was too strong a word. Here he was, a vagabond in smart clothes: unshaven, wearing his crumpled suit, and his shirt sticking to his back.

He wandered down the long passageway and up the creaking stairs, the narrowness surrounding him like a secret tunnel. The bedroom door was ajar, voile curtains hung limpid against the arched window, which opened on to a small veranda. Overall, the shabbiness, created by her (and so unlike her), belonged to 632 Elysian Fields, the temporary abode of Blanche DuBois, or, in their world, a set. Before he focused his weary gaze on the bed, he detected her shallow breathing. If they had been following a script, the description might have been as thus: *Clothes lay on the floor, over the chair and spilt from the chest of drawers. A lamp had fallen over and pages of the mediocre* Elephant Walk *script were strewn across the room.*

Larry began to speak, his voice suspended in disbelief, thinking she was pretending to be insane. Then it hit him: she had been expecting someone else.

'Is something the matter?' he asked.

'I'm in love,' she said.

'Who with, darling?'

'Peter Finch.'[1]

All his instincts told him he should have been furious. Had it been five years ago, he might have belted her, hard across the face, as he had done in Australia when she made a scene about having misplaced her red slippers and refused to go on stage as Lady Teazle in *The School for Scandal* until they were found.

'Get up on that stage, you little bitch,' he had said, slapping her.

'Don't you dare hit me, you – you bastard,'[2] she had retaliated.

But they were too far gone for such passionate displays. He had his own dalliances; they were self-pitying indulgences and a tonic for his sorrows.

Now that the initial surprise of what he might have found had lapsed, he was overcome by the smell of stale cigarettes and gin. She sat up in bed and laughed, a shrill note scoring the manic scene. Or was it the blue piano from *A Streetcar Named Desire*? How much were they both play-acting? Further still, the stage director in him wanted to set the scene, to control every aspect of what was unfolding. The room looked as if it had been ransacked. He hated mess. He went to the window once more and pulled open the curtains, forcefully as though he were stripping bare the scene. She continued watching him, the pupils of her blue eyes dilating from the assault of sunlight, just as when Mitch, in *Streetcar*, rips the paper lantern from the light bulb.

How did he know she was there?

Clearly, Vivien could not remember the departure of the Finches, who left for an apartment in Wiltshire Drive after she had threatened to kill their child. It was only a turn of phrase, hardly a serious threat to the infant's life. The servants left, too, with one housemaid admitting she was scared of Vivien's behaviour and the rituals she had begun to carry out: blasting Indian music and trying to exorcise her soul. In that sense, their fever dream had come to an end and Larry's was only beginning.

Nor did Vivien remember the intervention carried out by David Niven and Stewart Granger, their close friends and colleagues who were part of the English expatriate community in Hollywood. Granger, known as Jimmy – his birth name – to his friends, appeared with Vivien in the play *Serena Blandish* at the Gate Theatre in 1938. In the early days, the unknown Granger idolised Larry and was awed by Vivien, whom he thought was very ambitious and hard-working.

In the present day, Granger was demoted by Vivien to an errand boy and he made arrangements with the studio's doctor and collected her prescriptions from Schwab's all-night drug store. It was Niven who served as her gatekeeper until Larry arrived, but when Niven passed out from exhaustion, it fell to Granger to coerce her into taking sedatives and chase her around when her impulses took hold. In short, they had kept her alive until Larry's arrival. Suffice to say, she hated them both and Granger never got over the deranged look in her eyes or forgot the verbal abuse she spat at him.

Confronted by everything that had taken place and short bursts of lucidity from Vivien, Larry revealed that the studio had told him of her whereabouts. In moments of clarity, he was Larry and she was Viv, the spouses at odds with their circumstances, not the glittering couple who sold a myth to their fans – who little knew they were all being written into the fable. She bought the story and reached for a packet of cigarettes and sparked the lighter. He walked to her, through the blueish smoke, as if he had been conjured.

Looking at Vivien's tiny frame, perched on the bed, he could not fathom the story he had been told. That she had somehow lost her mind and was wandering through the house naked, throwing money out of the window and threatening to jump out of it herself.

The final straw came when she propositioned the young secretary the studio had sent over. He suspected it was less about answering fan mail and more about chaperoning, just in case she tried to kill herself or succeeded through misadventure. There were whispers she had also made a pass at Tamara Finch, who reckoned it was done for shock value. Nobody could confirm any of it, it was all hearsay and rumours.

'But isn't everybody [gay]? Larry is inclined that way too,' Vivien remarked to her friend Bevis Bawa, in Ceylon, when he confided that he was a homosexual.

'Good Lord, I am gay too,'[3] Peter added for the sake of camaraderie.

Still, Larry reminded himself that it was the secretary's word over Vivien's and possibly a ruse for a handsome settlement. He had been the victim of such rumours; it followed people in their profession – this, having to have a dual personality – it came with the territory and he used effeminate terms of endearment towards his fellow men, 'Baby, Darling,' and so forth. 'I went through choir school, I went through public school, I was the prettiest boy in any school always, there wasn't a prefect who wasn't after me,'[4] Larry said of his appeal to other men.

The studio executives warned Larry of Vivien's behaviour. Her madness ricocheted off the celluloid screen during the rushes. It was the era of McCarthyism, there was a witch hunt going on: Communism in Hollywood. William Dieterle, the German-born director of *Elephant Walk*, supported the Marxist writer, Bertolt Brecht, and the production was delayed for three months as the State Department would not allow Dieterle to travel to Ceylon.[5] In short, the studio system wanted its stars to conform to their sterile American dream. The phone was slammed down and a telegram followed. '*Come immediately.*' The telegram said other things but in the bright, blinding sunlight in Ischia, Larry had crumpled it in his fist and forgotten about his marital discord.

The bedroom was a mess, with Vivien's clothes discarded on the floor. At convent school, she was taught to fold her clothes in a neat pile and to hide them under a satin square. The heat was stifling and a stationary fan glared down from the ceiling. He was positive that, by now, the neighbours knew a star was living among them. Certainly, her English accent singled her out and her Pierre Balmain clothing – when she wore it – in the blazing sun. It had gone beyond eccentricity: she was mentally ill. 'She's super nuts; she babbles like an idiot,' an insider said. 'When she has those attacks she drinks a lot, gets all puffy, a total wreck.'[6]

Larry was angry because she had taken him for a fool. She had led everyone in a merry dance and was exhausted from her bad behaviour. But it was more than that; a deeper malice lurked behind her feline eyes.

'No.' She drew back as he moved towards her. 'You stay away!'

'Vivien,' his voice was softer. He held out his hand, coaxing her to calm down.

'You're not going to call them, are you?'

Them? Who and what were *them*? He agreed to follow her wishes. She eyed him suspiciously, cowering into the corner of the mattress.

'Liar!'[7] she yelled.

The week before Larry's arrival, Paramount had telephoned a psychiatrist, Dr Greenson, who was well known among Hollywood stars and a disciple of Sigmund Freud. There was nothing he had not seen before and no psychosis he could not treat. Dr Greenson and a nurse banged on the door and were about to leave when David Niven answered. Niven had to tear himself away, to outsmart Vivien and invent an excuse to answer the door. Paranoia had been festering for days. They found her in the bedroom, the window wide open, the fan swirling overhead, blowing the pages of her *Elephant Walk* script around the room.

An old boyfriend was in town – John Buckmaster – a companion from her days when she was the young wife of a middle-aged barrister. The year was 1935: she was 22 and with a child at home, and he was only 20, with a flat in Chelsea and a theatrical star – Gladys Cooper – for a mother. He was the first man with whom she had an extramarital affair and he introduced her to Larry one night at the Savoy Grill.

Troubled by schizophrenia, Buckmaster's star burnt bright and fast, and he moved between institutions, this time in New York, a place far enough away from his respectable family. Social standing and money meant that such things could be hidden. Buckmaster had chased a man down Second Avenue with a carving knife and, having failed to stab his victim, he tore off his clothes and was arrested for committing indecent exposure. He then left the concrete landscape of Manhattan for the desert planes of southern California. All hell had broken loose.

Nivien and Granger had found Vivien in a compromising position with the former thespian. But, as the doctor reminded Niven, it was nothing that he had not seen before. To Niven's relief, Buckmaster fled the scene and ran off into the night to his rented bungalow at the Garden of Allah.

'By the way,' the doctor eyed Niven, 'how's the sex thing between you?'[8]

Alfred Kinsey's book, *Sexual Behaviour in the Human Female*, had just been published to the astonishment of the American public – though almost every woman (and man) could privately resonate with the findings. However, a great hysteria took hold and there was a fear that women might be sexual beings, and some, like Vivien, who followed their biological instincts, were considered barbarians.[9]

'She'll offer it to you. If you accept it, it'll make matters worse. If you refuse, she'll make matters worse,' Dr Greenson continued. 'I don't envy you.'[10] He explained that, given Vivien's mental state, sexual activity was heightened and patients did not discriminate when it came to partners.

Given Dr Greenson's explanation for Vivien's promiscuity, it might have explained her attraction to Peter Finch in Ceylon. Or perhaps it was wishful thinking for Larry, as he could not understand why Peter would betray him by sleeping with her. Where the hell was Peter, he wondered. And why did Larry place so much emphasis on Vivien's affair when he, too, had cheated – he was the first to cheat with Dorothy Tutin, his Polly Peachum – but kept it a secret? He was a hypocrite, in that sense.

Although Peter was indebted to them both, they had almost missed seeing him in Sydney, had it not been for the persistence of his colleague and co-founder of the Mercury Theatre, who sent Larry several letters, imploring him to come to a lunchtime performance of the play. The general impression was that the Oliviers thought they were above the theatrical company, and, by then, Peter considered it a dead-end job.

To everyone's surprise, Larry and Vivien came to O'Brien's Glass Factory and sat among the ordinary patrons, many of whom were workers at the factory and dressed in their overalls with sawdust at their feet. Afterwards, they looked for Peter; Larry invited him to England, which Vivien thought was a spur-of-the-moment proposal.

They were to meet once more, at a drinks reception, before Vivien and Larry left Sydney with the Old Vic Company. Once more, Vivien clung to Larry, while he held court with Peter. This time, he made Peter promise to come to England. 'A talent like yours is wasted in Australia,' he said, offending everyone in the room. Peter kept his promise and a passage was booked on *The Esperance*.

When Peter arrived in London, he telephoned Larry and Vivien and was told they were in America and would be home the following day. They met once more, over sherry and biscuits, and Vivien seemed restless: they were going to be late to a party. Half an hour later, they rose from their drinks and bid Peter farewell before Larry advised him to look up their agent, Cecil Tennant.

'You're all right, aren't you?'[11] Larry asked Peter, as he put on his overcoat.

There was a brief moment of silence, followed by a confusing glance from Peter who had travelled so far and waited for two weeks for their invitation, only to be dismissed like a footman.

'Give us a ring sometime,' Larry said.

'Good luck,'[12] Vivien added, on her way out.

Inside the house at Hanover Drive, Vivien remained unaware of the passage of time. She had not slept in days, nor had she dressed. A cough rattled through her chest, a reminder of a tubercular-scarred lung from bouts of the illness during the war. Perhaps it was true what the Sinhalese said, that the Ceylon night air would bring out any fever that lurked inside someone. She smiled at the blank television screen, praising the phantom figure only she could see.

Larry followed Niven's example when trying to care for her. The patient remained unresponsive. Step by step, they mirrored each other. In the small refrigerator there was some cottage cheese and little else, but Larry had to find an inventive way to disguise her sleeping pills. Vivien stood in the doorway; the light from the kitchen window emphasised the makeup streaked down her cheeks and smudged under her eyes. 'You won't let them send me away, will you?' she had asked Niven. The same question might have been asked of Larry.

'Who?'

'Oh, they will be coming for me. But you won't let them take me. Promise?'

'I promise.'

'You're the only one I can trust.'[13] She turned and walked away.

Larry telephoned the head of Paramount. They had washed their hands of the whole situation and replaced Vivien with Elizabeth Taylor. Furthermore, they revoked Vivien's $175,000 fee and refused to pay for her living expenses. He asked for Dr Greenson's number and the mocking silence from the other end of the line answered his question. It was very clandestine and somewhat sordid. Dr Greenson would be on his way, but first, he needed payment for previous visits and refused to even look at Vivien unless the $1,500 bill was settled. 'The girl's health is far more important,' the studio head said, putting the onus on to Larry to care for her.

Larry did not feel like going into detail or explaining the journey he had undertaken, except that he was desperate to solve the problem at hand. Bed was on his mind and the promise of sleep evaded him.

The doctor moved towards Vivien; like a spectre, his shadow slipped along the wall. She jumped from the bed and fell to the floor naked, as the nurse restrained her.

She kicked and screamed, shifting her head from side to side in an attempt to bite the nurse, who held her arms behind her back. 'Oh Larry,' she said, her voice weakened by the noise. She raised her head and looked up at him, and he turned to acknowledge her command.

'Yes, Vivling?' His eyes scanned the various scratches along her body, his pet name betraying the unfolding horror.

'I hate you.' Her eyes were dead and her voice was cold. The words wounded him more than finding her in bed with another man. He knew that she meant them.

'I know who you are,' said the nurse.

'You do?'

'Why, yes!'

Vivien smiled.

'You're Scarlett O'Hara, aren't you?'

The doctor manoeuvred around her, pricking her flesh with a needle, the liquid travelling quickly through her veins, numbing her body.

'No,' Vivien said as she swayed her head, overcome by the sedative. 'No, I'm not.'

'Then, who are you?'

'I'm Blanche DuBois.'[14] Her eyes rolled back, a quick release of the sedative, and then she was gone.

They stood up, abandoning her limp body on the floor. The doctor retrieved a pen from his pocket and unscrewed the lid. He needed to write papers for a civil commitment – or the involuntary hospitalisation – of a mentally ill patient against their will. Dr Greenson asked to be shown to the telephone so he could phone for an ambulance to transport Vivien to an institution.

Larry appealed to Dr Greenson and asked if he could take Vivien to England and have her institutionalised there. He had little faith in Hollywood psychiatrists who, like a false psychic medium, clutched at straws until a common bond was struck. The last assessment, from 'the psychiatrist to the stars',[15] Dr Martin Grotjohn, suggested Vivien would make a full recovery at home and in the care of her mother. Laughable, to say the least, she would as soon have knocked her mother out as listen to her,[16] but there was a sensible solution cloaked, albeit, in the generic advice.

Surprisingly, Dr Greenson did not put up a fight and told Larry he would require a nurse to accompany him on the journey to England. Larry looked at Vivien's still form, like a corpse laid out on the floor, and wondered how she could ever recover.

For two days, Larry and Vivien remained at the house; he was her jailer and she was a vision of the walking dead. Dr Greenson had given him a bottle of pills, which she had become wise to and so they improvised a cunning game with each other. Niven had been there before, and now it was Larry's turn.

Each time, she asked what it was. He pushed the pills into her hand before handing her a drink to wash them down. It was all explained in the simplest of terms as if she were a curious child.

As with Niven, she agreed to take the pills but only if he kissed her first.

Kiss. Kiss.[17]

She threw back her head and laughed. The pills went under her tongue and she smirked with her mouth closed, full of water from the glass. On another occasion, she threw the pills into the swimming pool. He had fallen asleep, his body finally succumbing to the pent-up exhaustion.

The splash woke him up.[18]

In her manic phase, she was drawn to water and immersed herself in it. Under the water, the sound of white noise drowned out the chaos of the outside world and inside her mind. In *A Streetcar Named Desire*, she, as Blanche DuBois, explained it was called hydrotherapy. It has been said that cold water in the right ear can temporarily alleviate depression and cold water in the left ear can ease the symptoms of mania.[19]

She told Larry that the nurses who tended to her in his absence had wrapped her in cold, wet sheets. It sounded barbaric, but it was undertaken to activate the sympathetic nervous system and, as her body adjusted to the cold sheets, she would be sedated.

Later, having succeeded in convincing Vivien to take her pills, he placed an international call to Laurence Olivier Productions, to book two airline tickets to London but he did not want to connect in New York, as it meant a long stopover and he was unsure if Vivien's nerves could handle the stress. He tried to charter a direct flight and charge it to the company, along with her medical fees. More mounting debt for the board to scrutinise – Vivien was fond of the expense account – and he would barely earn £20,000 from *The Beggar's Opera*.

In a moment of clarity, she saw him as her protector and asked if he loved her. To her mind, it was a simple question and it deserved a straightforward answer. Not so, in recent days, he struggled to accept the stranger she had become. He once read that individuals who suffered from mental illness lashed out at those they loved the most. Trapped in the chaos and confusion of the situation, he took comfort from the analogy. 'It's obvious,' he said, 'she must love me to death.'[20]

Chapter Three

'It's not in the stars to hold our destiny but in ourselves'

Julius Caesar, William Shakespeare

1953

Thick fog surrounded the airfield at Croydon as the aeroplane made its descent and the wings dipped from side to side at one or more of the abortive attempts to land. Death in the air seemed a dignified end for Vivien, as she stirred in her seat. They had almost died in a plane crash in 1946 when they were rushing from New York to London. On that fated journey, Larry remembered the choking of the engines as they caught fire and the tormented look in Vivien's eyes as she faced death. They belly-flopped on to a field in Connecticut and miraculously lived to tell the tale.

Before taking off from Los Angeles to New York, Vivien had to be restrained and sedated. She was lumbered into the back of an ambulance, tied to a stretcher and buried under a blanket. The reporters caught her on the airfield at LaGuardia as the doors opened; her skeletal face and hollow eyes cast dark shadows in the photographs. In the car at the airfield on the West Coast, she had delayed the flight to New York by an hour, after she began to cry hysterically and refused to board it. Eventually, Larry dragged her out of the car and she climbed up the steps.

'So sorry, folks,'[1] she called to the waiting reporters.

The experiences at both airports were much the same, as they crossed the two time zones and coasts, ahead of the connecting flight to London. All rationality seemed to evaporate into thin air when it came to Vivien and logistics. The reporters in Los Angeles believed Larry's explanation that she was afraid of flying and obeyed his request not to take photographs, so as not to startle her before take-off. A rare victory for him but the gossip columnists in Hollywood were already reporting on her nervous exhaustion.

Hours into the flight to New York, Larry awoke in his seat and felt someone watching him. 'You look exhausted. Are you all right?'[2] Vivien asked him. He engaged her in idle chit-chat until he noticed her eyes starting to close.

On their final journey to London, the sedative failed to work and Vivien insisted she could not leave the United States, she had a contract with Paramount. Nobody knew what to do, and if she managed to break loose, the waiting reporters would have had a field day with the story. Larry pointed to the injection in the nurse's hand and said, 'Give her another.' She was forcibly sedated once more and carried to the back of the plane and watched by the nurse. Those words and the coldness of his voice would haunt Vivien for years to come.

At Croydon Airfield, the English reporters followed the scent of blood, though were more orderly than their American counterparts. Larry looked out of the window, detecting dim headlights in a sea of fog, and he looked to the nurse who sat upright in her seat, exhausted from the transatlantic flight. The brakes screeched to a halt, like a drill before the curtain rose and the players dashed to their marks, ready to go.

The nurse went to Vivien's side and checked her vital statistics and wrote in her diary. Larry kept his gaze on the window as the headlights drew closer.

'I really am sorry for being such a nuisance,'[3] Vivien announced, as if addressing an audience in the theatre.

Forty minutes later, the door opened and they were blinded by flashbulbs, which frightened her and she held on to Larry's arm.

'Welcome home, Lady Olivier,' the voices called, testing the waters.

'We really are home, aren't we?'[4] she asked Larry.

As the car drove to Netherne Asylum, Larry must have tried to piece together what Peter, and then Vivien, had told him about their affair. For Peter, it all happened quite suddenly; however, for Vivien, it was a slow burn.

⤜⤜⤛

It was two o'clock in the morning and snowing a blizzard in the empty streets of Pimlico. A Rolls-Royce pulled up outside a block of flats in Dolphin Square and Vivien opened the car door before the driver had a chance to do it. She ran to the front door and pressed the buzzer, holding it until someone answered, their voice barely audible from exhaustion.

'Peter, Peter, it's Vivien. You must let me in,' she said.

Vivien walked into the small flat occupied by Peter and Tamara. The living room was filled with children's toys and debris from the Finches' busy lives. Tamara walked around, picking things up and apologising for the mess. An improvement on their last dwelling: they had moved from a dingy flat in Notting Hill, around the corner from the serial killer, Reg Christie, who was hanged for murder in July 1953. Standing in the middle of the room, Vivien said the flat was smoky and airless and rushed to open the windows, allowing the cold air and snow to spill inside.

Tamara offered to take Vivien's mink coat and was surprised by the flimsy dress underneath. Later, as the story grew, it would be said that Vivien wore nothing beneath her coat, as she sometimes did. Her hair was soaked from the snow, which dripped from the fur on to the floor. A stirring child interrupted the scene with repeated calls of 'mummy'.

'The child does not want to sleep,' Vivien said. 'She was born under the sign of Scorpio, like me – if she chooses not to sleep, she should be allowed to get up.'[5]

Sometimes, Peter hated Vivien's haughtiness but he felt indebted to her. She smiled euphorically before announcing the news: she was going to Ceylon to make *Elephant Walk* for Paramount and Peter was coming with her.

Peter was overwhelmed. He looked to his wife for a response, and then his eyes met with Vivien. He asked about his contract with Laurence Olivier Productions.

It was all settled, she assured him.

Tamara implored him to think about it first.

'I know what's best for your career,'[6] Vivien said, undermining Tamara.

'What about a screen test?' Peter asked.

There was nothing to think about: Vivien was a star and it was all arranged for Peter to be her leading man. She could not abide his and Tamara's questions and instead focused on their shabby décor: the lining of the curtains was badly sewn and their furniture was marked by wet glasses. 'You should put placemats under your glasses,'[7] she scolded them both, as if she was the landlady and they were her tenants.

Less than a week later, Vivien and Peter left for Ceylon.

'Goodbye, Vivien. Take care of her, won't you, Finch?' Larry said to Peter on the tarmac at Heathrow.

'Don't worry, I will,'[8] Peter promised.

Vivien and Larry shared a clumsy goodbye kiss. Vivien pulled her hand from Larry's and took Peter's arm. Drizzle moved across the airfield and their polite small talk was drowned out by roaring aeroplane engines. They each smiled once more; there was nothing else to say.

From the aeroplane window, Peter gave Larry a reassuring wave and Vivien blew him a sad little kiss.

The Comet disappeared into the grey skies.

Larry was no stranger to the passageways and wards of Netherne Asylum in Surrey, where he had overseen the committal of his older sister, Sybille, five years earlier. After Sybille's breakdown, she wrote an authorised biography of Larry, a sort of rehabilitation project, mentally and financially. The facts startled him and he crossed out several parts of her manuscript and wrote corrections. He could not abide the cold truth and reminded her that his childhood beatings were given for telling lies.

Now, he committed Vivien to the walls of the same redbrick building. Lying to others had become second nature and Larry censored much of the truth when speaking to Dr Rudolf Freudenberg. Dr Freudenberg, a German psychiatrist who had fled Nazi Germany in 1935, went first to Vienna to refine his methods in psychiatric care, which later manifested as an insulin coma. Before sending Vivien into an unnatural sleep, he probed Larry for facts, perhaps looking for emotional pitfalls in his story. David Niven once said, 'Larry and Vivien complement each other like tea and cake'[9] but it was hardly a psychiatric evaluation.

If the doctor were a biographer, such as Felix Barker,[10] the latest to write an authorised biography – though 'authorised' should be used very loosely – Larry could have dazzled him with greatness and steered the story so it was favourable to both himself and Vivien. 'Art is a little bit larger than life – it's an exaltation of life – and I think you probably need a little touch of madness,'[11] Larry would say.

If they had been following a script and Larry had been the director, instead of a bewildered bystander, the scene might have played out as such. Vivien was led into the room by two nurses; her eyes pierced through his soul. Somehow, she looked smaller – a frail creature who was foreign to him – and he wondered if she was lost forever. She moved in a dreamlike state, the same state Larry had found her in at Hanover Drive and thought she was putting it on, the way people do when they re-enact a mad scene in the theatre.[12] On the stage, there would be markers and prompts. Real life was not so different: there were various objects around the room, taken in with quick glances, as though her eyes were a camera and she had to capture each thing before she forgot. The window. The desk. The door. She took a deep breath, suddenly, and her chest expanded. It dawned on her where she was and she mumbled an objection before jumping from the chair and making for the door. In the world of Blanche DuBois, the doctor and nurse would have been standing guard, expecting this move, before wrapping her in a straitjacket.

She screamed for help, over and over.

Something ceased inside Larry and he no longer felt the urge to react or to follow her from the room. He stood still, letting them take her away, listening to her screams; her obscenities. He knew she blamed him. Years before, when she was in poor physical health, he told her that her sorrow was his worst fear.[13] Sinister as it was to let her scream and struggle, he knew it was part of the course and trusted that strangers could help her.

'She's all wound up,' Dr Freudenberg said. 'We will put her to sleep for three weeks and let her unwind slowly. It will be better if you are not with her at this time.'[14]

The endless stretch of a hospital corridor represented universal feelings of loneliness and despair for those who had walked it, regardless of their status. Behind the doors of the rooms, patients were enduring treatments that were supposed to restore them to their old selves, at least enough to rehabilitate them back into society. For the recipients of ECT, ice baths and cold packs (wrapped in wet sheets), it felt like a form of dehumanisation and many would suffer from trauma, even if it was not acknowledged in those days.[15]

At the time and later on, it was suggested that Vivien's breakdown was 'a manifestation of the rejection she felt when her parents sent her to England to be educated when she was a child'.[16] Rejection and abandonment were two separate issues in the grand scheme of things: she was removed from the loving arms of her Ayah and placed into the care of the nuns. The old cliché, 'cruel to be kind', would be thrown around by well-meaning friends, but some felt Larry was cruel to leave her at Netherne.

Had Vivien's parents, Ernest and Gertrude Hartley, wrestled with their conscience before sending her to the Convent of the Sacred Heart in Roehampton when she was 6 years old? Did her mother hold her hand as they approached the neoclassical mansion, and holding in the other hand, the school booklet with a portrait of Our Lady of Sorrows on the cover? In India, they used to do everything together and Vivien, as a child, accompanied her parents to the Bangalore racetrack. Larry maintained that Gertrude treated Vivien with an air of indifference and only became interested in her after her fame. With the Hartleys' newfound wealth, they were play-acting at being aristocrats before the economic crash of 1929 depleted their fortune. A rich man in India was a poor man among the British gentry and little Vivien was often reminded that her father was 'in trade' – he was a stockbroker with Pigott Chapman & Company. Not the same as the ruling classes – bloodlines were their currency – but at least the Hartleys could afford the school fees.

It was a contrast to Larry's upbringing and he said, 'We were what was called gentry, though we lived in a slum in Dorking.'[17] In his father's house, there were masses of china sitting on shelves and the silverware was unpolished. A chimney sweep lived next door and was richer; his daughter had a pony and cart but the Olivier children could not ask for rides, as they were considered superior to the sweep's family. 'We were very, very poor,' Larry said. 'I always had to use my father's bath water after him to save water.'[18]

Little Vivien wanted for nothing, except her mother's love and the companionship of siblings, but all of hers had died. There had been a stillborn girl, born in 1912, and twin girls, Clara and Katherine,[19] who died hours after their birth in 1915. After their burial in St Mary's churchyard in Ootacamund, nobody spoke of them again. Practicalities aside, Gertrude had brought Vivien from India and duly enrolled her at the convent, where she was the youngest child and, as such, Mother General let her keep a kitten. Vivien had never before felt cold weather nor tasted heavy, boiled food and bland meats such as mutton. In India, children were given *chota hazri*; a banana or a glass of fruit juice prepared by the servants. Even as an adult, she favoured oily food and anything cooked in wine.

Gone were the endless summers in India; her muslin dress and *topee* framing her petulant face, and the clicking of Gertrude's Kodak No. 2 as her chubby legs ran across the lawn of their hillside home in Ootacamund. '*Roti, makan, chini, chota baba nini*,' the Ayah sang, dipping her finger into opium to send her charge to sleep. '*Bread, butter, sugar, little baby sleep*.'[20]

It would be two years before Vivien saw her mother again and six years before she reunited with her father. During their absence, they sent her bangles with coloured-glass beads and shawls which arrived in boxes, shipped from the port of Calcutta. On her birthday, there was a doll whose porcelain face had cracked in transit. There would be postcards and letters from Gertrude as she travelled across Europe and, later, invitations to spend the summer holidays in Connemara in western Ireland, where Vivien rode horses and waded upstream, catching minnow with her bare hands.

Perhaps the lack of a maternal figure in Vivien's life marked her, for she felt nothing of the sort towards her own daughter except a feeling of entrapment. Did Gertrude feel a sense of relief after leaving Vivien at the convent? Is that how Larry felt after he signed Vivien into Netherne?

Later that night, having come from Netherne, Larry dined with Ernest and Gertrude and relayed to them the facts of Vivien's breakdown in Ceylon and Hollywood. He asked if insanity ran in the family.

'Good God, no!'[21] Ernest shouted.

There would be family secrets and traits dismissed as idiosyncrasies. Gertrude's paternal uncle, Gabriel Yackjee, suffered from 'chronic mania'[22] and was committed to an asylum in India. Gertrude, herself, was prone to dark thoughts and low moods and delusions of grandeur. Ernest, a philanderer, viewed life as a performance and was a great storyteller – in other words, a liar. How Dr Freudenberg would have had a field day with them.

'She's not a sleepy baby,'[23] Gertrude said, excusing Vivien's cyclic disturbances.

The subject was closed.

In the clinical setting of Vivien's hospital room, a nurse administered injections of Pentothal to induce her into a coma. They had stripped her without her consent and she recalled feeling exposed: her naked flesh was cold but she could not push them away, or protest for them to stop. She had made herself submissive; there was nothing else she could do. The nurses had undertaken this ritual a thousand times before and they did not see a famous film star but another patient; an anonymous body, like a corpse. Later, when she learnt of the indignities at Netherne she would be relieved to be dead to the world.

The last time Vivien had felt such an intrusion was when she gave birth to her first and only child, Suzanne Mary Holman, on 12 October 1933, at the Rahere Nursing Home. She described childbirth as humiliating and nicknamed her baby 'Toosoon' to punctuate the upheaval in her life. As with pregnancy, she treated her newborn with an air of detachment and offhandedly chose the name Suzanne because, to her mind, it sounded French, and she later came to regret it. More than likely, she was depressed and it explained the lack of bond with her baby: she felt hopeless when Suzanne cried, until blue in the face, and was at a loss to comfort her.

At Netherne, each day resembled the last. Vivien was fed by tubes and given daily ice baths and was mummified in damp sheets to keep her nervous system sedated. Had the nurses recognised their famous patient? Did they care? Vivien did not know. They unwrapped her each morning, and plunged her into the deep bathtub, with a nurse on either side, holding her body in a dead man's float. Her body did not react to the icy water seeping into her ears, drowning her chin, the coldness reaching the back of her neck. At the Sacred Heart, she was made to undress in the dark and to wear a linen shift in the bath; weighed down by the water and confined to the tin tub, it had felt like a shroud.

Afterwards, the nurses placed her on a bed and wrapped her in towels, rolling her to and fro; her arms stuck to her sides and her legs were not as restricted but not exactly free. It was a pointless exercise, she was too far gone to put up a fight. And so it began again, the next day and the next. Every evening, a needle topped up the sedatives, and a nurse took her pulse.[24]

Two weeks later, Vivien opened her eyes and took in her surroundings. The stretch of white. White walls, white ceiling, bright lights. The doctor's white coat. The nurses' white hats. The white cups of tea. The whites of the doctor's eyes – not strained with pity but with scientific logic. The colour white was symbolic to Blanche DuBois; a filmy cover to hide her sins. She went for a walk and wondered why all the patients wandered aimlessly, looking out of the windows, with no hope of leaving. 'I thought I was in an asylum,'[25] she later said, unaware of the true nature of her stay.

A needle was administered and another wave of drowsiness swept her up in its darkness. When Vivien opened her eyes, she was not in the room she had been in before. The doctor was familiar, but the two nurses were not. Her jaw ached; an instrument, a block of some sort, had been shoved between her teeth. Two straps were holding her wrists in place; the same apparatus was applied to her ankles. A light hanging overhead was switched on, blinding her. Her temples were damp, where a metallic liquid had been applied. The doctor walked behind her; his white coat could be seen in her peripheral vision. Fear washed over her. A sharp jolt through her temples, slamming through her skull. Her body lifted off the bed. Again and again, until it was over. She was limp; a dead weight, left to be untied by the nurses, who talked to one another in medical jargon as if she did not exist. They held on to her as she convulsed. The final twitch told them it was over. They fixed her on to a hospital bed and wheeled her out of the room.

When the ECT was over and she came round, she decided she wanted to leave Netherne and demanded the staff to telephone Larry, to order him to come at once and take her home. 'Psychiatrists cause more trouble than any other people in the world,' she said. 'I don't believe in them.'[26]

There was no address for Larry; not even her parents were in the country and her teenage daughter, Suzanne, was in Paris. Her first husband, Leigh Holman, came and spoke to Dr Freudenberg, whom he trusted. She saw Leigh as a means to escape and tried to convince him that she was better and needed to go home. 'Maybe you can spirit me away some time,'[27] she once wrote to him early in their courtship. She hoped he could spirit her away once more.

The only alternative was to section her and Dr Freudenberg did not want to do that. So, Leigh, who continued to love her in spite of everything, convinced her to recuperate at University College Hospital at Gower Street in London.

At the new hospital, she managed to have something of a social life while confined to her bed. It was remarkable in itself that she convinced her visitors to make appointments for her from the outside world. Noël Coward sent daily gifts of flowers, powder and bottles of Dior scent. She asked Bumble Dawson, her old school friend and costume designer, to arrange for a beautician to come and pluck her eyebrows and use an epilator on her legs. The mood in the room changed as soon as Vivien asked about Larry. Those friends were her only sources to the outside world – an exclusive world – but they, despite their collective talents, could not tell a convincing lie. Privately, they thought Larry was a louse to leave her alone in the 'loony bin'[28] like that.

In reality, Larry wrestled with his guilt, but his reasons were justifiable, as he physically removed himself from the situation to process all that had taken place. In his mind, something terrible had happened to her, to them both, which he struggled to articulate, much less understand.

~~~❦~~~

The first time Vivien saw Larry was no accident but a carefully staged plan; she claimed it was serendipity which made their paths cross. No, she was the mistress of her own fate. Or, as some believed, an expert manipulator. At 18 – almost 19 – she had orchestrated her first marriage to Leigh Holman in a similar way when she stole him from her friend's sister, Dulcie Martin, to whom he was more or less engaged.

'That doesn't matter,' Vivien told her friend, Clare Martin, who reminded her that Leigh was otherwise taken. 'He hasn't seen me yet.'[29]

Vivien and Leigh were married on 20 December 1932 at the Catholic Church of St James in London in a service that was short and casual.[30] She had just turned 19 and her girlish face was framed by a Juliet cap. During the reception, she went to the bathroom, followed by her mother and bridesmaids, and took off her wedding ring to wash her hands. 'Bad luck!' a bridesmaid shrieked, foreseeing it as an omen of a broken marriage. Vivien herself had no sentimental attachment to the ring, bought from Mappin and Webb in Regent Street, which in her opinion was a decidedly unromantic place.

A few years later, Vivien possessed the same self-assurance when she declared she would marry Larry one day.

'Ridiculous. You're both married already,'[31] her friend reminded her.

'It doesn't matter. I'll still marry him one day,'[32] she replied.

She had spied Leigh at the Dartmouth Hunt Ball and first glimpsed Larry on the stage in *Theatre Royal* in 1934, the tickets bought from the money she earned from modelling for photographers. At 21, her star was slowly in ascent and she popped up in quota quickies – the studio's description for films shot in a few days on a low budget – as a decorative girl with a few lines. In the film *Things Are Looking Up*, she was initially cast as part of a crowd scene. The girls who had lines were known as 'special girls' and they earned extra money and had a studio car to take them home at night. 'I decided I wanted to be a special girl,'[33] she said, her eyes fixed firmly on the prize.

It was the stage that swept her away, despite her voice being too weak to fill the house. She had an agent, John Gliddon, who was half in love with her, and Sidney Carroll, the theatrical director, read her palm and convinced her to change her name from Vivian to Vivien; she adopted Leigh as a tribute to Leigh Holman. Her first stage role was Giusta in *The Green Sash*, which ran for two weeks at the Q Theatre, followed by an overnight success in *The Mask of Virtue* at the Ambassadors Theatre for which she was paid £10 a week to play Henriette Duquesnoy, a prostitute masquerading as a virgin. After her celebrity soared, she assured everyone, 'There *isn't* any change and there never *will* be.'[34] She had her first extramarital affair, with John Buckmaster, around that time, too.

At the Savoy Grill, she was formally introduced to Larry, as he dined with his wife, Jill Esmond, a stage actress from an important theatrical family. They were celebrating the news of Jill's pregnancy, but Vivien did not know it at the time. She sat with Buckmaster, far enough away to spy on Larry.

'Doesn't Larry look odd without his moustache?'[35] Buckmaster remarked.

Leaning forward in her chair, Vivien watched Larry's wife holding court with the patrons who stopped to greet them. She implored Buckmaster to introduce her to them – to Larry in particular. Buckmaster was not anyone special in her life; she was also having a casual fling with the film producer Alexander Korda, to advance her film career.

Buckmaster rose from his chair and walked to Larry and Jill. He pointed in Vivien's direction and waved for her to join them. They both congratulated Vivien on her performance in *The Mask of Virtue* and asked what she was going to do next. Nothing of importance, she said. *The Mask of Virtue* closed after twelve weeks and her career had stalled but she was memorising the script of *The Happy Hypocrite* and would play the part of Jenny Mere, a dancer who wore veils and chiffons, hooped earrings and bells on her wrists. For a time, Vivien adopted this look in the 1930s, wearing luxurious fabrics in dramatic colours and gold rings on almost every finger. 'The Little Gypsy', British *Vogue* called her in 1936.

Vivien's eagerness enchanted Larry; Jill merely smiled, perhaps nauseated from the scent of lobster being carried to and fro by the waiters. Vivien told Larry how realistic he was in his latest play, *Romeo and Juliet*, at the New Theatre and that she went to the matinee whenever she could. He invited her to call backstage and she did, going into his dressing room as he removed his makeup. She leant down and kissed him on the shoulder before leaving.

Smitten by her, Larry would later write, 'Apart from her looks, which were magical, she possessed beautiful poise.' He studied her appearance in the mirror and from their brief exchange, he noticed that her neck looked too fragile to support her head. But, to him, she had something else: 'an attraction of the most perturbing nature I had ever encountered.'[36]

In the hospital bed, Vivien was self-conscious. Her temples ached, she felt the raw skin where she had been singed by the ECT and her hair was burnt along her hairline. Later, as the ECT treatments became commonplace, she resorted to wearing wigs to disguise her hair loss. The beautician had not been in weeks, nor a single visitor from her theatrical orbit. A part of her was missing – she was certain of it. Like a puzzle, she tried to slot everything into place, to push the words from her brain into her mouth. In order to understand how she ended up at the hospital, she had to remember how she got there. Any rationale was lost; she only cared about Larry.

At first glance, the body in the bed meant nothing to Larry; there was no spark of familiarity. The pale face, marked by the ECT, and the colourless eyes were that of a stranger. A current of shock and fear surged through him but he could not express it. Everyone, including society, wanted him to be strong and to face the challenge head-on. There could be no platform to convey his feelings; everything within the confines of their marriage, and beyond, was to be buried from public view.

Above all else, they were to resume their lives as if nothing had occurred and her mental breakdown was to remain a secret. He would tell everyone that Vivien had to convalesce from tuberculosis, a dark shadow which had plagued her since the Second World War. To be afflicted by tuberculosis was far more respectable than mental illness: a consumptive was more socially acceptable than a lunatic. Even cancer, she said to the horror of others, was a clean, respectable illness.

As much as Larry lied to the outside world, he could not deceive himself. To outsiders, he still referred to her as Baba – their pet name for each other – and perhaps he could only speak of his love for her in a disengaged way. Not to her face. He realised that something terrible had happened, far beyond anything he could fix. She was no longer the girl he had fallen in love with. He loved her that much less.[37]

Chapter Four

'I am sure,
Though you can guess what temperance should be,
You know not what it is'

Antony and Cleopatra, William Shakespeare

❧

1953

The publicity machine had gone into overdrive, despite Larry's best efforts to mask Vivien's breakdown as a bout of tuberculosis and exhaustion. 'A star in eclipse,' journalist and writer Alan Dent wrote. 'Your lamp had been turned too high, but it has been skilfully and in good time turned down again by your devoted Larry.'[1]

In the present day, Vivien felt the role of Larry as her great protector was exaggerated. She had not forgiven him for leaving her in the hospital and going to Ischia. He tried, but failed, to make her understand it was the only way for Dr Freudenberg to treat her. It was the lesser of two evils. The other was being sectioned in America and with an enormous medical bill to pay. Meanwhile, in England, her treatment was covered by the National Health Service, something that surprised her friends and they thought it was mean of him. 'It's just that I hate waste,' he would say. 'Petty economy, not sensible economy, is my sin.'[2]

The ECT created vast gulfs in Vivien's brain and she struggled to remember what had taken place in Ceylon and Hollywood, nor could she sympathise with Larry's predicament and the burden she placed on him. It was a relief, at least for Larry, that she did not mention Peter Finch, with whom she remained enthralled. As with the Victorians who believed a camera would steal their souls, the treatments at Netherne had snatched the best parts of her. Ravaged by her spell of illness and with the fading ECT scars on her temples, it was difficult to recall John Betjeman's description of her as 'the essence of English girlhood'.

In recent years, there was anecdotal evidence to suggest Vivien lost parts of herself to the characters she played. Or perhaps the truth was she gained part of their identity in place of her own. Scarlett O'Hara, the Civil War heroine in *Gone with the Wind*, wasn't so much acting, it was a study of Vivien's haughtiness and ambition. And Blanche DuBois was a Southern belle looking for beauty in a sordid world, fighting to survive, and descending into madness. A child of the Raj, the faded grandeur of the American South struck a chord with Vivien: she could see something in those women that she, too, repressed. Those long days of filming, labouring under hot studio lights, and the immersion into the characters. Young Vivien and older Vivien: so convincing that she had won Academy Awards for both portrayals.

'When had Vivien first gone mad?' Larry might have asked himself. He recalled an episode in 1937, when they performed with the Old Vic in *Hamlet* at Kronborg Castle in Helsingør (Elsinore, as Shakespeare wrote), Denmark. It was tense for everyone involved; nobody wanted Vivien as Ophelia and they thought she was a weak actress with a poor track record. Her recent play, *Bats in the Belfry*, a comedy by Diana Morgan and Robert MacDermott concerning a meddling aunt, had passed without fanfare. The Old Vic Company felt the part of Ophelia should have gone to Jill Esmond, but Larry demanded Vivien be cast or the play was off. *Hamlet* was being performed for the Silver Jubilee of King Christian X of Denmark and the guest list was awash with aristocrats and minor royals from Europe. What could anyone do except let him have his own way? Interestingly, Lilian Baylis, the manager of the Old Vic, exerted control by stopping the clock in the courtyard of the castle, as she felt the striking interfered with the performance. Metaphors would come later.

Aside from the importance of the occasion, Jill accompanied Larry and the Old Vic, and Larry was torn between preserving his wife's dignity – if not her feelings – and tending to his mistress. Everyone knew of his affair with Vivien and most sided with Jill, who was still revered in the theatrical world: he was the louse who moved in her shadow. It was as stifling as a hothouse and the danger thrilled Vivien: she lured Larry into an inconsequential world of playing games and hoping to be caught in bed together. She continued to write to Leigh in London, calling him *darling* this and *darling* that, and made no mention of her little girl in the nursery. There was only Larry, in the here and now. 'Love,' she said, 'was an all-embracing and overpowering emotion.'[3]

Then one night, before a performance, the tension became too much and Vivien flew at Larry like a demon. A few moments later, she stopped and stared into space; the eruption was forgotten. She put on her makeup, dressed in Ophelia's costume, and went on stage and acted in the mad scene. He was too frightened to mention it, but it was etched in his mind. It would be several years before he saw violence such as that in 1937. 'Vivien was barking fucking mad from the word go,'[4] he later said, realising the clues were always there.

Only when she was in Hollywood filming *Gone with the Wind*, in 1939, would she have another erratic episode without the violence. By then they had both left their spouses and were, according to the morals of the day, living in sin. He had finished making *Wuthering Heights* with Merle Oberon, another dark beauty of Vivien's calibre and she was driven mad with jealousy. But there was a darker force at play, and when he left for New York to do *No Time for Comedy* on Broadway, she had a breakdown.

It's worth noting the strange appearance of June bugs,[5] sent in the post from fans in Georgia. They were sent to Vivien after she admitted, in a magazine interview to publicise *Gone with the Wind*, that she had no idea what they were. Regardless of her whimsy interviews, she was disenchanted by the publicity machine and her morale suffered at the hands of the picture's director, Victor Fleming, who worked her into the ground. Cue a plague of June bugs: some mounted on pins, some squashed, and some alive. They were symbolic: 'not only do they have great intuition but they are also grounded as they

bury themselves into the earth. If your life has somewhat been chaotic lately this is a sign from the universe telling you to work on
grounding yourself just like a June bug.'⁶ She released them into the
shrubbery at the bottom of her garden, much to the horror of the
California Agricultural Commission, who warned her of their capac-
ity for destruction.

One night, her secretary, a young Texan woman named Sunny
Alexander, found her in the living room, half dead from taking four
sleeping pills, staggering around naked and falling over the furniture.
She had tried to centre herself amid the chaos of her mind, and failed.
Tears streamed down her cheeks as she rambled incoherently about
Larry. Sunny dragged her to the bathroom and held her under a cold
shower. The following day, she apologised to Sunny for causing a fuss
and promised to never again take sleeping pills. In his own way, Larry
was touched by the extremity of her devotion and admonished her,
by letter, as one would a naughty child.

Larry could not relax until they reached Notley Abbey, the eleventh-
century manor house in Buckinghamshire he had bought in 1944. The
purchase and subsequent renovation – it was left in ruins after a bomb-
ing raid during the Blitz – had almost bankrupted them both during
the process. Surprisingly, given its dilapidated state, the frescoes painted
by monks on the beams in the attic were preserved. He planted lime
trees along the avenue and raised dairy cattle in the grounds; the farm-
ing venture was handled by his brother, Dickie, who would bring his
17-year-old bride, Hester, to live there. The dairy cows were named
after Vivien's characters: Sabina, Blanche, Juliet, Cleopatra, Anna
Karenina, and so forth. She had a folly, Vivien's Folly it was called;
an arrangement of cypress trees with a fountain in the middle. At her
most manic, she swore the trees were women dressed in ball gowns and
crinolines, swaying to music and bowing to greet her.

Vivien loved Notley but not as much as Larry did. She had a rose
garden and filled the rooms with bowls of white roses and burnt
Guerlain scent and hung dried lavender from the open fireplaces
which failed to heat the house. There were no framed photographs

in the rooms: 'We can't stand photographs of ourselves displayed in our home,'[7] she said in an interview.

The first winter she had spent there, during the war, saw her recuperating from tuberculosis and, later, a miscarriage. Every night she detected the rustling of a nun's habit and heard phantom footsteps outside her bedroom door. Larry refused to believe Notley was haunted; they lived in a world of make-believe, not the supernatural. Now, she would rest in the Blue Room, which had a view of the garden, and listen to the news on the wireless.

During Larry's time abroad, he received a mountain of bills from his dependants. 'My God, how can Eton possibly send up the fees?'[8] he said of his son's school fees. There was also a letter from his ex-wife's accountant, asking for an increase in her alimony payments of £3,500. He offered an increase of £450, but Jill's lawyers sent a court order demanding £750. Resentful of his financial ties to Jill, he did not consider the depth of their marriage to warrant such debts – his explanation was that they had only slept together seven times in total. Besides, she was a lesbian and living happily with a female companion, and he felt it was time for her to move on.

Vivien, too, had one foot in the past and another in the present. 'Who must I apologise to?'[9] she asked. It would become a familiar question in the aftermath of a manic episode. As she regained her clarity of thought, she would feel deeply ashamed of her behaviour and try to make it right.

His concerns were graver: in addition to his ex-wife's maintenance and son's school fees, Notley was haemorrhaging money and his accountants warned the bank would repossess it. Years earlier, in 1940, when he and Vivien had lost their savings on an American tour of *Romeo and Juliet*, their financial straits had seemed romantic, even comical in hindsight. At one point, they had $17 between them. At the time, however, it was anything but a joke and their confidence was destroyed by negative reviews, his more so than hers. The critics poked fun at his spindly legs padded beneath his tights and his protruding stomach and false nose, all wilting under the heat of a New York summer. Queues snaked around the 51st Street Theatre, formed of patrons demanding their money back and gangsters threatening the box office if it did not comply. One night, the audience laughed as Larry, drenched in sweat, was too exhausted to manoeuvre around Juliet's balcony. They lost $5,000 a week and, in the end, the play made a loss of $96,000.

How he envied Vivien, her mind understanding nothing of his problems and living only in the moment. In the present, she cared little about their financial hardship. She was apt to wander off in the direction of the library, calling after her cats. More than ever, he resented her. Everyone knew of her episode but none of their London friends believed him when he spoke of its severity. 'Poor darling, stuck in the loony bin,'[10] a friend said and blamed him entirely for her mental collapse. He tried to defend himself by saying that he, too, had suffered a breakdown in Ischia and a small notice was printed in the press: 'Sir Laurence Olivier ... is himself now close to the same illness on the Italian isle of Ischia. He is seeing nobody.'[11]

There were rumours of Vivien waking from her insulin coma and Larry being nowhere to be found. That was only part of the story. The fact was that Dr Freudenberg promised to keep her comatose for three weeks but brought her around a week early.

Regardless of who was in the right or wrong, there were more bills to pay. Dr Greenson and the nurse who tended to Vivien at Hanover Drive and accompanied them to England charged Larry $3,356 and he only realised, then, the nurse had a name: Doris Cotchefer. He refused to pay, saying that Nurse Cotchefer had been sent by Paramount and, therefore, the responsibility was theirs. It would mean more legal letters, more solicitor's fees to pay, and the risk of an exposé in an American newspaper. All in all, Vivien's breakdown had cost him more than his fee for *The Beggar's Opera*.

The next piece of news perplexed and pleased him in equal measure. He had succeeded in transferring Notley Abbey to Laurence Olivier Productions, allowing him and Vivien to remain there as employees of the company. Now they really did live on a set.

⟪⟫

In the autumn of 1953, Vivien and Larry began rehearsing for *The Sleeping Prince*, a play set in the Edwardian era and written by Terence Rattigan to coincide with the coronation of Queen Elizabeth II. A few months prior, Vivien watched the coronation of the young queen on television, listening to Larry's narration over the ceremony. Larry had pre-recorded it in May – an easy task, as the coronation's rituals were known in advance and so he, and they, kept to the script. Perhaps that was where Vivien had gone wrong: she veered from their invisible script for living and nobody, not least her husband, knew what to do. Rumours of a divorce were being printed in the newspapers and both were quick to deny it, stating they were happy together, even if they did not believe it themselves.

In the play, Vivien was Mary Morgan, a plucky showgirl from Brooklyn, and Larry was Prince Charles of Carpathia, the Prince Regent of a fictional Balkan country. They both knew it was frivolous and he felt it was beneath him but they needed the money and, more than ever, the prestige. Her dressing room was filled with flowers, enormous wreaths and posies from fans – an overwhelming sight, it seemed as if she were lying in state instead of partaking in a first night.

They had appeared in superficial productions before, capitalising on their love story. Before they were married, they starred in *21 Days* in 1937, a picture directed by Basil Dean and so terrible it was not released until 1940, after they had become Hollywood stars. 'Oh, we just don't mention it!'[12] Vivien later said. A scathing review in *The New York Times* wrote, among other things, that 'Miss Leigh, as the party of the second part, is required to devote her charm and talents to nothing more constructive than making the apparently inevitable parting from poor Mr Olivier seem exceedingly painful, indeed'.[13] Only they knew of the tension that existed behind the camera lens: the tormented look in their eyes was the result of the consequences of their affair and the uncertainty of their future. 'I wish we could go on forever,' her character, Wanda, said. 'Forever's a long time,'[14] his character, aptly named Larry, replied.

Likewise, their past work mirrored social events; they had acted in propaganda pieces before, namely Jean Anouilh's *Antigone*, adapted from Sophocles' classic Greek tragedy, with Vivien in the titular role and Larry producing and playing the part of Chorus. Although staged in 1949, Anouilh's modern retelling corresponded with the British war effort and its resistance against Nazism and enemy threats, still the mindset of post-war Britain. Four years later, it would seem Larry had developed a phobia of her appearing in bleak tragedies, knowing, more than anyone, the depths she could plunge to.

In *The Sleeping Prince*, when Vivien and Larry first walked on stage as Mary Morgan and Prince Charles, the audience broke into cheers and the *Daily Express* noted, 'The phenomenal kitten is back ... Sir Laurence Olivier is a minor stage prop.' From the stalls at the Phoenix Theatre, Kenneth Tynan loomed with his poison pen, ready to plant a dart in Vivien. She had first met Tynan at a party a few years earlier and noticed he stood off to the side, observing the revellers. Mistaking his reluctance as shyness, she and Larry offered him a lift home to his flat in Hyde Park Gardens. 'He didn't want to be too pally,'[15] Larry said of their first meeting with Tynan.

Nevertheless, she was terrified of Tynan, a gangly figure from Fleet Street who had a fetish for her husband's talent and resented her for, as he viewed it, getting in the way. 'Vivien was an interloper between myself and my fucking genius,'[16] Larry said of Tynan's attitude towards her. Tynan looked down on Vivien's skills as a stage actress and this time, in a review for *The Daily Sketch*, he mocked them both:

> Once upon a time there was an actor called gruff Laurence Olivier, whose wife was an actress called pert Vivien Leigh, and a playwright called clever Terence Rattigan wrote a play for them, called *The Sleeping Prince*, with a gruff part for him and a pert part for her, and to nobody's surprise it ran happily ever after, with twice-weekly matinées.

Larry was irritated by the uncharacteristic criticism of his acting but he tolerated it, as he thought Tynan represented the younger generation of playwrights and theatre-goers, and by associating with him, he would be 'on the side of thinking people'.[17]

Although buoyed by the comeback, Vivien began to feel like Larry's charity case and guilt consumed her. 'His stricken lady', Tynan called her, a dig at the 'burden' she had become to Larry. 'I always used to worry so much when I acted with Larry in case I let him down. He is a genius you see, and I didn't think I could keep up with him and so it was a strain,'[18] she said. She would carry that inferiority complex, always.

Only two years before, Vivien and Larry appeared together in the West End and on Broadway in alternative productions of George Bernard Shaw's *Caesar and Cleopatra* and William Shakespeare's *Antony and Cleopatra*. She was in her dressing room at the Ziegfeld Theatre in New York, listening to the radio, when she heard she had won the Academy Award for *A Streetcar Named Desire* and he took her in his arms and kissed her. They were on the cover of *Life* magazine and in the photograph she gazed adoringly at him, befitting Caesar's appraisal, 'They will know Cleopatra by her pride, her courage, her majesty, her beauty ...'[19]

Larry remembered the period differently: she became paranoid about their social status, of missing parties, and was worried the newspapers would report on it. The press called her portrayal of Cleopatra 'smouldering and sensual, wily and treacherous ... and when destiny turns against her she does not go down whimpering but with pride and glory, looking grand in her regal vestments, looking cool, grave and triumphant'.[20] Those words did not resonate with Larry and their predicament. In the evenings, he found her in the horrible grey bedroom he loathed so much, huddled into the corner of their bed, sobbing and wringing her hands. She was inconsolable. After several episodes, he took her to a psychiatrist, which only heightened her hysteria, and she feared the presence of photographers catching her comings and goings.

They were going through the motions during *The Sleeping Prince*, a hit for them both, but Larry was thinking of other projects worthy of his talent. From the 'gods', she looked like an impish girl, but up close, in her mirror lit by industrial lights, the glare of age was catching up with her. Deep lines formed around her mouth and eyes – she had become, what Noël Coward called, 'papery'.[21]

She knew the gentle pace of the play was deliberate: he was terrified she would break down again. From the wings, her young understudy, Greta Watson, chosen by Larry and paid £5 a week, watched her every move. Perhaps Miss Watson had jinxed her; five minutes after the curtain call, Vivien fell and broke her left wrist in two places, giving the ingenue her big chance before the footlights. But not for long. Vivien returned with a sling fashioned from a silk scarf and the show went on. 'You have to be so terribly strong to be an actor,' she once joked. 'Why, I had to have my neck untwisted by a masseuse every week.'[22]

One night, Peter and Tamara Finch came to a performance and visited Vivien and Larry backstage. Why, given all that had taken place in California? Peter would claim it was the 'done thing' and Tamara reluctantly followed him, knowing too well that Peter owed his career to Larry. They could not bite the hand that fed them – an idiom they kept to when there seemed to be no way of cutting all ties. Peter hastily greeted Vivien and moved on to the supporting cast, leaving her with Tamara. The two women came face to face after Vivien's spectacular breakdown.

'I feel very sorry for you,'[23] Vivien said. She pulled Tamara by the arm and introduced her to the cast. 'I want you all to meet the most courageous girl I know. She has just had an operation on her nose to try and look more glamorous. I think she is wonderful.'[24]

Far from a dismal apology for her behaviour in Ceylon and Hollywood, Vivien was forewarning Tamara of a defeat. In recent days, however, Peter had been busy filming *Make Me an Offer* and Vivien was restricted to her drawing-room comedy, which ran for 274 performances. The monotony was killing her and she missed the danger of losing herself to a character, of immersing herself entirely in a new world. There had been no artistic fulfilment since her portrayal of Blanche DuBois.

Vivien first became interested in Tennessee Williams's play, *A Streetcar Named Desire*, as early as 1948, which had opened on Broadway in 1947 and was directed by Elia Kazan. It centred around Blanche DuBois, a fading Southern belle who seeks refuge with her sister Stella and her chauvinistic husband, Stanley Kowalski, only to find herself falling into the depths of despair having lost her family home, Belle Reeve, and turning to prostitution to survive. Blanche's nerves were tested by the Kowalskis' rough living conditions in the neighbourhood, Elysian Fields, and the torturous abuse she endures from Stanley, who succeeds in breaking her spirit when he rapes her.

The role of Blanche was to offer Vivien a career milestone; a real challenge as an English actress to lay bare her soul on stage – the part was carnal and the most shocking to date. She wanted to push herself as hard as she could, to be seen as something more than Scarlett O'Hara and the haughty girls she had played before. Larry agreed with her sentiments and she asked him to direct the British production.

'You're mad to try it,'[25] friends warned her. The explicit themes of sex and domestic violence were far from her repertoire.

'But Blanche is such a real part, the truth about a woman with everything stripped away,' Vivien argued. 'She is a tragic figure and I understand her.'[26]

They came up against the English censor and the Lord Chamberlain ordered certain parts to be changed: the suggestion that Blanche's young husband was homosexual had to be toned down and the 'Christ' profanities were changed to 'God'. There was also a warning that no undressing should occur on stage, so Vivien moved around in a slip.

'English people perhaps are so sexually repressed that the play may have brought out the worst in them,'[27] Vivien said. It was true: when her biopic on Emma Hamilton, *That Hamilton Woman*, was released in 1941, *The Observer* wrote, 'These are not days when we have much patience for looking at history through the eyes of a trollop.'

The rehearsals for *A Streetcar Named Desire* were rough and Larry manhandled Vivien throughout, trailing her to and fro, and shouting at her to dig deeper within the crevices of her psyche. It was part of their game: she would say she needed brute force to drag the performance out of her. For the part of Blanche DuBois, she spoke in a Mississippi accent and dyed her hair blonde, which washed out her pale complexion and gave her the haggard look she wanted. In her everyday world, she wore a plain black dress and the celestial belt she had worn when she signed her contract for *Gone with the Wind*. On the stage, her slips and flimsy costumes emphasised more than Blanche's prostitution; she wanted to portray her as moth-like, flitting from darkness to light and perishing in the process.

Night after night, the Aldwych Theatre was packed with an audience thriving on the sex and sensationalism of the plot. It did nothing to silence the puritans who compared the show to that of the Windmill Theatre, where its patrons wore flasher coats and went solely for the nude girls. They cheered when Stanley hammered Blanche and raped her, lapping up what they viewed as something sordid instead of harrowing; a public execution rather than a tragedy. She continued trembling after the curtain fell. It was not a portrayal, it was an exorcism. 'I feel as if I'd been bulldozed and can't believe I have to go through it every night,'[28] she wrote to Leigh Holman.

Instead of going home, she went for late-night wanderings through Piccadilly. In the guise of Blanche, she befriended the young prostitutes plying their trade, talking to them in a Mississippi drawl and hoping they viewed her as one of them. Their expressions, their body language as they eyed a punter, and the glimmers of shame and vulnerability made an impression on her.

She had played a prostitute in *Waterloo Bridge* in 1940, a picture directed by Mervyn LeRoy about a ballerina, Myra, who believes her fiancé, Roy, played by Robert Taylor, is dead. Myra is forced into prostitution to make ends meet and subsequently takes her own life. The Motion Picture Production Code sanitised the topic of prostitution and, as a remedy to her immorality, Myra kills herself on Waterloo Bridge. A nod to the title: the bridge was reputed to be the last stop on the road for socially unassimilated women.[29] Blanche DuBois was different: there was no end to her suffering, nor Vivien's.

After nine months of playing Blanche on stage, Vivien resurrected her on screen for Warner Brothers, directed by Elia Kazan, and was paid $100,000 for the privilege. It had been a decade since she last acted in a Hollywood production and the press were not kind when she stepped off the plane into the glare of the flashbulbs. 'The picture was to show off a cute hat she was wearing. Actually, it showed up cruelly a distinct flabby chin and tired lines around her eyes,'[30] they wrote. She was 37, not an ingenue but not a crone either. Already the callousness of the tabloids and the artifice of the publicity machine were testing her nerves.

Larry followed her to California to star in *Carrie*, directed by William Wyler, which became a box-office flop. He was accompanied by Suzanne, Vivien's estranged daughter with whom she never had an easy relationship. Suzanne was almost 17 and old enough to resent the decision her mother had made in leaving her to pursue an affair with Larry. Still, they had spent a few holidays together in the company of others but never really connected as mother and daughter. They were so different, physically: Suzanne with her father's fair hair and features, but with Vivien's little nose and petite frame. Attempting to forge a maternal connection, Suzanne announced her plans to become an actress and enrolled at RADA, as Vivien had done before becoming pregnant in early 1933.

In the evenings, at their rented home in Coldwater Canyon, California, Suzanne observed Vivien strung out from having played Blanche all day. 'Now she's in command of me,' Vivien said of the character, and the possession. Suzanne felt pity for her mother but not quite sympathy; she was tired of the Hollywood set eyeing her with curiosity, loudly remarking that her homely looks were so unlike Vivien's. Perhaps Vivien enjoyed it; she was the belle of the ball wherever she went, even for an ageing actress with lines on her face.

The time spent filming *A Streetcar Named Desire* on location in the French Quarter in New Orleans was something of a spiritual awakening for Vivien and she was living as Blanche in her natural habitat. Or, rather, in a place that seemed to be suspended from Vivien's reality and, therefore, connected her to Blanche. The Crescent City was like none other, with its macabre practices of voodoo and the violence of segregation in areas such as Bourbon Street.

In a way, Blanche is connected to the supernatural. There is her casual interest in astrology, more so in the stage adaptation of *A Streetcar Named Desire*, when she asks Stanley what star sign he was born under and summarises his personality traits. Blanche reveals that she was born under Virgo, the virgin, though nobody is convinced of her purity of mind, body or soul. Stargazing is a passing hobby for Blanche and she looks for the Pleiades, also known as the Seven Sisters, and references a place called Moon Lake Casino. There is also her repetitive singing of the popular song, 'It's Only a Paper Moon', the tone changing as her circumstances close in on her. This, of course, might quietly point to the lunar effect or, to put it bluntly, Blanche's madness.

One day on the set, Marlon Brando, who played Stanley Kowalski in the Broadway production and in the picture, asked her, 'Why are you so polite?' There was hostility between Vivien and several members of the supporting cast, who were together on Broadway and felt Jessica Tandy, the original Blanche, deserved to reprise her part on screen.

'I believe in good manners at all times. It's terribly important,'[31] Vivien said, drawing on a cigarette and observing him intently.

She received letters from Larry, who was miserable on the Paramount sound stage, filming *Carrie* with Jennifer Jones. To Vivien, he called Jones degrading names pertaining to the female anatomy and reiterated his original stance, that screen actors were 'dumb animals'.[32] When he had filmed *Wuthering Heights* for Wyler in 1938 he had shared a similar animosity with his leading lady, Merle Oberon, and spat on her while reciting his lines.

Holding Larry's daily letter in her hand, Vivien closed her eyes and listened to Brando looming closer, imitating her husband's monologues from *Henry V*. 'You never know what he's going to do next, where he's going to be or what he's going to say,'[33] she complained about Brando at the beginning of rehearsals. One day he came to the set and proudly announced he had chlamydia. Now, she was intrigued by his crooked nose, broken during a sparring match with a member of the crew between the acts of *Streetcar* on Broadway, and the pet racoon on his shoulder. At that moment, he was Stanley and she was Blanche.

On her return from New Orleans, Vivien seemed more tranquil than before, but Larry realised it was the calm before the storm and the metaphorical sand timer of sanity was running out. She professed a fondness for eating avocados and going square dancing,[34] though God knows how the two were interrelated. 'Square dancing seems the best possible way to get exercise,'[35] she remarked. To appease the publicity machine, she judged the Duke University Chanticleer Beauty Queen competition, selecting a photograph of Miss Love Lindsey as the winner.[36] It was all so wholesome, for the time being, at least.

In the garden at Coldwater Canyon, a tarantula crept across the lawn and was bottled up and removed by Larry, who released it far away from home.[37] A believer in omens, she knew the tarantula was the oracle of fate, misfortune and even death. Given how things petered out, she was not wrong.

They returned to England, without Suzanne, on a French tramp steamer. There were three other passengers on board the small freighter, which took a month to reach Tilbury docks. The seafarers were listless, it was hardly the second honeymoon Vivien had envisioned. If Larry had thrown himself into the part of a sailor, he might have reached for a sunstone and held it to the overcast sky, searching for her light. He felt claustrophobic due to the confines of the vessel and his expectations of Vivien's moods: would she be high or low or indifferent to the point of emptiness? There seemed to be no in-between. Instead, his greatest fear was the realisation that, aside from their work and his keeping tabs on her behaviour, they had nothing to talk about. Their marriage was dead; Vivien, the girl he had fallen in love with, ceased to exist. Suicide crossed his mind, but it was his theatrical way of thinking. A melodramatic ending, hurling himself from the ship's rails into the dark Atlantic as it raged beneath him. All that needed to be said remained unspoken:

He: 'Our lives together had been supported ... by the glitter of our position.'[38]

She: 'Sometimes I dread the truth of the lines I say. But the dread must never show.'[39]

Chapter Five

'Words, Words, Words'

Hamlet, William Shakespeare

⚜

1954

Vivien and Larry reached a point in their relationship where their lives together revolved around work and nothing more. At home, Vivien gave parties and surrounded herself with people as if to avoid being alone with Larry. Or perhaps it was the other way around: Larry brought associates – producers, investors and their ilk – to Notley and threw them into the ring, expecting Vivien to entertain them. And she did. He immersed himself in projects, looking for a familiar spark of excitement that was often lacking in his latest endeavours. They were drifting ...

In the summer of 1954, they went to San Vigilio and kept up appearances for the paparazzi, who snapped Vivien in her enormous white sunglasses, driving Larry in a convertible, and sailing on Lake Garda. Outside her natural habitat of the theatre, there was something prim about her appearance, more so when she spoke conversational Italian with an English accent. In a photograph, she wrapped her arms around him and turned her face to his, but he looked straight ahead, smiling at the camera, to the voyeurs who believed in the myth of the Oliviers in love.

What bonded them together in the first place? It had been nineteen years since they first met, albeit platonically in the beginning; she stalked him from the stalls and he was flattered by the heroic part she had cast him in. She was always the more exciting of the two; the one who lived on the edge and was tempted by danger. In a lucid moment, she asked him how they could ever be happy when the foundation of their happiness was built on the misery of others. For that, he gave no answer, nor did he care to accept any morsel of responsibility for the pain he had caused.

When their affair began in 1936, Larry was not the sexual swordsman his matinee image portrayed him to be, but he was under Vivien's spell and enraptured by whatever dimension she had taken him to. There would be no return. He had insignificant affairs before Vivien with the actresses Peggy Ashcroft, Ann Todd and Greer Garson. And whispers of homosexuality followed him throughout his schooldays and career, notably an on-and-off flirtation with Denys Blakelock, an actor six years his senior and the son of a clergyman. Henry Ainley was another would-be paramour who sent him explicit letters and he responded, enjoying the idea of a homosexual affair – his sadistic side liked pushing people to the brink for his own amusement – but he was already involved with Vivien.

Jill knew of such temptations or 'devilments', as she called them, and she herself dodged rumours of lesbianism for years. 'I thought I could cure her,'[1] Larry later said of Jill's sexuality. They were virgins when they met and, after their marriage, their clumsy attempts at passion were few and far between. After Jill became pregnant, the low, flickering flame had well and truly burnt out.

In a way, his ambition to wed lent itself to cruelty, for he did not find Jill attractive but decided, after their first meeting during a rehearsal for *Bird in Hand*, that she would do. Jill, in turn, was capable of wounding him and three weeks before their wedding, in 1930, admitted she was in love with somebody else but would marry him anyway. 'I was dying to get married so that I might, with the blessing of God, enjoy sex, the thought of which was beginning to obsess me unremittingly,'[2] Larry said, upon reflection. In those days, he was religious and afraid of his father (known as Fahv), the Rev. Gerard Kerr

Olivier, a high Anglican priest in charge of St Gabriel's in Dorking. After his marriage to Jill, he lost his religion, and his morals.

For Vivien, there was no mystery when it came to sex and she was guided by her instincts rather than her morals. At the age of 17, she shocked her mother Gertrude when she confided she had two boyfriends, both of whom she had promised to marry, and then over lunch she kissed a German waiter. *'Du verdienst es geküsst zu werden,'*[3] she said, giving him fair warning. Gertrude slapped her across the face.

It was hypocritical of Gertrude, for, despite being a devoted Catholic, she was involved with a family friend named Tommy (born John Lambert Thompson) until his death in 1938. The difference was, Gertrude was not the first to break her marital vows – that responsibility lay with her husband, Ernest, who had once loved her so much he resigned from the Bengal Club. His resignation was a way of renouncing his social status,[4] as the club prohibited its Caucasian members from having wives of a different race. As with all good families, and indeed good Catholics, Gertrude and Ernest remained married in name only and his affairs continued until he died in 1959.

Perhaps too much emphasis was placed on the kissing incident and the adolescent crushes Vivien had formed during her time at convent schools in Paris, Biarritz, Sanremo and the Bavarian Alps. In Paris, she attended the opera with a school friend and their chaperone and sneaked to the lavatory to put on lipstick and powder, a scandalous thing to do. Her act of rebellion was considered 'fast', a label affixed to immoral women in the 1920s. Nevertheless, she denounced promiscuity and told friends she was waiting for the 'real thing'. In confession, however, she listed her sinful thoughts and deeds – she had read *Lady Chatterley's Lover* – and peered between the grill at the priest, delighted by his discomfort.

Was Vivien a fantasist or merely prophesying her future? Gertrude, who lacked a sense of humour, always found her unreasonable and difficult to manage and long into adulthood she scolded her: 'Now, miss, you mind your manners.'[5] But Gertrude was nobody's fool, she was a headstrong woman, who saved her family from financial ruin and founded beauty academies, the Academy of Beauty Culture, with its headquarters on Dover Street in London. If Vivien could be impulsive and, at times, thoughtless, then Gertrude could be calculating and cruel. A pursuer of perfection, Gertrude warned, 'One cannot help getting old, but one can help getting old and ugly.'[6] And, she added, 'Going to bed with a greasy face ought to be grounds for a divorce. It's horrible, most unattractive and quite useless.'[7]

All her life, Vivien subconsciously heard the critical voice of Gertrude and tried to be picture-perfect. It was not enough. Gertrude wanted her child's mind to be as impressive as her beauty and would play Kim's Game with her, a memory exercise used by British Intelligence and the military. At bedtime, Gertrude arranged objects in a pattern on a tray, then removed them, and had Vivien recreate the pattern in the morning.[8] All through the night, her little brain ticked over with images of the pattern, a snapshot that became a photographic memory, but it did nothing to control her impulses.

There was an incident in India, when Gertrude told the story of Daniel in the lion's den to a group of children, and Vivien crawled along the floor and bit her on the leg. The high spirits – then described as being naughty – and the crashing melancholy were heightened after Vivien, as she called it, entered 'womanliness', around the age of 14. Not enough understanding was, or is, given to the changing brains of adolescent girls and, in those days, an equal amount of neglect was placed on women's health as they progressed towards menopause. Around that time, Gertrude was having injections of homoserine before a gynaecological operation, which, reading between the lines, was a hysterectomy.

The disturbing thing about Vivien was that she could appear helpless, and yet, like her mother, came to possess a cruel streak. It was different for men. 'Ah, well, all men are pigs,'[9] Larry said, justifying his lustful shortcomings. The physical side of Vivien and Larry's affair reached its height during *Fire Over England*, an Elizabethan melodrama filmed in 1936. After being in the arms of Vivien before the camera and behind the scenes, he went home to Jill who was heavily pregnant and 'looking her worst',[10] with a blotchy complexion and varicose veins. The excitement sustained Vivien: she filmed during the day and at night performed as Anne Boleyn in *Henry VIII* in the open-air theatre at Regent's Park; her voice was muffled by torrential rain and she had to shelter under an Ulster (a caped overcoat) between acts.

They were three weeks into filming *Fire Over England* when Jill went into labour. After fourteen hours, a son, Tarquin, was born, and both almost died in the process. Exhausted as Jill was, she detected Vivien's scent on Larry's clothes and a smudge of lipstick on his face, but she said nothing.

The following day, Larry brought Vivien to visit the baby. In that moment, Jill felt defeated and succumbed to the situation that was bigger than all of them put together. Real passion, she realised, was a force to be reckoned with. 'If you are ever hit by it, God help you,' Jill said. 'There is nothing you can do.'[11] Having gone through the physical transformation of pregnancy and the pain of childbirth herself, Vivien was alarmingly cold to Jill's situation. She declared the newborn baby, bruised from its delivery, as enormous.

Where was Leigh Holman in all of this? He was often away sailing in the Baltic or at his chambers at Middle Temple but could never forget his responsibilities and his moral compass would always guide him home. Some considered him an unsuccessful barrister – his heart was not in it – and his first ambition was to be an athlete, but he suppressed those dreams to follow his father and brothers into law. At weekends, he could be found in his friends' country gardens, digging trenches and planting shrubs, and his skills included carpentry. He taught Vivien how to drive a car and their joint interests extended to fine art and antique furniture. In the early days of their marriage, she was dependent on Leigh and sought his validation. The clinginess, in hindsight, might have been the first sign of mental illness, as women suffer from bouts of depression before mania sets in.

All Leigh wanted from Vivien was loyalty and discretion. He was no fool, nor was he a passive bystander during her infatuation with Larry, when both couples met in drawing rooms across Mayfair. Leigh and Jill, the two would-be injured parties, made small talk while Vivien and Larry only had eyes for each other.

As with so many of his generation, Leigh quietly carried the grief of losing his brother, Paul, from a stray bullet in the First Battle of Ypres. Later, in 1934, his sister, Hester, was fatally thrown from her horse while out hacking with him. In between losing his siblings, his beloved mother, Sophia, died shortly after his marriage to Vivien. Some might have portrayed him as a philistine with no knowledge of Vivien's artistic world – Larry considered him a bore, at first – but that was not true. As the youngest of six children, Leigh's older siblings were talented and independent: his brother, Paul, had been an amateur operatic performer at Cambridge before taking the bar, and his sister, Hester, had studied at the Slade School of Fine Art, and another, Dorothy, worked as a Red Cross nurse in Egypt during the First World War.

Ironically, for all Vivien's single-mindedness, she absorbed the personality traits of those she loved or wanted to impress. With Leigh, a Devon man, she proclaimed to be a country girl interested in England's green and pleasant land, and followed him to his home in Holcombe Down, in Teignmouth, purchased by his late father in 1898. How did she appear to his headstrong mother, who was in poor health, and his intelligent sisters, a generation above her? Her foreign birth and schooling abroad might have impressed them or did they detect her longing for stability, found only through marriage to an older man? She charmed them instantly and made a friend of Dorothy, who would follow her career with interest and collect mementoes of her stardom.

At the time, Vivien was living in the countryside with her father, Ernest, in a cottage belonging to the Mills family, while Gertrude stayed with Tommy in Biarritz. The family's finances were depleted and they could not afford to launch Vivien into society or give her a coming-out party, as they had no permanent address or the means to support it. A nomadic life might have seemed bohemian to the Holman women, who lived between Lancaster Gate in London and their country retreat in Devon.

For Leigh, the appeal must have lay in Vivien's unconventionality – she had no memory of the First World War nor had she been affected by it – and the social mores of his bourgeois background meant nothing to her. He was of the lost generation of men, too young to fight but old enough to feel the loss of their brothers and fathers who were killed on the battlefields in France. When the German Zeppelins were flying over England, Vivien was a toddler in Ootacamund while her father trained horses for the Indian Calvary in Bangalore.

Born under the sign of Scorpio, Vivien's chameleon-like qualities were second nature to her. So much was true when, after she met

Larry, she began using explicit language – until then, 'damn' was her favourite expletive – and shocked everyone when she punctuated her speech with four-lettered words. 'Oh, fuck,' she said one day, surprising everyone, including Leigh. The first tell-tale sign was in that exclamation, but not everyone took heed.

In Leigh's absence, Larry took Vivien to the ballet and tended to her while she recovered from a sore throat. Two months later, Vivien showed her prowess as an adulteress and followed Larry and Jill to Capri with the motive to take him from his wife. Jealousy was consuming her and she roped Leigh's friend and fellow barrister, Oswald Frewen, into accompanying her in the guise of a chaperone. They descended on the island, checking into the Hotel Quisisana for two nights, where the Oliviers resided and, adding to the farce, they took an adjoining room and each party came and went as they liked without locking doors or knocking before entering.

Amid the surprised chatter and friendly kisses, Jill sensed Vivien's determination as she greeted Larry and wrapped her limbs around him. They were children of the theatre: they had no inhibitions. They were hiding in plain sight. Even then, there was something forbidden about Capri – 'the homosexual paradise'[12] of the 1930s – and the spectacle of lovers living openly was sophisticated, unlike in England, where such things were a scandal and accepted only within the close-knit theatrical circles.

They went boating and swam in the Tyrrhenian Sea. Vivien's handbag fell into the water and Larry dived off the boat to retrieve it. The scent of mimosa, bergamot and bitter fruit trees hung in the air as they explored Mount Solaro and looked through binoculars at the Bay of Naples. Oswald snapped a photo of the trio, their pale skin scorched from the Neapolitan sun; Vivien, wasp-waisted in slacks, turned her body to Larry, who was equally receptive to her as he held on to Jill. Two days later, Vivien was in Rome and sobbed when Larry telephoned her from Naples, with the news that he wanted to send Jill back to London and have Vivien join him in Capri. His mad, impulsive plan was quickly forgotten and Vivien sobbed all the more, knowing how tempting it would have been to throw caution to the wind.

In London, Vivien was confronted by Jill who called at her home in Little Stanhope Street, Mayfair. The tiny house, in a Queen Anne style, had once been inhabited by Lynn Fontanne and Vivien thought it was a good omen for her stage career and asked Leigh to buy it. The minuscule rooms were filled with chintz fabrics and antiques, and Jill was overwhelmed by the intense energy of Vivien, which consumed every corner of the space. Vivien was drenched in Joy, the scent all the more potent in the small space, where burning sticks of incense also wafted through the air. She had a phobia that, for some inexplicable reason, her natural odour might offend others and so she moved in a perfumed haze as heavy as a storm cloud. Little Suzanne was out with her nanny and a housekeeper lurked nearby. There was a sense of orderliness in the doll's house and Vivien, as fine as a Dresden figurine, sat crossed-legged, glaring at Jill, who was swollen and nervous.

The plan was for Jill to crush her competitor but she found herself succumbing to Vivien's spell. Or was it a curse? Vivien disarmed Jill by asking about the intricate details of Tarquin's birth and how the baby was feeding. Overcome by emotion, Jill confessed she felt like a failure: she did not produce enough milk and had to give her baby a bottle.

'Not as much a failure as me,'[13] Vivien pointed to her bust and accused Suzanne of ruining her figure, shuddering at the idea of pregnancy and childbirth. Besides, she barely saw her child and entrusted her to a nanny, a disciplinarian called Oake, who complained about her charge's behaviour. 'Silly bitch,' Vivien had called the nanny and said it was her own fault for spoiling Suzanne.

The christening provided further pain for Jill when Larry rushed to Chelsea Old Church, having come straight from Vivien's bed. His dishevelled appearance gave him away and everyone pretended otherwise, except for his mother-in-law, Eva, who glared at him. In the photographs, Larry looked proud of the son he had sired even if he had no real interest in fatherhood, and Jill, moon-faced and exhausted, smiled through the pain. She had since developed a bond, or dependence, that was lacking when they first married and might have regretted her early appraisal of matrimony: 'Marriage, if it is to be better than slavery, must mean perfect freedom of thought and action on both parties.'[14]

Later that day, Larry brought Vivien to the christening party and she stood next to him, wearing trousers and a red sweater, having come straight from the studio, where she was filming *Storm in a Tea Cup*, a comedy with Rex Harrison, who was in love with her. Standing off to the side, she refused to mingle with the guests and soon left with Larry. He returned without her and everyone saw the traces of her lipstick on his face.

It was no good: they could no longer live a lie and so Vivien and Larry confessed to their spouses that they were in love and had been for almost two years. 'I was only half alive before I met Vivien,'[15] Larry told Jill.

Leigh, in particular, took the news badly; part of him wondered if it was a cruel joke or the dialogue from a script she was learning. He had taught her to play Call My Bluff,[16] a game in which the players (she and him) shared two true statements and one lie about themselves and in the end, each had to figure out which was the fib. Everything she said was true and he implored her to think of their child, to reconsider her plan to elope with Larry.

'But you wouldn't give up your baby, would you?'[17] her friends asked.

'No, not exactly, but she's more with her nurse than with me,'[18] she answered.

When the day of reckoning came, Leigh went to his chambers and Jill travelled to the south of France; neither could face the finality of it. Personal feelings aside, the shame and stigma of a broken home would be a blot on their families, especially their offsprings' childhoods. Gertrude over-compensated for her wayward daughter and became the only mother figure Suzanne would know. Vivien wanted Leigh to understand that she tried to resist hurting him and had packed her bags before, but Oswald Frewen talked her out of it. In a rare moment of temper, Leigh destroyed her final letter to him.

After endless discussions and pleas from Leigh, Vivien could not be persuaded otherwise and packed up her things while the house was empty. Her dressing gown was left on a hook behind their bedroom door and Leigh kept it there, telling her she could come home when her fixation with Larry ended. It pushed her further away from him and everyone who told her it was just a phase: marriage was forever.

Vivien and Larry were to live together at Durham Cottage, a house tucked behind a high wall off Christchurch Street in Chelsea. The transition was not easy for her and she lived with the insecurity that

Larry would leave her for somebody else, or, worse yet, return to Jill. And so, she began to shower him with affection, building him up as a man and actor and making him feel invincible. His presence on set, when she was doing *St Martin's Lane* with Charles Laughton, distracted her to the point of unprofessionalism and during the close-ups, Laughton fed her her lines. The moment the director, Tim Whelan, called 'cut', she and Larry would escape to her dressing room and someone would be sent to find her. Perhaps he felt overwhelmed, for he complained to a friend that Vivien was wearing him out, having demanded sex four times a day. Or was he boasting of her eagerness to please him?

Her greatest insecurities were realised when Larry sailed on the *Normandie* to America on the day of her twenty-fifth birthday. She saw him off on the boat-train at Waterloo Station and cried all the way home. Two days later, she received a telegram from him, asking her to plant daffodils on the lawn at Durham Cottage. Of course, he was as devastated by their parting as she was but the spoils of film stardom were too tempting to ignore. They had, since eloping, squandered their joint income and owed a small fortune in tax to the Inland Revenue. 'We'll only be separated a little while. I'll join you by New Year's Eve, I promise,'[19] he told her.

The temptation had come from the Hollywood director, William Wyler, sent by Samuel Goldwyn to convince Larry to play Heathcliff in his screen adaptation of Emily Brontë's *Wuthering Heights*. Yes, Larry said, but only if they cast Vivien as his leading lady, Cathy, and they both held on to that dream. They all went for drinks at the Florida Club, a nightclub off Berkeley Square with a glass dance floor and telephones at every table. Wyler brought them down to earth with the news that Merle Oberon would play Cathy. Vivien could have the supporting part of Isabella, if she wanted it, but she declined and surprised Wyler with the proclamation that she would play Scarlett O'Hara in *Gone with the Wind*.

Nobody, except for Vivien, took the announcement very seriously, least of all David O. Selznick, who had spent a fortune and two years searching for his Scarlett. 'I have no enthusiasm for Vivien Leigh,' Selznick reputedly said, after she sent him unsolicited portraits of herself taken by Angus McBean.

From Selznick's perspective, she had little to no acting experience when it came to playing against type – how could she, a spoilt English girl, embody Scarlett, a Southern belle whose privileged life disintegrated as the Civil War raged on? How could she possibly channel the breadth of emotion into Scarlett as she marries three times, is widowed twice, and lusts after the meek-minded Ashley Wilkes? In the process, she rebuilds her fortunes but loses a child and her husband, Rhett Butler, walks out on her, leaving her wailing but, ultimately, gathering the strength to survive once more.

Yet, Vivien saw herself as the physical embodiment of Scarlett, brought to life in Margaret Mitchell's bestselling novel. In a way, her appearance as Elsa Craddock in *A Yank at Oxford*, produced by Metro-Goldwyn-Mayer and starring Robert Taylor served as a prelude to Scarlett, wherein she played the scheming flirtatious wife of an Oxford bookseller. But the complexities of Scarlett ran deeper than petulance.

Before Larry's departure, Vivien asked Leigh for a divorce and he refused, thinking she would eventually return to him and their unconventional routine of her rushing out to parties and climbing into their bed as he was leaving for work. There would be notes scribbled on paper, telling him of her nocturnal plans, and to Daisy, the housekeeper, advising her on how she liked things done. In Leigh's eyes, it all went wrong when she left him in Denmark to sail back to England for her small part in *Things Are Looking Up* at Lime Grove Studios in 1934. A letter made his feelings clear: if the studios were going to monopolise her time, she would have to stop it. He wrote, 'There is one thing I want you to be very careful about – that is not to be away when I get back.'[20]

Maybe, for Vivien, it was a turning point in her marriage; she knew she wanted more. But so did Leigh, for whom affection and sentimentality did not come easy and was received by Vivien with indifference. 'You put nothing in, darling, when it was most necessary,'[21] he reminded her. Leigh knew he was losing her to her career but he was prepared to fit into this new life, if it meant saving their marriage.

After she eloped with Larry, she realised Leigh held on to the false hope of her coming home, even if she could not meet his expectations as a wife and mother. Was it his unconditional love or was he exerting

The Double Life of Vivien Leigh

his power over her? As far as the Catholic church was concerned, she would always be his wife. Or maybe, it was neither: he felt enough responsibility towards her to try and stop her from ruining her life, in the long term, it would seem. 'I think I could have helped you. But you did not tell me what was happening, and I did not guess,'[22] Leigh wrote to her, perhaps viewing her sexual attraction to Larry as fleeting, almost like an illness that could be cured.

In a bid to preserve their nuclear family, Leigh let Vivien have Suzanne for a few days overnight; a dull visit for both mother and daughter. Vivien discouraged Suzanne's rough-housing and took her to her friends' homes, where she chain-smoked and nervously spoke of Larry, asking if they thought he'd be faithful or not, and doing nothing to censor her explicit language when speaking of adultery. When he did call, his voice crackling down the line held her attention more than her child did.

It would be cheaper to join him, he told her; after all, the two phone calls alone had cost £50 and their 'desperate gabbling'[23] across the static line was redundant when they could be together for less. Caught in limbo and driven by lust, Vivien packed her things and sailed to America to be with Larry, her 'worshipping seducer'.[24] She also cancelled her contract to play Titania in Tyrone Guthrie's staging of A Midsummer Night's Dream, a part she had played the year before, wearing Oliver Messel's headdress of the fairy queen.

The long journey to Los Angeles would have seemed futile to a sane person but for Vivien a week of stolen moments between filming Wuthering Heights was worth any pangs of loneliness in London. Samuel Goldwyn was furious about her arrival and the studio's publicists leaked a few stories, claiming Vivien was a 'close friend' of Larry's and often visited him on set to watch him brooding over Cathy in purple heather up to his waist. A stalker, to say the least. At the end of each day, he went to Vivien's suite at the Beverly Hills Hotel, then a shabby establishment with wicker furniture which failed to evoke a colonial look. 'If you invested in a suite, nobody asked any questions,'[25] Larry said of their clandestine arrangement.

Coincidentally, or not, Larry's American agent was Myron Selznick, the brother of David O. Selznick. 'I think we ought to take her along to meet David, don't you, Myron?'[26] Larry suggested.

81

They arrived in Culver City just as the old studio sets – notably the wooden gate from *King Kong* – were being doused and set alight to replicate the burning of Atlanta. Two stand-ins, dressed as Scarlett O'Hara and Rhett Butler, were filmed in a horse and cart escaping the fire.

'Hey genius,' Myron called as the flames roared around them. 'Meet your Scarlett O'Hara.'

It was said that the flames illuminated Vivien's dark hair and flashing eyes – now reported as green, like her heroine's – and at that moment, she was mesmerising. Indeed, the logistics of this star part seemed too good to be true. David O. Selznick claimed he would never recover from his first look of Vivien and invited her to take a screen test as Scarlett. There were so many girls being tested and Vivien remembered the costume she wore was still warm from its previous occupant. She was hoping to forge connections in Hollywood and was taken by Myron to United Agents and to meet the director, William A. Wellman, who was casting for his adaptation of Rudyard Kipling's novel, *The Light That Failed*. None of it mattered any more, she was the girl Selznick wanted and after having cast Paulette Goddard in the part he terminated their agreement due to her cohabitation with Charlie Chaplin. It was a flimsy excuse, given Larry and Vivien's affair, but it had paved the way for her. Well, of course, recollections would vary. That was the Hollywood way.

⤞⟆

At Notley Abbey, the pulse of everyday life eluded them both and he seemed to love her more in retrospect. Vivien continued to hero worship Larry, calling him the greatest actor who ever lived – and she believed it. The bolstering of his ego made it hard for him to leave such a loyal servant; after all, hadn't they both cheated? And what was a betrayal of the mortal flesh when their art was so great?

Vivien was now 40 and the years of physical and mental illness told on her face and body. Acting was essentially disguising oneself and pretending to be somebody else, but the intrusive glare of the camera could not hide the ravages of real life. It was not her fault: she, like all women, was at the mercy of Mother Nature. He, although six years her senior, was considered to be in his masculine prime; he was still a god.

Instead of acting with Vivien, Larry began to cast actresses who looked like her and she no longer felt part of the magic circle. 'The school of Vivien', as one observant friend called it. First, there was *Hamlet*, released in 1948, in which he cast Jean Simmons as Ophelia. He knew talent when he saw it; likewise, Gabriel Pascal went to a dancing school in Golders Green to scout someone to play the harpist slave girl in *Caesar and Cleopatra*, his wartime picture with Vivien. Simmons stood out from the group of girls and he told her to say goodbye to her friends; she was going to be a star.[27]

It was a part which Vivien felt was hers, she had thought of nothing else. As a consolation prize, Larry then offered Vivien the part of Gertrude, Queen of Denmark, Hamlet's mother, which eventually went to Eileen Herlie. The incestuous undertones were not lost on Vivien: in early 1939, while she was filming *Gone with the Wind*, he had sent her rapturous letters, calling her 'mummy darling' and immersed himself in a swimming pool, imagining he was a foetus inside her womb.

The mother issue was always present: he had lost his mother, Agnes, when he was 12 years old and idolised her as the perfect specimen of womanhood. The last time he saw Agnes alive, she was in bed having become paralysed down her left side and he did not know she was dying from a brain tumour. He was leaving for All Saints, a choir school where he boarded, and stood in the doorway, with his cap in his hand, smiling at her. 'Goodbye, darling,'[28] she said to him. After Agnes's death, he contemplated suicide by throwing himself in the Thames but resisted, perhaps thinking, as he was religious in those days, it was a sin. No, Vivien would have said it was because he was a coward.

For Vivien, it had to be Ophelia or nothing, and so it was nothing. Instead, her fur coat would be draped over a bass drum and a member of the crew tapped through it to make the sound of muffled heartbeats.[29] Jean Simmons was only 17 and fresh from the Rank Charm School when the picture began and was 18 when she was nominated for an Academy Award for Best Supporting Actress but lost to Claire Trevor. Larry won an Academy Award for *Hamlet* and the irony did

not escape Vivien: in 1940, they had both been nominated – he for
Wuthering Heights and she for *Gone with the Wind*. She won and he lost
to Robert Donat, and on the way home he threw her award from the
car window. She would use it as a doorstop ever after.

The casting of Simmons was a knock to Vivien's confidence and
she resented their rehearsals together, his feeding Simmons her
lines and training her for the part. On the set at Denham, he forced
Simmons to do her drowning stunt, lashing her with buckets of cold
water until it was unbearable and she gasped for air. Ophelia was dead
and like all corpses, she craved the earth. He had schooled Vivien for
her debut in their stage production of *Hamlet* in 1937 and they read
their lines in the back of the car on the way to Shepperton Studios.
She wrongly suspected Larry was sleeping with his young ingenue
and spread the rumour that he was. Every other day, she came to the
studio and watched the filming, standing next to the camera as an
extra set of eyes.

'Goddam Larry is fucking his Ophelia,' Vivien confided to a friend.
'I'm losing him to a bloody child. I was barely out of my teens when
Larry started fucking me.'[30] The battle that Jill once endured had
come full circle and Vivien thought only of her own distress as
opposed to the heartache she had caused others.

Larry's next foray into Shakespeare was to be *Richard III*, co-
starring Claire Bloom as Lady Anne, a part Vivien hoped to play
on screen. Bloom, like Jean Simmons, was a carbon copy of Vivien
but had the girlish youth – she was 25 – that Larry depended on to
bolster his screen image. They were to have an affair for the duration
of the filming and he brought her to Notley at the weekends; the
first visit instilling nervousness in Bloom, for she admired Vivien and
was intimidated by the legend of the Oliviers. He calmed Bloom's
anxiety by telling her that Vivien had given their affair her blessing;
furthermore, Bloom was not in love with him and knew they were
both using each other.

From Bloom's perspective, Vivien's energy lingered in the rooms
and she found her to be a mercurial presence, unlike Larry, who was
'plodding, full of theatrical mannerisms and false charm'.[31] There
were her chintz curtains, antique furniture, paintings, and dressing
table adorned with bottles of Caron's Bellodgia, Tabac Blond, Worth's

Dans la Nuit, and Marcel Rochas's Femme. Although Vivien turned a blind eye to Bloom sleeping with Larry, she must have realised how easily she had given up her territory. The *other woman* was in her house – in her bed – the way she had shamelessly gone to Larry and Jill's home in Burchett's Green.

Unnerved, Vivien went to Shepperton Studios and sat, bundled up in a scarf and wearing dark glasses, watching Larry directing the scenes and them reciting their lines. The line, 'Dispute not with her; she's a lunatic,'[32] might have hit too close to home. Still, she sat motionless, watching the two, unnerving Bloom more than her affair with Larry did.

Their lives, on and off the screen, had become trivial. Vivien went into her next picture, *The Deep Blue Sea*, Terence Rattigan's screenplay based on his play of the same title and produced by Alexander Korda. Directed by Anatole Litvak, whom Rattigan thought was the wrong choice, Vivien's character, Hester, was a judge's wife who leaves her husband for a young and penniless pilot, who ultimately treats her badly, thus destroying her confidence and provoking a suicide attempt.

It was another descent into madness without the polish (and budget) of a Hollywood production. On this occasion, would life imitate art, as it had done in *A Streetcar Named Desire*? Perhaps not. Vivien was only half-committed to Hester's breakdowns and swung between aristocratic restraint and hysterical outbursts. Above all else, she complained that the widescreen Cinemascope process made her look like 'a rather strange apricot balloon'.[33]

To Larry, it might have been a relief to know that Blanche DuBois had been exorcised at Netherne Asylum. For the time being, at least. When it came to filming his death scene in *Richard III* – stabbed in the head at the Battle of Bosworth – he drew on a kitten he once owned with Jill, called The Enemy, and its accidental death while sprinting through a door that closed too quickly on its neck. 'All actors are cattle,' Alfred Hitchcock said, though Larry went so far as to compare film acting to prostitution. It was true to a degree: they sold themselves for money.

The truth was that Vivien was difficult to insure and so was to be paid £65,000 with a payment of £5,000 upfront. The remainder was to be paid from the net profits, which did not materialise as the picture was a flop. Her leading man, Kenneth More, was critical of her as a woman, finding her untrustworthy and vain, whose confidence was boosted by phoney praise and attention. As an actress, he could not fault her: a nuanced view, given the criticism Larry directed at her when his insecurities took hold.

Nobody worked harder than Vivien and not even her naysayers could, or would, deny the force with which she drove herself on stage and in front of the camera. If her earlier work in film was forgettable and treated with frivolity by her – *The Village Squire, Gentlemen's Agreement* and *Look Up and Laugh*, each made in 1935 – then *Gone with the Wind* was a turning point in her professionalism on the set. She had early starts and long days, with only two days off each month coinciding with her period, as cinematographers long believed an actress's face was not photogenic during that time. Otherwise, she remained focused on the part as chaos on the set unfolded and the original director, George Cukor, whom she loved, was replaced by Victor Fleming, a gruff taskmaster. Exhausted and overworked, her nervous system eventually collapsed and she began to have outbursts between takes, shouting and swearing, and losing her patience.[34] Olivia de Havilland, who played Melanie Wilkes, remembered seeing Vivien on the last day of filming and being shocked by the change in her appearance; she had given something to Scarlett that she never got back.

Nevertheless, Hollywood directors found Vivien more interesting than Larry on screen. It was true: she was a film star, a title she rejected. 'Being a film star – just a film star – is such a false life, lived for false values and for publicity. Actresses go on for a long time and there are always marvellous parts to play,'[35] she said. The film star, however, could not entice audiences into the cinema, and given *The Deep Blue Sea* was filmed in Cinemascope, it was shown in only one in eight British cinemas as the others did not have the necessary equipment.

Somehow, she was caught between two worlds, playing women who defied social mores and yet she was restricted in her execution. Nowhere in society could she expose her shadow self: highly sexed, mentally ill, with all of the so-called sordid qualities of Blanche DuBois. Her place in the modern world was still conflicted. 'I am part prude and part non-conformist,'[36] she said of her duplicity.

Behind the scenes, Vivien and Larry tried to rebuild their lives together and spent their days walking in the woods and sitting in the dovecote. The dialogue was strained and each had little to say when veering off-script. Larry spoke of his livestock, particularly the sows, who he confided had a disease of the uterus.

'Don't be disgusting,'[37] Vivien said.

She had been trying to conceive a baby, a task which she undertook half-heartedly when Larry suggested it as a remedy for the stagnation between them. It failed to materialise and she felt something lower than depression; something emptier than despair. During times of hopelessness, she was like 'a thing, an amoeba, at the bottom of the sea'.[38]

On cue, their friend Glen Byam Shaw, director of the Shakespeare Memorial Theatre in Stratford-upon-Avon, came to Notley one afternoon and spoke of the season ahead. *Macbeth, Twelfth Night, Titus Andronicus* ... 'Tragedy you can wallow in,'[39] she said.

Chapter Six

'I say there is no darkness but ignorance'

Twelfth Night, William Shakespeare

꒰⚬꒱

1955

In the spring of 1955, Vivien's mental health was on a downward spiral. The tell-tale signs were there but Larry chose to ignore them. She always needed a passion project and so did he. Otherwise, who were they? 'I haven't the faintest idea,' he said of himself. 'I certainly don't wish to know myself.'[1] In terms of his identity, he was a vessel for the characters he played – a chameleon – but Vivien was always herself, hence the reason critics believed her range to be limited. Her fixation, now, was on Peter Finch and she was determined to entice him back. Having been separated, romantically, for over a year, how did they manage to reconcile?

During the festive season of 1954, Vivien and Larry did the rounds of seasonal parties and they inevitably crossed paths with Peter and his wife, whom she summoned to Notley for Christmas. The Finches went together and, despite appearances, their marriage was failing and Tamara blamed Vivien. To onlookers, Peter's dancing with Vivien seemed harmless, but Tamara knew she was a viper in their nest. Larry treated them aloofly, moving around with half-closed eyes and talking with restrained politeness. As they gathered on the lawn to watch the fireworks, Larry pointed a rocket at Peter, whom Vivien stood close to, shivering in the freezing night air. At the last moment, Larry changed his aim and the rocket shot up to the sky. An explosion of colours rained like a meteor storm, reminiscent of the night the stars fell and the innocent onlookers thought Judgement Day had come.

In the New Year of 1955, Vivien began her assault on Peter and bombarded him with telephone calls, which Tamara answered, and, upon hearing her nemesis's voice, hung up. Then, Vivien began to arrive at the Finches' flat in Dolphin Square and pressed on the doorbell until she disturbed the entire household. Having failed to get an answer, she stood on the street and shouted for Peter to come outside and go back to Notley with her. Silence eventually came; a relief to those indoors.

The strain was too much and Peter began drinking again, not that he needed an excuse to return to the bottle. He vanished for long periods and often ended up sleeping on his mother's sofa at Bury Walk in Chelsea. His mother, Betty, who had abandoned him in childhood, came back into his life when he was on the brink of stardom and expected him to pay her debts and become the protector which she had failed to be. Vivien knew where to find him and she wormed her way into his mother's heart and home, becoming a sympathetic friend to Betty and winning over her affection, and pity. She would sob her heart out to Betty, who would hold her in her arms like a child, comparing her to 'a taut spring that you felt at any moment might burst into pieces'.[2] They both agreed that Tamara was trying to suppress Peter's free spirit and Vivien compared him to 'a wild, sensual Pan'.[3]

The connotations of the mythical figure of Pan had perhaps taken a sinister turn and Peter's libertine way of life reflected occultist Aleister Crowley's ramblings:

PAN: Duality: Energy: Death.
Death: Begetting: the supporters of O!
To beget is to die; to die is to beget.
Cast the Seed into the Field of Night.
Life and Death are two names of A.
Kill thyself.
Neither of these alone is enough[4]

The changeable nature of Peter was beyond Tamara's control and she recognised, but could not resist, the destructive force of Vivien. As a child, Tamara had supernatural visions which disturbed her sense of peace: a spectre appeared in her bedroom, transforming into a lion and it rose on its hind legs, towering above her, protecting her from evil spirits, devils and witches.[5] When it came to Vivien, Tamara had no talisman and she accepted her fate. 'I couldn't fight Vivien,' she said. 'It would have been like trying to fight the Queen of England.'[6] Was Tamara being defeatist or merely recognising the power Vivien wielded? The melodrama had played out before, on screen, in *Caesar and Cleopatra*:

'Is it sweet or bitter to be a queen?' Claude Raines, as Caesar, asks. 'Bitter,' Vivien, as Cleopatra, answers.

For the season at Stratford, Vivien and Larry lived at Avoncliffe, a regency house with a garden sloping down to the River Avon. Much like its temporary inhabitants, the house had seen better days and in modern times it was used to accommodate visiting actors. Far more impressive to Vivien was its historical connection to the family of Emma, Lady Hamilton. Having played Lady Hamilton in the biopic *That Hamilton Woman*, she thought it gave the house a romantic air. Larry, who was Lord Nelson in the picture, took a jaded view of the love affair. 'Lady Hamilton?' he remarked. 'She was the tart who fucked Nelson?'[7]

The production of *That Hamilton Woman* was filmed at General Studios in Hollywood, a cheap location which contrasted with Alexander Korda's lavish period drama, equipped with a mechanical set mimicking a boat. Between takes, Vivien threatened to be sick, as she suffered from motion sickness, and had to be given Dramamine. Larry and Vivien played their parts for romance, rather than historical accuracy. The two had never looked so attractive on screen, her face illuminated by her love for him – they had married before filming began. After its release in 1941, it became Sir Winston Churchill's favourite picture.

Larry's flippant comment about Lady Hamilton was replaced with sobering attention to the Shakespearean parts he would play at Stratford. He knew his portrayals were far more superior to anything Vivien might attempt, and with his heavy makeup and artificial features – he had a penchant for false noses and chins and pretend limps – he convinced the audience and the critics of his greatness. Vivien had to work harder for their praise and the critics seldom noticed when she did anything brilliant on the stage, especially when she was with Larry.

From their points of view, her Viola in *Twelfth Night* was passive and dull: she wore an Eton crop and winged eyeliner and looked like a pixie, going against the director Sir John Gielgud's warning, 'Vivien, dear, don't make Viola twee.'[8]

On the opening night, she called Trader Faulkner, a young Australian actor who played her twin, Sebastian, into her dressing room.

'Darling Trader, how much are you paid here?' she asked.

'£25 a week,' he replied.

'When Sebastian and Viola kiss at the end as long-lost twins reunited, if I made it up to £27, do you think you could hold on to our kiss?'

'Oh, Viv. To hold a kiss with you for every performance? I'd need thirty quid!'[9]

The lightness soon evaporated and the production seemed to be vexed with minor annoyances, mainly from Gielgud's point of view and he asked Vivien why she did not cry, as all of his leading ladies cried on stage. 'Oh, I do,' she said, 'but only when I have to go home to Notley with Larry afterwards.'[10]

The critics, particularly Kenneth Tynan, continued their onslaught of negativity towards the Oliviers, especially Vivien. As Lady Macbeth, Tynan wrote she was 'more niminy-piminy than thundery-blundery, more viper than anaconda ...'. She played Lady Macbeth's sleepwalking scene in bare feet, and her maid and dresser, Ethel, would clean her feet before she put on her slippers. 'What, will these feet ever be clean?'[11] Ethel muttered furiously as she rubbed them with a towel.

Vivien wondered why Tynan was obsessed with tearing her down and Larry agreed. 'It affected her very badly. She took it bravely and with gallantry, though it would affect her gravely. It was mortifying.'[12] Was there a psychological aspect to Tynan's bullying, aside from his worshipping of Larry? In his youth, Tynan had wanted to be a theatrical director and he was engaged to direct *The Cocktail Party* but was fired by the show's star, Fay Compton, who hated him. Humiliated, Tynan gave up on his dream of being a director and pursued the life of a critic. 'I was ready to kill him,'[13] Larry said of Tynan.

Larry warned Tynan that his hostility to Vivien would push her towards a nervous breakdown. He told Tynan that he was, in fact, responsible for at least one of Vivien's breakdowns. A shattering of her confidence, really, as she tried, night after night, to impress the sadistic critic; the self-confessed bastard of Fleet Street. She could expect no mercy from him; he revelled in sadomasochism and was part of its underworld, having formed relationships with like-minded individuals.

Friends and theatrical types tried to lift her spirits and they praised her Lady Macbeth as being the greatest of their generation. Larry agreed and chose his words carefully when appraising her in public:

> Vivien is not ambitious. It is her natural disposition that drives her at full pressure all the time. Like any great actress, she always wants to do better. Vivien has no fear of slipping, no fear of losing her public. I think she works too hard and tell her so, but she is a very difficult person to advise.[14]

As Lavinia in *Titus Andronicus*, Vivien disgusted the prim audiences when her hands and tongue were mutilated and portrayed with streaming red ribbons. Some believed Tynan's criticism was justified when her performance failed to convey the horror of the scenes unfolding. Echoing Tynan, a critic from the *Daily Express*, John Barber, wrote: 'I hate the phrase "The Oliviers", which kowtows to the pair royally known as Larry-and-Viv. Look beyond the gloss.' Gielgud agreed with the criticism. 'Poor Vivien who seems in a bad way. She is utterly ineffective on the stage – like paper, only not so thick, no substance or power – and off stage she is haunted, avid, malicious and insatiable.'[15] Larry, who was proud of her Lady Macbeth, was embarrassed by her turn as Lavinia.

The reviews put her in a foul mood and she worked herself into the ground trying to match Larry on stage at Stratford. Noël Coward observed that her incipient tuberculosis and awareness that she could 'never be as good an artist as Larry, however much she tries, has bubbled up in her and driven her on to the borderline'.[16] As was evident, the harder she tried, the more she was criticised and slowly but surely her mental decline escalated.

For Larry, the first sign of disharmony was the photograph of Peter Finch on Vivien's dressing-room table. 'I believe that if you want something with all your heart, you get it,'[17] she had once said. Now, it seemed, she was manifesting Peter into existence on her makeshift altar. Much like the old saying that you are never more than 6 feet away from a rat, Finchie was always lingering somewhere, often – from Larry's perspective – unwanted. In recent days, Peter had moved into Notley to recover from the breakdown of his marriage to Tamara and his excessive drinking, and he was adhering to temperance and trying to lose a stone in weight by eating curried eggs.[18]

At Vivien's request, Peter came to Stratford and the two were closer than ever, united in their dysfunction. Both insomniacs, they slept for four hours at a time and filled the waking hours partying with the cast and crew or drinking sessions with only the two of them. He, the underdog, saw them both as victims of circumstances that were beyond their control. They held hands in the full glare of Larry and did nothing to hide their affair. In defence of her adultery, she said, 'I am an actress. A great actress. Great actresses have lovers. Why not? I have a husband and I have lovers.'[19]

In her spare time, she read *The Crack-Up*, an essay written by F. Scott Fitzgerald and, in the rambling prose, she found it resonated with her situation. 'The test of a first-rate intelligence is the ability to hold two opposed ideas in the mind at the same time, and still retain the ability to function,' Scott Fitzgerald wrote. 'One should, for example, be able to see that things are hopeless and yet be determined to make them otherwise.'[20]

What could Larry say or do about it? Words failed him when he reflected on her adultery and instead, he accused her of losing touch with her craft.[21] For him, his passion for acting came at an early age and he nurtured it into a vocation, a way of life. As a young boy, he caught the attention of Ellen Terry who came to his school to see a production of *Julius Caesar*, in which he played the part of Brutus. 'The little boy ... is already a great actor,'[22] Terry noted in her diary.

Vivien's desire to act came at an early age but compared to Larry, her approach was far more flippant. 'What do you want to be when you grow up?' Maureen O'Sullivan asked her. They had been class-mates at the Convent of the Sacred Heart in Roehampton and O'Sullivan would go on to have a successful film career in the 1930s. 'I'm going to be an actress,' Vivien replied. She was not sure why she answered the way she did. 'I like dressing up, I think.'[23]

For Vivien, her early success, which happened overnight, was due to a clever press campaign. She hadn't the first clue about stage direction or vocal projection and moved around in *The Mask of Virtue* looking pretty and saying her lines in a sing-song voice, and getting laughs for her (unintentional) comedic timing. The morning after the glowing reviews, she invited the photographers into her tiny living room and ran back and forth, changing her clothes for a series of photographs of herself alone, holding Suzanne, and so forth. For the final one, she had an idea to change into a short playsuit and remove her shoes, to sit atop a pile of cushions and play the ukulele. Hours later, she tried to stop the photo from being printed, but it was too late. A moment of silliness, but she felt she had gone too far in casting herself as a barefooted bohemian.

Acting to Vivien, in her younger days, was viewed as a party. At the beginning of 1936, she played the Queen in *Richard II* at the Oxford Dramatic Society which lasted for one week and nobody received a fee. Going to parties with the undergraduates was far more exciting than recreating the House of Lancaster.

Even her training was seen as something to do – a novelty, emphasised by her devil-may-care attitude to her studies at RADA. In April 1932, she successfully auditioned for Sir Kenneth Barnes at RADA and was taught Shakespeare by Ethel Carrington, the actress and wife of the Shakespearean actor, Murray Carrington. She was to perform as Rosalind in *As You Like It* but the production was sabotaged by her trying to keep up with a temperamental spotlight. Her last play, *The Young Person in Pink*, was ruined when she recited the wrong dialogue. Five days before her wedding to Leigh, she left RADA at his behest.

Leigh's sudden aversion to acting must have surprised her and she did not realise they both could be different people, depending on their environments. In the countryside, Leigh was informal, even rugged, with his tanned skin and unkempt hair, riding his horse and cart through Holcombe Down. To him, she was somebody else, too – his Vivvy,[24] a bright jewel with tales of the Raj and who conversed in foreign languages, little phrases collected here and there during her travels abroad. Maybe she was always play-acting – over-compensating for her roving childhood and then, barely out of convent school, she was married and pregnant and did not know how to be a wife and expectant mother within their four walls. She had never experienced the stability of family life with everyone under one roof, of being considerate to another person day in and day out, or the putting down of roots in a permanent place.

However, a fortnight after their honeymoon in Germany and Austria, just as Nazism infiltrated the Reichstag, Vivien asked Leigh for his permission to return to RADA for French lessons with Mademoiselle Alice Gracet. The long days of waiting for Leigh to return from his chambers were monotonous and she needed a distraction. She negotiated a way out of her gilded cage and back on to the stage. Months into her resumed lessons, she was pregnant and fighting against time, and so, in a French production of *Saint Joan*, she awkwardly manoeuvred around the stage in chain mail and boots that were too large and the toes remained pointed upward. The criticism started early and her reports from RADA were negative: 'Why are you so bad? Is it because you have too much sense of humour?'[25] All in all, her training lasted for six months and she did not complete the course.

⚜

At Stratford, the mental anguish took a toll on her body and she began to swell around her face and neck, a strange occurrence which happened before a manic episode.[26] She was drinking heavily, contributing to her bloated appearance. It turned out she had pleurisy, which explained her shortness of breath and weakened voice, which was never penetrating in the first place. Perhaps the manic episode that was gathering momentum had staved off the fatigue often associated with the virus, and during energetic bursts, she telephoned friends and invited them to her nightly parties for the cast and crew.

Exhausted from the proverbial merry-go-round of performing and partying, Larry convinced Vivien to see Dr Freudenberg for an informal chat and, to his surprise, she agreed. 'Poor Larry, he's over-anxious, that's all; it's easy to understand when you think of all the terrible dances I had led him, but, you see, I've never really been or felt better,'[27] she told the doctor.

She succeeded in tricking Dr Freudenberg and, to her relief, he denied her a course of ECT. To Larry, the doctor explained that under the circumstances it would have been dangerous to shock her brain. Was it genius acting or manipulation on her behalf? If she had been of a clearer mindset, she might have argued it was neither. It was a survival instinct against her phobia of ECT: once, in 1953, she had awoken during it and the procedure frightened her.[28] What could Larry do? An intervention was out of the question; in the first instance, nobody believed him and, in the second, he could not risk upsetting Vivien and ruining the Stratford season.

They drove, in silence, back to Avoncliffe. Vivien drifted in and out of sleep and his resentment festered into something deeper than anger; it was fatal to their lives together. The dialogue from *Macbeth* rang truer than ever:

Macbeth: How does your patient, doctor?
Doctor: Not so sick, my lord, as she is troubled with thick-coming fancies that keep her from rest.
Macbeth: Cure her of that! Canst thou not minister to a mind diseased, pluck from the memory a rooted sorrow, raze out the written troubles of the brain, and with some sweet oblivious antidote cleanse the stuffed bosom of that perilous stuff which weighs upon her heart.
Doctor: Therein the patient must minister to himself.[29]

For Larry, there was a sense of relief in knowing Peter would be waiting at Avoncliffe, ready to do his bidding. Always the faithful servant, Peter never quite evolved from the grateful protégé, despite having replaced his mentor in the marital bed. 'For God's sake, go up and see Vivien,'[30] Larry coaxed Peter, who, without a backward glance, took her to bed.

When Larry was not acting, he was directing and so it was to be the scene as he envisaged it. As sadistic as it seemed to an outsider, it gave him time to reflect on his circumstances and to restore his energy levels: he was carrying on with several good-natured women whose kindness he understood as pity towards an ageing actor, miserable in his private life and sleeping in his dressing room. Then, his clarity of thought was restored and his eyes were opened to the situation: he realised that his life with Vivien was no longer forever.[31]

Although conflicted by his responsibilities towards Vivien and his art, he must have known that undertaking a theatrical season with her was a mistake. There was also the promise of an Eastern European tour with *Titus Andronicus* but it was months away and he could ignore it in the interim. Still, audiences invested in the glamour of the Oliviers and believed in their love, but neither could sustain him.

During the Old Vic tour of Australia and New Zealand back in 1948, Vivien and Larry had performed together in *The Skin of Our Teeth*, *School for Scandal* and *Richard III*. The public was convinced of their love, even if Larry had an unsettling feeling that something had gone wrong with Vivien. The only difference was they could still hide behind the prestige of their image, evident in having been invited by the British Council to complete the tour. They were the king and queen of the British theatre and Vivien was at the height of her film stardom. Untouchable is perhaps too much of a cliché, but it was true, at least on British soil. In hindsight, arrogance might have been a better description. Their colleagues from the Old Vic called them God and the Angel.

In the New Year of 1948, the company sailed from Tilbury Docks on the SS *Corinthic*. From the deck, they watched the fanfare of press photographers on the quayside taking photographs and shouting in their direction. Vivien, who was dressed in a Dior suit, accepted a bouquet of flowers and obediently smiled for the cameras. 'The sun will be pleasant,' she said. 'But I love England. I am not really content away from it, and I am always very happy to come back.'[32]

For the duration of the crossing to Fremantle, Vivien learnt the words to Bush Paterson's *Waltzing Matilda* and the company rehearsed in the ballroom of the ship. They stopped in Las Palmas de Gran Canaria and Cape Town, coming ashore for two days to break the monotony of the voyage.

There was an element of snobbery that was reflective of the imperialistic attitudes of the time. 'Why are you, the greatest actor in the world, taking a touring company to Australia of all places?'[33] Samuel Goldwyn asked Larry. It was assumed that Australia, then considered a new country and, therefore, uncivilised, would fawn over the stars. Not so, in the cities, the sophisticated people received the Oliviers with an air of indifference and suspicion. In Melbourne, the press thought their visit was patronising and unnecessary, given the undiscovered talent there. 'We have better Richard III's here,' a local newspaper wrote. Many Australians, however, were used to travelling over 100 miles to watch a play and others came to the theatre for the first time to see the Oliviers. Not far from Larry's mind was the fact that it was their celebrity, and not their art, which attracted the public.

In Perth, Adelaide and Tasmania, the public received the Oliviers with enthusiasm, mobbed them after each performance and followed them to their hotel. Larry and Vivien, basking in the glory, waved to them from the balcony of their hotel. At functions, they played the part of pseudo-royals and raised their teacups in a toast to King George VI, which Vivien thought silly as she disliked tea and considered it 'a ridiculous waste of time'.[34] Perhaps the adoration went to Larry's head and before each reception given in their honour, he requested the National Anthem to be played. At the Capitol Theatre, he made sweeping speeches in support of the Food for Britain appeal, as unlike in Britain, post-war rationing was not enforced in Australia. So much for the 'old country' being superior.

The vast landscape and changing climate of Australia became overwhelming. They were exhausted from the airless heat and mosquitoes, and the tropical rains that once flooded their dressing rooms in Perth. The Australian crew, who adhered to strict labour laws, refused to rehearse longer than necessary, as they received no extra money for it. Vivien and Larry rehearsed to the point of exhaustion. 'You are looking at two corpses,' Larry told the press.

From Brisbane, they flew to Auckland, New Zealand, where Vivien, who was terrified of flying, had to be placed on oxygen to restore her levels. In New Zealand, Larry had his knee operated on and enjoyed the dramatic scenes of being lowered by a hoist on to the ship. As with Larry blatantly asking for food from the Australians, Vivien was equally candid and to those in her circle, she declared the New Zealanders far more cultured than Australians.

In the press, however, she said New Zealand was comparable to Italy but Australia was 'absolutely individual, like no place on earth'.[35] Playing to the gallery, the role of ambassadors, as opposed to actors, suited them. Vivien visited hospitals and flower shows, and Larry gave speeches and again raised a toast to King George VI at almost every luncheon or dinner.

It was not the productions that stood out to Larry, but the series of unfortunate events marring the ten-month tour. His tearing the cartilage of his knee; the exhaustion they faced. Her bronchitis; and the news of her beloved Siamese cat, New Boy, who was run over and killed by the milkman at Notley. He still called her 'Baba' on the tour, both in person and in his diary – surely a sign that he adored her.[36]

Then came the time for a serious talk and he pleaded with her to stop flirting with their male colleagues. To his surprise, she apologised for humiliating him. On the voyage home, it was rumoured that she had a fling with the actor Dan Cunningham and did nothing to discourage the whispers. In the swimming pool onboard the ship, she swam close to the young men; slithering past them in her bikini, so close they reached out and touched her. Of course, Peter Finch had made his mark but was not yet a threat. His entrance would come later. During that period, in Larry's eyes, Peter was just 'a clever young Australian actor ... a very, very bright boy'.[37]

'I lost you in Australia,'[38] Larry told Vivien.

In December 1955, Vivien and Peter escaped to Paris to spend an illicit few days in the city before heading to the south of France, staying at La Reine Jeanne, a villa in Le Lavandou. At first, Vivien arrived alone, followed by Peter, and the two were trailed by Larry in a bizarre game of cat and mouse.

Days later, Larry caught up with the lovers and they spent five days at the villa in a haze of pretence. When Larry was uncertain about something or someone, he would become feminine in his manner – a shield against the brutality of others – and it would be difficult to chastise him because he exuded softness.[39] 'Dear boy, I forgot to get you a Christmas present,'[40] he said to Peter, as he removed his tie. Vivien watched the half-hearted scuffle with a smile: her two men were willing to duel to the death. But it wasn't as serious as all that.

A few days later, Larry spirited her away to San Vigilio to stay at their old haunt, the Locanda Hotel. The small hotel was cloistered by cypress trees with a view of the lake and rolling hills planted with olive groves, a lyrical landscape suited to a sentimental novel.[41] Later, she went on to Bavaria to take the cure.

Divided in their personal life as Larry and Vivien might have been, in public they were united: 'False face must hide what the false heart doth know.'[42] They were to star in a screen adaptation of *Macbeth* for Alexander Korda, and Larry had gone to Scotland to scout locations and the script was almost completed. The prospect excited Vivien and she longed to play the ruthless Lady Macbeth on screen; it was a picture she could sink her teeth into after the dismal failure of *The Deep Blue Sea*. All hopes were dashed when, in the New Year, Korda died of a heart attack. There was also talk of Peter appearing with Vivien in *South Sea Bubble*, Noël Coward's latest play. Given the tension in France, Peter decided otherwise and cried into his brandy, saying, over and over, how much he worshipped Larry.

It was a period of transition for Vivien and Larry, domestically and professionally. They sold Durham Cottage to Lady Irene Curzon, Baroness Ravensdale, the daughter of the former Viceroy of India, and leased Lowndes Cottage in Lowndes Place. Despite Durham Cottage having so much romanticism tied to it – it was their first home together – Vivien had recently fallen down the stairs and suffered minor injuries. An omen, maybe. She received poison-pen letters in the post from individuals who wished she had broken her neck.[43]

Never before had she been the recipient of such vitriol and Larry sensed the tide was turning in terms of their popularity. He was looking for new, independent projects to fulfil his artistic needs and she was preparing for rehearsals of *South Sea Bubble*. Or, as Noël Coward put it, 'Larry and Vivien have decided to present a united front to a deeply concerned world'.[44]

Trouble was never far away, and before long, Peter was back at Notley and playing the country squire on Larry's turf. Being in Larry's home and sleeping with his wife gave the young Finch an air of arrogance, which made everyone uncomfortable, but they were too polite to challenge him when he assumed control of the room. 'After you've been to bed with Vivien, nothing else matters,'[45] Peter said. Their passion afforded him a sense of bravado, as it had done to Larry decades before.

Spurred on by Peter and her mania, Vivien became impossible for Larry to reason with. Larry knew the routine as well as any script, but each performance depended on his own psyche at the time. Peter, had he an ounce of common sense, should have removed himself from the sorry state of affairs. All the blame fell on Vivien, who was drinking more than ever – gin, a depressant, was her poison – and violence now factored into her outbursts. Alexander Korda's nephew, Michael, had been madly in love with her – a harmless adolescent crush – and sailed with her on Korda's yacht, *Elsewhere*. Even Michael, with his youthful lack of experience, spotted the signs of instability early on and became afraid of her when she was drunk: he thought she turned into a monster.[46]

No longer interested in dealing with Vivien in a sympathetic way, Larry became complicit to her behaviour. One night, before the company left Stratford, she burst into the library at Avoncliffe wearing a flimsy nightgown and made grand theatrical gestures towards Larry and Peter. 'Which of you is coming to bed with me tonight?' she demanded to know. Later, Larry would claim it had been part of a ruse and that he, Peter and Vivien laughed about it until dawn. It was not quite the drawing-room comedy Larry portrayed it to be;

it was a betrayal and confirmation that her feelings for him were as changeable as her moods.

Years before, when they returned from Australia, Vivien disturbed the foundation of their lives together and planted seeds of doubt within Larry. They were sitting in the small winter garden at Durham Cottage, having finished lunch. The blinding sunlight made everything seem all the more ethereal. She, without warning, turned to him and said, 'I don't love you any more.'[47] In a state of shock, he hoped that his ears were deceiving him or that she was playing the part of a sinister game. 'There's no one else or anything like that,' she continued. 'I mean, I still love you but in a different way, sort of, well, like a brother.'[48]

Later, he would express his innermost thoughts on the matter. He should have kicked her out; he should have left her; he should never have endured her thoughtlessness for the sake of keeping up appearances. He should never have suffered the humiliation.[49]

Instead, they went on a painting holiday to Opio, a village in Provence, having been inspired by Sir Winston Churchill's book *Painting as a Pastime*. They rented a Castello for three weeks – an old house on the edge of a hill with a studio across the courtyard and a small garden with a swimming pool. During their stay, they locked the gates to the courtyard and stripped the orange and fig trees of their fruit.[50] Their own paradise; their own Book of Genesis – two gardens, two betrayals.

It was only recently that Larry had been able to bear to leave Vivien indefinitely. So, he shouldered the burden of her illness and relied on close friends to kill any gossip before it was printed in the newspapers. Despite his flings, which he thought were far less consequential than Vivien's affair with Peter, he had a sense of not only loyalty, but duty. Familiarity kept them together: he knew she liked the colour white, collected china, was fond of crossword puzzles, and possessed a startling thoughtlessness that jarred him at times, such as forgetting her daughter's birthday. They both loved *Chants of Auvergne*,[51] the collection of folk songs sung by Madeleine Grey. He knew of her superstitions: she forbade him from whistling in her dressing room, as it was unlucky, and was afraid of seeing a new moon through the glass.[52] There was also the worry he felt when she was under the weather, physically, and he whisked her away for chest X-rays to ensure the dreaded tuberculosis was not coming back. Nevertheless, he could no longer gather the strength nor the interest to defend the image he held in his mind.

Strangely enough, it was Peter who was the more poetic of the two and said, 'If ever there was a flawed masterpiece, it was Vivien.'[53]

Chapter Seven

'True hope is swift, and flies with swallow's wings'

Richard III, William Shakespeare

ళ∘⦿ఆ

1956

'We think Etna is choking and are hoping for an eruption any minute. But apparently, he often smokes for want of something better to do, and it never comes to anything really big,'[1] Vivien had written to Leigh Holman from Sicily in 1936, before leaving for Capri to be with Larry.

The significance of expecting so much and receiving so little might have rung true in her subconscious as she packed her bags, ready to elope with Peter. One night, they plotted their every move: they would leave without a trace, go to New York City, and begin anew. Some argued she was manic when she agreed to the idea. Or had she proposed it? Others might have said she was always impulsive and irresponsible.

During that time, Peter was rarely sober and easily manipulated, according to Tamara, who had paid a £1,000 deposit – borrowed from her mother – on a family home, big enough to turn into flats to rent to tenants for an additional income. Peter, despite his success on the stage and screen, had squandered every last penny and plunged his family into poverty, to the extent that Tamara had no money to buy a pint of milk. He told Tamara he was only helping Vivien. 'Helping?'[2]

Tamara questioned him, disbelieving his excuse. She knew Vivien and Peter were still 'carrying on', as she called it.

As Vivien had done to Leigh in 1937, she was ready to pull the rug from beneath Larry to fulfil her own happiness with Peter. However, as in Shakespearean plays, the weather was to become a prophetic omen and it dictated their fate. They went to Heathrow and were stalled by the thick fog which grounded the aeroplanes. It was impossible to take off. She sat, waiting and waiting; every announcement over the tannoy was like her inner voice – her conscience – telling her it was a bad idea. To go home. To abandon this foolishness. Eventually, the fog lifted and she regained her clarity of thought. Peter wanted to board the plane but Vivien told him it was over: she was going back to Larry. 'But you know, there was really never any question that Vivien would give up being Lady Olivier to become Mrs Finch,'[3] Peter would later say, his ego bruised and his heart broken.

To her surprise, Larry was waiting at Notley and neither mentioned the incident. In fact, Vivien only ever confided in one person, Terence Rattigan, who later developed it into *The VIPS*, a picture starring Elizabeth Taylor and Richard Burton. Art and betrayal – the two had become intertwined in her life. As was Larry and Vivien's wont, their feelings were conveyed through the works of the Bard:

Life's but a walking shadow, a poor player
That struts and frets his hour upon the stage
And then is heard no more. It is a tale
Told by an idiot, full of sound and fury
Signifying nothing.[4]

Larry did not try to romanticise the episode and he realised they were trapped in a desperate cycle of trying again for old times' sake. She seemed more balanced than ever before and became obsessed with showing her devotion to him, and he played along, happy that in some way she had come back to him. It was reminiscent of an incident during their failed run of *Romeo and Juliet*, in 1940, when Vivien and Larry were entertaining Jack Merivale, the stepbrother of her former lover, John Buckmaster. Vivien and Merivale played a game of Chinese Checkers and he won; she teased him about his victory and then turned violent, screaming that he had cheated. Embarrassed, Merivale pleaded his innocence and implored Larry to intervene but he remained unmoved by the scene. 'Don't you try to come between us,' she menaced. 'We've been together for years. Nobody's coming between us. Don't you try!'[5]

❦

In the meantime, Larry took steps to ensure nobody would come between them, and they, in the spring of 1956, attempted domestic bliss – but it fooled nobody except themselves. It had been Larry's idea to give Vivien a child, thinking it would stabilise her moods and provide her with a long-term focus. Not to mention he was looking portly and older than his 49 years, and the critics thought he had 'lost his way ... he is an ageing matinee idol desperately fighting to win back his old reputation'.[6] What else could they do except play to the establishment and create a family? Vivien could retire to Notley with her baby and allow a nanny to do the rest. At least, those were his expectations. More than ever, the words of Leo Tolstoy rang true: 'Respect was invented to cover the empty place where love should be.'

The idealism, however, contradicted Vivien's plans and she continued as before. She shirked the confinement, advised due to her fragile health, and pushed herself harder than ever, despite being 42 and with a history of miscarrying. In June, she performed in *Night of 100 Stars* in aid of the Actors' Orphanage at the Palladium and rehearsed her dance routine for a total of thirty-four hours. 'Oh yes, I knew about the baby,' she remarked to those who were surprised by her physical activity. 'It was tiring but apart from that, I didn't suffer any ill effects.'[7]

For the past two months, she had been performing in Noël Coward's *South Sea Bubble*, as Alexandra, Lady Shotter, the flirtatious wife of Sir George Shotter, the governor of Samolo, a fictional South Sea island. The play toured the provinces before heading to London to open at the Lyric Theatre, and tickets were sold out in advance. The majority of the notices were positive, even if the plot was frivolous, and Coward knew the comedy would have faltered without her celebrity. After its opening in London, she revealed her pregnancy to

Coward, who was furious and felt betrayed. In his opinion, Vivien was a 'terrible little bitch' and he wrote to his friend, the author Nancy Mitford, telling her of Vivien's impulsive decision to have a 'dear little baby'.[8] More than anything, he resented Vivien leaving the play at the height of its success.

On a high, Vivien gave a press conference to deliver the news. Sitting on a loveseat with Larry standing behind her, she said:

I feel wonderful and terribly excited. It's been so long – twenty-two years – since my other baby was born. I'm going to have to learn to be a mother all over again and I'm not good at knitting … No, I don't take extra orange juice or milk. I carry on normally.[9]

'I just adore babies,' Larry added. 'But what's all the fuss about? Is it because of my great age?'[10]

Ahead of the baby's birth, she wanted to move to a Georgian house with five bedrooms in Chelsea or Belgravia. She also spoke of designing a yellow and white nursery, and her maternity wardrobe was to be custom-made by Balmain. Their unborn child would be a girl, she was certain of it, and they would name her Katherine. A photograph was taken of the Oliviers: he looked down at her lovingly – he was the world's greatest actor, don't forget – and she looked off to the distance, somewhat disengaged after all she had said.

A short time later, Vivien told Peter that he might be the father but she could not be certain, as in recent months Larry was more attentive than before. Peter then told Tamara, who felt suicidal by the news; she imagined newspaper headlines and a scandal. Tamara might have cast her mind back to Vivien's interactions with their daughter Anita – her god-daughter – and the consequences of those exchanges. 'Shut up and do as you're told,'[11] Vivien told the 3-year-old child when she refused to cooperate with something trivial. Another darker episode occurred when Vivien tried to force Anita to sit on a potty and, losing her patience, she turned to Tamara and said, 'Thank God you're here! I would have killed her if you hadn't arrived in another minute. I can't bear screaming and disobedient children. She didn't want to do what she had to do, and I was going to make her.'[12]

Perhaps it was naïve of Tamara to believe Vivien would publicly reveal the paternity of her child or that Peter would play a part in its life. The myth of the Oliviers would be preserved at all costs. A vortex gathered momentum, pulling them deeper into madness and deceit.

All the while, Larry was preparing to film *The Prince and The Showgirl* with Marilyn Monroe, with Monroe in the part which Vivien had played on stage in *The Sleeping Prince*. It was speculated that Vivien would reprise her role on screen but having seen Monroe in *How to Marry a Millionaire*, she thought to herself, 'Heaven help me, that she was very funny.' She turned to Larry and said, 'This girl is wonderful in comedy,'[13] and suggested that Monroe star opposite him, as she felt she was too old for the part. Repaying the compliment, Monroe said, 'I saw Vivien Leigh in *Gone with the Wind*, she was great.'[14]

Later, Vivien decided she wanted to be in the picture but Larry reminded her that she was too old. Such conflicting feelings about her age were apparent in 1952 when Dodie Smith wanted her to star as Cassandra in the play *Letter from Paris*, despite her being 39 and the character 17. A week later, after saying yes, she reneged on the agreement. She met Smith in person to deliver the news and gave her a bouquet of spider dahlias.

'You do forgive me, don't you?' Vivien asked.

'Oh no,' Smith replied, 'I shall go on liking you and admiring you, but I shall never forgive you. Because you would have been perfect as Cassandra.'[15]

Surprisingly to Larry, it had been love at first sight when he met Monroe in New York: he was charmed by her whispering voice and vulnerability. It soon turned to hatred when she failed to report to the set on time and insisted on numerous takes of every scene. He could just about tolerate Monroe's demand for a recording of *Londonderry Air* to be played over and over, forming part of the picture's musical score. Privately, he considered her a 'spoilt, contaminated fat slug'.[16]

It was believed that Vivien had announced her pregnancy to steal the limelight from Monroe, whose neurosis both she and Larry loathed. 'She will weekend with us – sometimes,'[17] Vivien said. Later, when her bitchiness was revealed, Vivien claimed to have been misquoted. As for Monroe, she was tired of acting and said, 'I'm going to make fewer films because I want to be a very good wife.'[18]

On 11 August, Vivien gave her final performance in *South Sea Bubble* and, after a farewell party in London, she left for Notley to await the birth of her baby. Hours later, the familiar pains began and she miscarried the next day – a gynaecologist came from London in the early hours of the morning, trying, in vain, to save it and told her nothing could be done. The foetus was a girl; he was so sorry. The death knell sounded at 5 o'clock in the morning and was recorded as such in her diary in fewer words – three words long – than she devoted to Suzanne's birth when she wrote, 'Had a baby, a girl'.[19]

Vivien and Larry were both grief-stricken and Vivien spent the day in bed, in tears and staring out of the window. 'We are bitterly disappointed but the main concern now is that Vivien should make a complete recovery,'[20] Larry told reporters. He suggested they try again, as soon as she healed from the necessary curettage. In that sense, he was clinging to any hope of saving their marriage and forging a permanent bond with her. She rejected his idea, not only was her age against her, but there were only so many blows she could stand. A day later, Larry's brother's wife, Hester, gave birth to a baby girl and said, 'Maybe … maybe Vivien might like to be the baby's godmother.'[21]

Vivien was no stranger to empty sentiments and the awkwardness in which they were spoken. In 1944, she had been pregnant with Larry's child and the timing could not have been worse. Her health was bad: she had just completed a gruelling tour of North Africa to entertain the Allied troops and came home with a racking cough and a fever, later to be diagnosed as tuberculosis. Despite those physical setbacks, she conceived and told everyone it was an act of God, a miracle, especially after her miscarriage in 1941.

At the time, Vivien was filming George Bernard Shaw's *Caesar and Cleopatra* with Claude Raines and Stewart Granger, and wondered how she would portray a 16-year-old Cleopatra while 'in the family way'. So, filming at Denham Studios was rushed to accommodate Vivien's condition and the threat of V-1 flying bombs dropping on London. Shaw, who had written the play and adapted it for the screen, considered her an 'idiot'[22] and thought poorly of her as his Egyptian queen. 'Vivien gabbling tonelessly such sounds as *cumminec-cho* and *oaljentlemin*! Does she always go on like that, or should I have had her here to drill her into the diction of the part?'[23] Shaw said, after watching the daily rushes. Gabriel Pascal, the director of the picture, was a ruthless taskmaster who worked her too hard and forced her to do laborious stunts. One such stunt, running across a marble floor on the set of Memphis Palace, caused her to slip and fall. She lost her baby a few days later. Larry told her the foetus had been a boy. 'There will be plenty more where that one came from,'[24] Vivien said, full of false bravado.

She was devastated and the emotional impact of the miscarriage was believed to have contributed to her mental instability. There was no evidence to suggest this, but Larry and others close to her made the connection between the trauma of losing her baby and the cyclic distur-bances that were to follow. Within a month, she would be high again, the rush of mania almost always corresponding with her menstrual cycle[25] and the crashing lows that crept in when the hormones fell.

Perhaps the feelings of lost motherhood when Vivien had wanted it most and the rejection of her firstborn child were hard to recon-cile not only within herself but from the point of view of others. In Hollywood in 1939, she surprised everyone with a party game called Ways to Kill Babies – her own invention – and improvised how one would carry out infanticide, such as throwing a baby from a car window. Undoubtedly, it was done to push the boundaries, to shock and entertain with something as taboo as murdering an infant. She had a pregnancy scare around that time – it was Larry's baby and she was yet to divorce Leigh Holman – and so the charade would have made sense to her.

Shortly after Vivien recovered from her miscarriage, Suzanne returned to England with Vivien's mother Gertrude, as they had been living in Vancouver during the war years. Suzanne was almost 12 and had last seen her mother five years earlier when Vivien flew to Canada after the filming of *Gone with the Wind* and brought with her Scarlett O'Hara dolls. During their informal meeting, Vivien must have seemed like a big sister or a playmate, and they both smiled in a photograph taken by Gertrude. Around that time, David O. Selznick wanted Vivien and Suzanne to star in *Jane Eyre* but Leigh rejected the idea, frightened by the recent kidnapping threats made on the child. Despite Vivien's strained relationship with Suzanne, she had an easy-going rapport with Larry's son, Tarquin, who lived in America during the war. At home, in England, he craved approval from his father and clung to any scraps of attention which Larry gave to him, their bond becoming something bigger and more magical in the child's mind. Larry himself was embarrassed by Tarquin; his feelings of guilt and shame were projected on to his son, though he did not address his neglect. When Tarquin stayed at Notley, it was Vivien who mothered him and tucked him into bed at night. In turn, the boy became besotted with her and they shared a bond, always. Was it easier to love Larry's son, a child who was not her own and who, on the surface, harboured no resentment for her breaking up his family? Might her own child, a girl, who would share so many stereotypical notions of womanhood, see right through her?

Some believed Vivien consoled Leigh by giving him full custody of Suzanne; an apology, as such, for hurting him. The truth was, she was immature and not cut out for motherhood, and she wanted to spare her child the pain of feeling unwanted. In her defence, and to soften the blow, Vivien claimed she did want to have children, in the future, but not at the age of 19, when she had given birth to Suzanne. Certainly not in the years that followed; she chose her lover, Larry, over her child and did not challenge Leigh's bid for custody. The consequences of her actions influenced Suzanne's upbringing and she was raised by a nanny, her grandmother and her father. In a way, the war and her subsequent evacuation to Canada spared the child any embarrassment when it came to justifying her mother's absence. Years later, Vivien said, 'I felt too young to be the mother of a child, and very lacking in the qualities of restfulness and serenity which a mother should have.'[26]

One day at Notley, Trader Faulkner remarked to Suzanne, 'You're not like your mother, are you?'

'No, thank God,'[27] Suzanne replied.

The reality of Vivien's behaviour came to the surface when she was filming *Anna Karenina* for Alexander Korda in 1947. At the centre of Leo Tolstoy's novel was the love affair between Anna Karenina and Count Vronsky, for whom Anna leaves her husband and son. On paper, the story was profound and sympathetic towards Anna and her unhappiness; however, on screen, Ralph Richardson played Anna's cruel husband, Alexei, as likeable. Kieron Moore was miscast as her passionate lover, Vronsky, with whom she had no chemistry. 'A common stick,'[28] Lady Diana Cooper said of Moore, after seeing the picture.

Before the first fitting for costumes, designed by Cecil Beaton, Vivien stood in the doorway wearing a mink coat and with violets pinned to her chest.[29] As there was no time to do numerous fittings for the period costumes, Beaton had her wear a linen shift and a plaster mould was replicated from her torso. There was something touching about her vulnerability. More so, behind the scenes, when she lazed about in Anna's corsets and bustles, wilting from the summer heatwave and reading *Is Sex Necessary?* between takes. And, again, when she viewed the rushes and saw the picture falling apart on screen.[30] Her appearance preoccupied her and she studied her face in the mirror, inspecting the spidery lines around her eyes and mouth, prematurely formed from sleepless nights and chain-smoking, and wondered if her turned-up nose could be improved upon. The news of Larry's knighthood reached the set and she was furious about the honour. 'Really, it's too stupid!'[31] she snapped at her reflection in the glass. She was in a bad mood: her dressmaker from Paris was waiting at the hotel and the studio forgot to send a car for her. To her, nothing was right and everything was beyond her control.

As the filming came to an end, she fell into a deep depression. Perhaps it was the parallel storyline between herself and Anna, both of whom had abandoned their children, only Anna had died by suicide by throwing herself under a train. The final result was a failure: it was 'a beautiful shell without a heart'.[32] Anna's last words reflected Vivien's feelings: 'Why not turn out the lights when there's nothing more to be seen?'[33]

⚜

Two weeks after her miscarriage, Vivien went house-hunting in London and travelled to Portofino to recuperate without Larry who was busy filming *The Prince and the Showgirl* at Pinewood Studios. The paparazzi, loitering in the Piazza Martiri dell' Olivetta, captured her coming and going from souvenir shops. Her middle, still swollen where her baby had been, could not quell the cruel whispers at home: they said it was a cry for attention – a publicity stunt.

In Vivien's absence, Larry had a casual fling with Maxine Audley, who appeared as Lady Sunningdale in *The Prince and the Showgirl*. Audley participated in their Stratford season and seemed as mad as Vivien in her antics. One day, Audley and Vivien stripped off their clothes and jumped into the River Avon.[34] Their liaison, Larry claimed, was nothing more than kindness on Audley's part, and she remained a friend to them both. It is worth noting, from the perspective of Larry and others, that Vivien's sexual affairs were described as promiscuous and her interest in sex was labelled as nymphomania. Whereas, he was forgiven for being lonely and at a loss – he would be 50 soon – and society was far more understanding of men and their needs.

During a manic episode, Vivien told Tamara Finch that when she was a child in India she walked in on her parents having sex. She thought her father was violating – hurting – her mother and it scarred her deeply. As she grew older and more aware of the adult world around her, she came to resent men: their selfishness, their superiority, their authority.[35] Was it possible, then, that Vivien's nymphomania, as it was labelled, and casual encounters – fuelled by her mental illness – was an exercise in self-loathing? Often, her sexual deviance was viewed through an onlooker's lens and never from her point of view. Therefore, has it become mythicised and part of her legend?

In truth, when gripped by a manic episode, Vivien propositioned people of both sexes. 'Two women together was the most pleasurable lovemaking,' she told Tamara, inviting her to go to bed with her. '*C'est pas pour moi*,'[36] ('That's not for me') Tamara replied, letting her down gently.

Contrary to gossip, there would be more rejections than conquests, as those close to Vivien recognised her lack of control and kept her safe, as opposed to exploiting her. It asks the question: why did some boast of sleeping with her when they were aware of her compromised mental state? Was it an ego boost on their behalf?

It was reminiscent of Vivien's time at the Convent of the Sacred Heart in Dinard, then aged 13, where she attracted the attention of the local boys. The boys loitered at the gate and followed her to the beach, waiting for her to come out of the sea in her wool bathing suit. She was viewed as the distraction, the one to blame; the little tempt-ress of the Côte d'Émeraude. At home, her beauty piqued the interest of Tommy, Gertrude's lover, who was old enough to know better and to remedy her mother's jealousy, she was sent away to school. It remains unknown if Tommy's behaviour extended beyond leering glances but throughout her life, particularly during a manic phase, she was terrified of being raped. Sexual assault was her deepest fear. Or was it a dark memory she repressed? Later, her fame did not protect her when 'a dangerous man'[37] – Herbert Wanbon – tried to kiss her as she left her car and attacked Larry in his attempt to reach her. Her penetrable beauty made her fair game and, in a way, dehumanised her.

Longing for a connection to someone, Vivien telephoned Peter and told him of the miscarriage. The coast was clear: there would be no baby with a dubious paternity and no scandal. It affected her more than she could say but she found little sympathy from others: they considered it a foolish endeavour at her age and with her health problems. Some (wrongly) suspected it was a phantom pregnancy. She had no control over her mind, her impulses and, as it were, her body. Everything within her had become inhospitable.

There was an element of control attached to Vivien's affair with Peter: she had the upper hand and he knew it. An incident in Hollywood, in 1953, stood out. Vivien had a headache and wanted to leave a party and she asked Tamara to take over the wheel of the car if she became too ill to drive. However, Tamara could not drive, nor could Peter, and Vivien, in a rage and with her hands on the wheel, berated them for their incompetence. In her words, they were stupid and selfish, and she asked why other people should have to chauffeur them around. The Finches sat in the back of the car, feeling like two powerless fools.[38]

Peter wanted to distance himself from Vivien and he accepted Rank's offer to film *The Shiralee* on location in Australia. He was financially and spiritually bankrupt, having accused her of pushing him to the brink and inspiring extreme behaviour which, at times, confused him. As for his marriage to Tamara, it was over, and he would rarely see their daughter during her childhood. In Australia, his old habits returned and he spent the duration of the production drinking and womanising. On the beach, he met Yolande Turnbull and was attracted by her legs, and she agreed to follow him to London – she would eventually become his second wife – and, in Rome, he fell for a teenager who looked like Gina Lollobrigida, and she, too, agreed to go to London. All of the women, and his second marriage, were on the rebound from Vivien. 'It's my own bloody fault. I hate myself for being fascinated. I'm a selfish bastard. I want to quit all of this and make a clean break!'[39] Peter said. Although he tried, he never succeeded in kicking against the current of Vivien's love.

Feeling adrift, Vivien went to Torremolinos, in southern Spain, with Larry and they spent their time fighting and trying to get away from each other. He retired to his bed on Christmas Day and remained there on Boxing Day, suffering from gout. Vivien followed, an unnatural thing for her to do, as she loathed to be idle. At times, however, she had no interest in anything and could not read or do menial activities to amuse herself. That was the depressive state – the low as it were – and Larry welcomed it. For Vivien, the most memorable Christmas Day was spent in Hollywood in 1938, when at George Cukor's party, she was given the news she would be cast as Scarlett O'Hara. 'I knew that my dream had come true,'[40] she later said. 'I have always believed that if you want something with all your heart and soul you get it.'[41]

Their time in Spain was futile and filled with arguments as they toured the towns and coves of the Costa del Sol. She was captured in photographs swinging between dreaminess and high spirits, her mouth opened wide, clearly delighted by something while Larry kept his eyes on her, stony-faced. No longer could his little Baba charm him. There were silly errors at the airport and a mixing-up of seats which irritated him. Minor issues turned into embarrassing scenes and he must have wondered if it was worth the effort; he was only ever miserable in her company and she seemed not to notice the melancholy and anger consuming him. 'I do have a self-detestation,' he once said, 'though you might not think it the way I talk around myself.'[42]

'If you're in love with something, it's comparatively easy but if you're not, then life is more difficult, isn't it?'[43] she said of her tiresome roles. In hindsight, perhaps one was being Lady Olivier; their partnership was redundant, even if she refused to admit it.

Larry was far more pragmatic and honed in on his senses, knowing by then, their marriage had expired. 'Keep your bloody eyes open, all your senses open. You never know what might be useful. It's like a disease with me,' he said. His real life merged with his acting, and vice versa. 'It's fatal to be too relaxed.'[44]

Chapter Eight

'*Your bait of falsehood take this carp of truth*'

Hamlet, William Shakespeare

 ❧❦❧

1957

Although Vivien and Larry were drifting apart in their marriage, they continued to move in the same direction. In May, they embarked on a three-month tour of *Titus Andronicus* with the Shakespeare Memorial Theatre Company, performing the gruesome tragedy in Paris, Venice and Vienna, and going behind the Iron Curtain to Belgrade, Zagreb and Warsaw. The play would conclude with a month-long run at the Stoll Theatre in London.

For Larry, the tour was a penance and he felt it was pointless to break his contract. He remained in turmoil about his responsibility to his craft and the role of caretaker to Vivien as she ricocheted from one extreme to the next. He had disappointed her earlier in the year: she wanted to play the part of Ann Shankland in the Hollywood adaptation of Terence Rattigan's *Separate Tables*, only if he would direct and star as Major Pollock in the picture. They both agreed to do it and a press release was issued, and then they dropped out at the first hurdle, a move initiated by him and deeply regretted by her.

As she had given a passive performance as Lavinia at Stratford, it was hoped she would revive the character with an air of detachment once more, if only for the sake of her mental stability. Having absorbed the character flaws of Blanche DuBois, Larry was afraid of Vivien taking on the darker, more sinister elements of *Titus Andronicus*: the brutality of Lavinia's mutilation and the trauma of being raped on her husband's corpse.

As with English audiences, the foreign audiences were disturbed by the visualisation of Peter Brook's staging and the chilling music scoring the production which sounded like a piano's chord being plucked. Furthermore, as in Stratford, they were shocked by the red ribbons, representing haemorrhages of blood, streaming from Vivien's mouth and arms, where Lavinia's tongue and hands had once been. There was also the bone-grinding noise of an axe coming down on Larry's hand and one member of the audience fainted on hearing the bone-crushing sound effect. The macabre tone of the play paralleled the darkness hanging over Larry's life with Vivien. A feeling supported by Brook, who said, 'Everything in *Titus* is linked to a dark flowing current out of which surge the horrors, rhythmically and logically related – if one searches in this way one can find the expression of a powerful and eventually beautiful barbaric ritual.'[1]

After each performance, Vivien was like an animal being released from its cage. She wanted to stay up and party all night, feeling energised by the young members of the cast whom she dragged back to wherever she and Larry were staying. She was the queen, with a court of young male admirers who found her game for anything, in contrast to Larry, who wanted to retire after each performance, all his energy spent. They partied without Larry, and Vivien took them shopping, to art galleries and on sightseeing tours. Like a sponge, she absorbed everything from her surroundings and transmitted it to other people who were willing to learn. At that particular time, she was reading a book on Buddhism, an endlessly fascinating subject for her to delve into; she adored mysticism and others would have agreed that she was quite magical herself. Fatigue never overtook her and when she did sleep, her usual three to four hours, she was haunted by nightmares. In a sense, she channelled her troubles into Lavinia, intentionally or not, and she walked through the part as if in a dream.

In Paris, Vivien was entertained by the richest man in France, Paul-Louis Weiller, a controversial figure who, it was believed, had sold fighter planes to the French knowing they would crash. Rumours prevailed, but it did not deter her and she enjoyed his hospitality, namely driving around the city in his Rolls-Royce and floating down the Seine in a river boat. Every morning, she went to Les Halles and revived herself with onion soup[2] and later purchased an entire wardrobe from Balmain. She had followed a similar course during the Australian tour in 1948 and bought a Jerboa rat which 'hopped like a kangaroo' and enquired about an Agile wallaby but rejected a platypus as they 'cost about £40 a week in worms'.[3] For Larry, however, those little acts were no longer funny; she was no longer charming.

The decadence told on Vivien's face and she was looking swollen and aged, something the Parisians noted in their reports, and they questioned the great beauty which had been affixed to her identity for years. Since childhood, she had been told she was beautiful and at convent school she was part of an exclusive clique known as The Exquisites. She was almost 44 and the image commonly held of her was of Scarlett O'Hara's 25-year-old face, preserved in celluloid. In the flesh, her complexion was a mass of tiny wrinkles, like porcelain when it cracks,[4] and she wore too much makeup – she deliberately overlined her lips – and most were surprised by how petite she really was.

At the Sarah Bernhardt Theatre, she disappointed the French audience, who thought her charisma as an actress was lacking and the false voice she used on stage, as trained to do so by Larry, shattered any illusions they had of her. Before she left Paris, she was awarded the Légion d'honneur, which she accepted with good grace – making a speech in fluent French with tears streaming down her face.

Then it was on to Venice, where Vivien was joined by Gertrude and Suzanne and the trio took in the tourist sites and posed, pigeons balancing on their heads and arms, in St Mark's Square. Vivien wore a hat which resembled a habit and, swarmed by the vermin, she looked like a novice. 'Get thee to a nunnery,'[5] Larry might have quipped in happier times. In Venice, she was in her natural habitat and nobody, not least the locals, passed judgement on her high spirits.[6] She was, to the Italians' amusement, *tempestosa*.

Despite the performances being poor in Venice, the audience was intrigued by the set and the cruelty on display: the perversity of the crimes and the hallucinatory aspects of the lighting and music, and Vivien 'pale and passing like a Poe ghost'.[7] The Italian newspaper,

La Stampa, wrote, 'A bigger appeal – intellectual and worldly – could not have been invented in Venice for the beginning of the theatre festival.' The Italian critics considered Larry a giant of the theatre and Vivien 'a very light and ardent actress, who entered the magic circle of [Larry's] art with a surreal sensitivity'.[8]

They pressed on with the tour and each stop was punctuated by whichever fixation Vivien had at the time. She accepted invitations to events at which she was to be the guest of honour and invited the entire company to join her, entering, as it were, with her faithful entourage behind her, a sort of mad Pied Piper. Naturally, surrounded by so many, the veneer of the Oliviers began to slip and everyone was privy to things that were otherwise kept behind closed doors. In Vienna, she and Larry had an argument in a restaurant, their shouting rising above the dense noise of the patrons.[9] Then, days later, on the Simplon-Orient Express, she woke her sleeping colleagues and demanded they look at the Italian countryside as it flashed past the windows on their way to Belgrade.

In Belgrade, the play was received enthusiastically, the horrors of the script – the war and mindless slaughtering of young men – mirrored the terror of the Communist regime.[10] The curtain call lasted for twenty minutes and the company had dinner with President Tito and were served White Lady cocktails. Everyone was worried about the censorship and espionage operating under the guise of everyday life and were, perhaps, relieved when Vivien behaved perfectly with Tito, who wore diamond cufflinks despite his ideological distaste for wealth.

In Zagreb, at a dinner with Yugoslavian academics, Vivien gave an impromptu speech and smiling sweetly at their adoring faces, she said, 'I think this is the most fucking boring evening I have ever had in my life.'[11] Lost in translation, her hosts nodded and agreed, thinking she had given a lyrical speech of gratitude. She repeated similar profanity during a children's matinee performance when Larry, as Titus, began to recite, 'I am the sea; hark! How her sighs do blow—' interrupting him with, 'Silly cunt.'[12]

She started to unravel, as Larry knew she would, though to onlookers she was simply filled with enthusiasm and struggled to burn off an adrenaline rush. As the temperature rose to scorching levels, so did her euphoria and she tore off her clothes in a public park. The night before they left, she stayed on a park bench before going to the railway station in the morning. She had sat on the same bench before her performance in Zagreb, having gone missing before the curtain rose, and was eventually found and brought in for the play.[13]

The train waited at the platform and she refused to board it, announcing she loved Yugoslavia and did not want to leave. The police chief, who had been assigned to look after her, lifted her and placed her on the carriage and she responded by punching him in the eye.[14] On the way to Vienna, the train ground to a halt in a cutting between two tunnels in the mountains. She opened the carriage door and got out, wandering along the tracks followed by Larry and others from the company, who tried but failed to convince her to board the train. It started to move and they left her, so she sat down on the grass, watching it pull away. Moments later, she walked along the tracks, following the train, which then reversed back and collected her. Nothing made sense to her, or the others, and she remained silent all the way to Vienna.

Having arrived in Vienna, she was met by a doctor and injected with a sedative. The descent began and slowly she regained balance. By the time she reached Warsaw, the final stop on the European tour, she was somewhat restored to her old self, albeit still reckless and with a longing to experience everything. After their performance, they were pelted with flowers. The momentum broke and she smashed a hotel window.

From Warsaw, Vivien took a flight to Krakow with the company and was mobbed by Polish fans, who recognised her as Scarlett O'Hara, and narrowly missed getting back to Warsaw on time, as neither she nor the young people in the company who followed her had a clue about the flight schedule. She made it, however, and spent her evening dancing in a nightclub with no money to pay the drinks bill, and charmed her way out of the perilous situation.

<center>~~~~~</center>

In short, Vivien was determined to get her own way and she made a scene when she did not. It might have been easy to suggest she had the presence of mind to manipulate a situation to her advantage. A survival instinct, psychologically speaking, but it did not endear her to those she hoodwinked. She could not stand other people exerting their power over her, evident in her litigation with David O. Selznick, who, in 1945, sued her for breaking her seven-year contract with Selznick Productions.

'I signed the contract on a Friday the thirteenth,'[15] Vivien said, an omen for the legal misery it would cause her. She knew what she was signing, even if she had no intention of fulfilling the seven-year clause. Even the flat fee of £4,000 did not concern her. In due course, she came to resent the lack of royalties, given *Gone with the Wind* had grossed millions at the box office.

There had been a legal tug of war for four years after Vivien hightailed it out of Hollywood and returned to England, telling Selznick she was needed for the war effort. 'I shan't leave this country again until the war is over. I am staying right here,'[16] she said. Finally, when there was no sign of her returning, he applied to the high court for an injunction, preventing her from doing Thornton Wilder's play, *The Skin of Our Teeth*, to be produced by Larry, who had also bought the British rights.

Presiding over Selznick's claim was Sir Walter Monckton KC, who told the court that a basic contract engaging Vivien for Selznick Productions was made in 1939 and a series of options extended over several years. Remuneration started at £321 a week, rising to £1,500. Sir Walter argued that her screen personality was the 'most valuable commodity and to be treated as an exotic plant'[17] and, therefore, Selznick, had a right to demand exclusivity.

The judge, Mr Justice Romer of the Chancery Division, asked, 'Would the granting of an injunction compel Miss Leigh to idleness?'[18]

Mr Valentine Holmes, who represented Vivien, replied, 'I don't suppose there is affirmative evidence that she would get a job as a charwoman or temporary cook.' Mr Holmes argued if Vivien had not participated in the play, she would have been subjected to factory work under wartime regulations and the idea did not appeal to her. In his closing argument, Holmes explained, that as Vivien did not like to be idle, she adopted the view that throughout the war, those who were English should work as much as possible in England.[19]

The injunction was dismissed by Mr Justice Romer and Vivien was free of her legal entanglements with Selznick. However, she did not take the claim seriously and even before it was settled, she was touring with *The Skin of Our Teeth* in Liverpool, Blackpool and Manchester before opening at the Phoenix Theatre in London. As Sabina, she was the coquettish housemaid to the Antrobus family in the first and third acts, and a beauty queen in the second, who among other things, survives wars, the Ice Age, Biblical floods and the murder of Abel. She was hailed as a sensation and steered the (intentional) chaos of the play with comedic timing. The screen siren was still there and she played the part wearing Revlon nail polish in the shade 'Bachelor Carnation'. 'Don't look at my nails,' she told an interviewer. 'They're all broken. It's the polish. I have to change it so often.'[20]

During the run of the play, she began to feel fatigued. A dull feeling of nausea and pains lingered in her chest, causing her headaches and other odd symptoms that came and went. A persistent cough and spots of blood on her handkerchief alarmed those around her, but she continued with the play until breathlessness overwhelmed her and she became frailer as the days progressed. When she was not participating in a scene, as such, she lay on a couch far downstage, close enough to hear the audience's criticisms. At a matinee performance, two elderly ladies were watching the play, unimpressed with its hare-brained plot.

'Are you going to take tea at the interval?' one asked.

'No! Don't let's give them one penny more!'[21] the other replied.

After seventy-eight performances, the play closed due to Vivien becoming ill with a tubercular patch on her left lung. She was forced to rest at home with a fire burning and the windows flung open to resemble a sanatorium. Each day resembled the last, reclining in bed doing *The Times* crossword and talking on the telephone to her friends. She wondered if she could pass the time by conceiving a baby and was firmly discouraged by her doctor, who considered it a foolish idea. Instead, her confinement was spent reading St Thérèse of Lisieux's memoir, *The Story of a Soul*. Yes, she would always get her own way and upset others in the process, but at what cost? It seemed she could only go so far without some uncontrollable force stopping her in her tracks. The words of St Thérèse resonated with her: 'Dear God! You alone know all that I endured.'[22]

As in Leo Tolstoy's *Anna Karenina*, the train would become a symbolic omen and deliver Vivien to her fate; a slow road to destruction before her inevitable demise, metaphorically speaking. She could not see that Larry had become tired of her behaviour; he felt no enthusiasm for the displays of affection she paid to him in front of their friends, calling him the greatest actor who ever lived and, in an interview, referring to him as her master.[23] Although her words were sincere, to him they sounded generic and meaningless.

Twenty years earlier, he had fallen in love with Vivien's devil-may-care attitude and it made him feel alive to experience her ever-changing nature. She was reflection and he was light, or was it the other way round? Now, having turned 50 in Paris during the European tour, he was exhausted and longed for the uncomplicated adoration of a younger woman. He knew he was going through 'the change of life', as he referred to it, otherwise known as the male menopause. Women his age repulsed him. 'See her? That woman?' he remarked to his son, Tarquin. 'She's my age to the very day. Fifty: and who wants her? What has she got to look forward to? Where's the sex in her, and who the fuck wants to be touched by her?'[24]

It was a relief to him when the 'gory but nice'[25] *Titus Andronicus* concluded at the Stoll Theatre in London, marking the end of his commitment to not only the play but to Vivien. Or, to paraphrase Kenneth Tynan's review of the production, he could no longer tolerate 'the piling of agony on to a human head until it splits'. The problem was, he could not bring himself to make a clean break. There was something which bound him to her: a sense of responsibility, guilt, or the realisation that, off stage, he could not emote in real life without some dramatic part forcing him to do so. Or was it a sadistic streak that reared its ugly head now and then, forcing him to experience her at her worst? Only in the fictional world of his characters could he rise to the occasion.

In that fictional world, he had fallen in love with Dorothy Tutin, an act unfathomable to Vivien when she eventually learnt of the affair. A month before their European tour, he had accepted the part of Archie Rice, an ageing music hall comedian, in *The Entertainer*. The play was written by John Osborne, a young playwright at the centre of the Angry Young Men, a movement which detested the establishment and its influence on English theatres. Larry, although alien to the movement, wanted to be part of it and reinvent himself in the latest genre – the 'kitchen sink drama'. It ran for a month at the Royal Court Theatre and he fell in love with Tutin, who played his daughter, Jean Rice.

Perhaps his feelings were the result of his pent-up resentment towards Vivien and her illness, the latter had become part of her identity and the two could not be separated. During the run of *Titus Andronicus*, they had goaded one other as they walked from the wings and crossed the stage. 'Fuck you, fuck you,' they spoke in stage whispers. The company members were not shocked, it was how they spoke in private, and they considered it banter,[26] a sort of warm-up for the blood bath unfolding on stage.

In recent times, Larry had become desensitised to all around him and longed to escape his obligations to Vivien and his traditional repertoire, as it no longer satisfied him. Suddenly, he found himself energised by his new play and colleagues, particularly Dorothy Tutin. Those feelings for Tutin had first stirred at the beginning of Vivien's illness in 1953 and now, in 1957, they overpowered him. Like a virus which had lain dormant, Vivien's behaviour pushed him back to Tutin, who had played Polly Peachum in *The Beggar's Opera* in 1953. As with Jean Simmons and Claire Bloom, Tutin was another variation of Vivien and shared the same arrangement of feline features, dark hair and soft voice. Somewhere, amid the chaos of his marriage, he was searching for the perfect image he held of Vivien, even if it meant its physical likeness was transferred to another.

At times, Vivien suspected Larry was having an affair or, at the very least, she was curious about the unusual hours he was keeping after the theatre. Feelings of doubt stirred as she watched the rehearsals from the dress circle and on one occasion she cried at Larry's performance but said nothing by way of praise, except that something disturbed the equilibrium within her. His incarnation of Archie Rice was an effigy: someone he was becoming, or someone he already was and could no longer hide. She would observe Larry, Tutin and

Osborne conspiring with the director, Tony Richardson, all huddled together like a murder of crows.

At night, when he did not return home, Vivien went to the Chelsea Embankment and got out of her chauffeur-driven car and walked up and down the road. What was she expecting to find? It remains unclear except that her instincts told her to do it. One night, her friend Trader Faulkner spied her from his houseboat, dressed in a leopard-print coat, and mistook her for a prostitute looking for business.

Tutin lived in another houseboat and this was where Larry spent his evenings after the curtain came down. Like his first love, Jill Esmond, Tutin seemed stable and dependable – her earthiness evoking the maternal spirit he so worshipped – she was a solid force in his otherwise unpredictable world. A piece of Staffordshire china rather than the Fabergé egg that was Vivien: extravagant, brittle and useless, at least to him. It spoke of his longing to portray himself as a man of the people. A realist. He started to go to the East End to see nude shows, which Vivien said was 'perfectly alright'[27] as he said it was to research the world of Archie Rice. Still, the idea that everything about their old world – her world – might repel him never occurred to her.

Nobody would take Larry away from her and she was determined to fight off any competition. From Vivien's point of view, no other actress could compete with her; no other woman represented the theatre as much as she did. She was the 'un-coroneted Peeress of the theatre which is, after all, the nucleus of the new aristocracy'.[28] Tutin was 27 and part of a bohemian theatrical crowd which Vivien did not understand, nor did she care to.

With Gertrude in attendance, Vivien received Tutin at her marital home and sized up her enemy, wondering, perhaps, how easy it would be to reap the spoils of war. After Vivien showed signs of distress, Gertrude chimed in and asked if Tutin wished to be known as a murderess, for Vivien would take her own life if she did not leave Larry alone. It was enough to spook Tutin into cooling her affair with Larry, even if they did go on seeing one another with less enthusiasm than before.

A short time later, Vivien broached the subject and asked Larry if he was in love with someone else. He admitted that he was. 'How marvellous for you,' she said, perfectly calm – which surprised him. 'And how marvellous for her.'²⁹

Despite Vivien's measured response, she could not process the betrayal. That spring, though it seemed like a lifetime ago, there had been scenes of domestic bliss at Notley with them both gardening and resuming their plans to adapt *Macbeth* for the screen. The eerie stillness of her mood was contradicted by her restless nights wandering in the garden and awakening from night terrors. Jars had been filled with syrup and placed all around for the wasps to drown in.³⁰ There was a sound of frantic buzzing and then a gentle lull as they became trapped and slowly died. Wasps were symbolic of his situation: Larry couldn't resist something sweet and became trapped, and felt he was slowly dying as a result.

Several nights later, Vivien reflected on Larry's confession and fury gripped her, as had another manic episode. She was determined to exert her control over him and forbade him from sleeping: she demanded he stay up with her all night. A sort of torturous exercise, determined only to break him. His sleep defied her, and she took a wet facecloth and whipped him across his eyes, violently awakening him. The lashing across the eyes, and not the face, was almost Shakespearean in its punishment: a blinding of his vision, exorcising the distorted way he now looked at her – she was no longer his darling. The words of King Lear were never so prophetic as they were now: 'Get thee glass eyes, and like a scurvy politician, seem to see the things thou dost not.'³¹

He managed to leave the room and escaped to a study down the passageway, where he locked the door. She stood on the other side, hammering with her fists, making a scene. He could tolerate it no longer and he opened the door, driven by something demonic and gripped by an inner strength which terrified him. Later, he would say he was afraid of killing her one day.³² Taking her by the wrists, he dragged her back to their bedroom and threw her towards the bed. Instead of landing on the bed, she hit the marble bedside cabinet and cut her left eyebrow, resulting in a wound close to her temple. He knew then he had to leave: if not, they would murder each other.

The following morning, she wore a black eyepatch and explained she had been bitten by an insect. The venom, however, remained somewhere deep beneath the surface, flowing through her veins. She was off to meet with an Equity deputation and the Minister of Housing, Henry Brooke, at the Ministry of Whitehall to discuss the fate of the St James's Theatre, a place she and Larry had run from 1950 until the Christmas of 1956. 'Hats off to Vivien Leigh my pin-up public figure of the week,' the *Daily Mirror* wrote. 'She has had the courage to know what she wants and to go for it with no holds barred.'[33]

Her fixation to save the theatre began during their month-long run of *Titus Andronicus* at the Stoll and she rallied her supporters to march along The Strand in protest of its planned demolition. She failed to take a pragmatic approach to the old building which needed a new roof, was structurally unsafe and a fire hazard, and was costing a fortune to maintain. To her, it represented their union together and it had to be saved at all costs. 'It's just one more thing I know we shall lose,'[34] Larry said. He supported her, to an extent, and admired her courage.

In response, Vivien threatened to chain herself to the stage door, warning that only a lunatic would pull down a theatre with a human being attached to it.[35] When her threat failed to rouse sympathy from the government, she said she would leave England, as it was no place for artists.[36]

Larry was on board with trying to save the St James's, even if he no longer had a say in its administration, until Vivien took him by surprise. In July, they had attended a debate in the House of Lords and she could no longer bear the peers' dismissive remarks on the arts. Rising to her feet in Black Rod's box, she interrupted Lord Bessborough's speech. 'My Lords,' she shouted, 'I wish to protest against the St James's Theatre being demolished!'[37]

There was absolute silence from the peers. She was shaking from nerves and temper; she knew she could not control her impulses.[38] The peers stared at her with fury and bewilderment: in her green floral dress and sun hat, she was the picture of Scarlett O'Hara, 'I'm the terror of Tara' – just as she had sung at a war benefit in Aldershot in 1943.[39]

'Now you have to go,' Black Rod, Sir Brian Horrocks told her.

'Certainly,' she snapped. 'I have to get to the theatre.'[40]

Larry left before she was escorted out: he had seen enough and knew she had gone too far. There could be no salvaging their

argument in favour of the theatre. Mania and anger fuelled her out-
rageous, though some say justified, outburst: 'Vivien Leigh is a lovely
lady with, if she will pardon the expression, guts.'[41] It was rumoured
that plain-clothed policemen and policewomen were placed at the
door and around the building, in case she returned. She did not.

From her dressing room at the Stoll, she posed with a portrait of
the St James's Theatre and told reporters:

> I think it is a disgrace for the theatre to be demolished. We have just
> all come back from a tour of Europe, where in every country we have
> been to they are building theatres as hard as they can go. Come back to
> England and what are they doing? Tearing them down! I saw British
> workmen tearing down the Gaiety even on a Sunday. I have a great
> personal attachment to this theatre [St James's], but it is more for the
> sake of England that I think it should be maintained.[42]

The fate of the St James's Theatre was inevitable: in October, its interior was stripped, and in December, it was demolished. It symbolised
more than Vivien could say and perhaps more than she knew. In
time, legislation was passed, stating if an old theatre was demolished,
a new one had to be erected in its place. The old way of life was
being destroyed; she would never act with Larry again. *The Entertainer*
had transferred to the Palace Theatre and Joan Plowright replaced
Dorothy Tutin and became the object of Larry's affection. Vivien
knew the sand timer was almost out of its grains but she continued
to fight, despite it all being a lost cause. In the words of Lady Diana
Cooper, she was a 'poor valiant little heroine'.[43]

Chapter Nine

'Defer no time, delays have dangerous ends'

Henry VI, William Shakespeare

❦

1958

When Vivien was recovering from her breakdown at Netherne Asylum in 1953, an intruder broke into Durham Cottage and stole her jewellery and her Academy Award for *A Streetcar Named Desire*. At the time, the news was kept from her, as it was feared she would suffer a setback, but she was told after her release. When she learnt of the robbery, it upset her immensely. The sense of intrusion and material loss was understandable, but it was something much deeper: the knowledge that a stranger wanted what she owned and had taken it for themselves.

'Vivien has had a dreadful shock. It is such a pity, because she was recovering so well from her illness. The thieves have taken every piece of jewellery Vivien possessed,' Larry told reporters. 'The poor girl has nothing left.'[1]

Now, Vivien remained oblivious to a similar intrusion, but the loss would be much greater. At the beginning of 1958, she said goodbye to Larry, who had gone to New York to perform in *The Entertainer* opposite Joan Plowright, with whom he had now fallen in love and who was also married. As in the early days with Vivien, his lingering Oedipus complex transferred to Joan and he remembered a kiss from his mother when he was 12 and said, 'I've been looking for her ever since and think I've found her in Joanie.'[2] The news, of course, was kept from Vivien and despite Larry wanting a divorce, he was afraid to discuss it with her. He had asked her, two years earlier, and she had threatened to take her own life if he followed through with it. 'I'd rather live a short life with Larry than face a long one without him,'[3] Vivien said. She meant every word.

There were times when she knew Larry still loved her and little sparks of familiarity flickered between them. He looked at her with adoration, even on the *Titus Andronicus* tour when he could no longer stand to be alone with her. There was something moving about his wife being adored collectively and he was proud when others showed their admiration for her.[4] Her lovely voice and the way she gazed up at whoever was talking to her, and the sudden, small movements like an elastic band snapping into place. It inspired affection within him and there were moments of stolen glances and smiles. Like a sedative, before it took hold, the placid feeling filtered to nothingness, and then he woke up.

'For four months, I lived in the dark. In a constant nightmare,'[5] she said after her breakdown in 1953. For Larry, the period of darkness lasted much longer, too long for him to continue living with only a faint spark to light the path ahead. After her hospitalisation, he had to learn to live with a stranger and to re-acquaint himself with the new person she had become.

To walk away would have been sensible, but it was the easy way out, as far as he was concerned. He drew on the 'very deep feeling'[6] they had for one another, nurtured from their determination to be together in the face of adversity. They first experienced the public's cruelty in 1939 when they became world famous and their affair was revealed: they received letters from strangers, and according to him, people spat at them in the street. 'It breeds in you a great determination,' he said. 'And that will outwear a lot of bad weather; it will stand constant in the teeth of the gale and in the drenching of the flooding rain.'[7]

To Vivien, he confirmed the longevity of their partnership, and months before his departure to America, he took a lease on an apartment at 54 Eaton Square and she decorated it to her exacting tastes, each room reflecting a different mood, a scene, including his study. Her touch was everywhere: chintz fabrics; clashes of colours; mirrored walls; pillars; and maroon velvet silk curtains. When they first moved to Durham Cottage, he tried his hand at gardening but his flowerbeds wilted and the creepers died. He filled the pond with fish and they, too, suffered the same fate. Their home, wherever it may be, was her domain. She missed him terribly.

Meanwhile, at the Algonquin Hotel, in suite no. 808, Larry was living with Joan and bracing himself for the ending of his momentary happiness. 'Helpless'[8] was how he later described their situation and Joan, unlike Vivien's demands twenty years earlier, understood his responsibility towards his wife. Did he even spare Vivien a thought? She was, after all, declared the most 'over-publicised lady of the year'.[9] Her presence was everywhere, but he was not tempted to go back. The co-dependency, on his behalf, had been severed.

'The definition of a star, though, Vivien, is a girl who can stare into a camera and convince every man out there that she needs him and cannot exist without him,'[10] Kenneth Tynan informed her.

'Well now, I don't think that applies entirely ... I don't think men are all that important,' Vivien replied,[11] cutting Tynan down to size. Did she really mean it? She thought Larry was the most important man – the most significant person – in her life.

Going home to Vivien was an obligation Larry no longer wanted and the misery of leaving Joan and the sense of entrapment in his marriage took a toll on his sanity. He feared he was having a nervous breakdown.[12]

At home, Vivien's days were spent wearing a purple housecoat and waiting for Larry to call. Alone, she telephoned friends, asking them to come to dinner or to stay, but who accepted her invitations? Everyone from her world was busy with their lives as they transitioned to the next phases: marriages beginning and ending; grown-up children; searching for work; leaving England, like Suzanne who had recently moved to Switzerland; and moving into a new world where she no longer belonged. Her contemporaries were going forward and she seemed to be regressing and found comfort in a platonic relationship with Leigh Holman.

꧁꧂

Months before, in August 1957, Vivien holidayed with Leigh and Suzanne at San Vigilio. A memorable trip for everyone involved; Suzanne announced her engagement to Robin Farrington, a Lloyd's underwriter, who had received the Military Cross for his service with the King's Royal Rifle Corps in Palestine in 1948. The trip, seemingly harmless between two friendly spouses and their daughter, provoked criticism from Jean Mann of the Scottish Labour Party, who declared it 'scandalous'. Addressing Vivien publicly, Mann said:

> If you accept my invitation to tea in Parliament, I will tell you what I think. Yours is a terrible example for today's youth. Modern youth might be led to believe that it is possible to mothball their first husband and go on holiday with him from time to time, or even spend Saturday and Sunday with him, dedicating the other weekdays to husband number two.[13]

In response, Vivien spoke to the press and, in a notebook, she drafted a paragraph in Italian before speaking the language: 'It is a statement which I have telegraphed to London for the English press. I repeat it here to you for the Italian press.' She wrote a few more words and scribbled them out. 'I don't know the spelling any more,' she snapped, before continuing with her statement:

> I find that Mrs Mann's criticisms are inconsiderate, and are not inspired by the rules of good courtesy. Every reasonable person should find in the presence of our daughter, Suzanne, the reason for this holiday. About Mrs Mann's gracious invitation, I must say that I rarely have time for a cup of tea.[14]

Arriving at the Locanda Hotel, Vivien detected the confusion among the staff, many of whom expected her to arrive with Larry. 'Maria, it's nothing,' she told the hotel receptionist, in Italian. 'I discussed this vacation with my husband. I wanted to see Suzanne and Larry wanted to see his son.'[15]

Her affection for Leigh resembled that of a favourite uncle, and the paparazzi, who spied on their excursions, wrote: 'Leigh Holman's appearance is downright disarming, he is a man of 59, thin, severe, ascetic. Rather than her ex-husband, he looks like Vivien Leigh's father, and his brooding countenance is not like that of a man who, at sunset, is set ablaze by amorous feelings.'[16]

The years of loss – the deaths of his siblings, his parents when he was a young man, and the shock of Vivien's leaving – told on him. Many were quick to cast Vivien as the tragic heroine, owing to her mental illness but nobody thought of Leigh quietly weathering the storms and remaining steadfast to those who needed him. When young, she found him boring and unromantic, compared to the mutual passion she shared with Larry. Perhaps now she realised that Leigh loved her unconditionally and it was the safest kind of love.

The Italian tabloids reported that Leigh was only interested in his garden and his mind was on his flowerbeds at his home in Wiltshire. Not so, he was supporting Vivien in his gentle way, while she pondered her circumstances, though she could not decide on a sensible course of action. Leigh felt it was in her best interest to separate from Larry – not file for divorce – but he did not tell her that. Instead, he analysed the current state of affairs and, legally minded, foresaw the ending before she did.

Still, Vivien and Larry went through the motions of a reunion and upon her arrival in England, she was greeted by him with five kisses. 'This,' she told the waiting reporters, 'is to reply to the rumours that we are getting divorced.'[17]

'As for me,' Larry said, 'I have no declaration to make about something that doesn't exist.'[18]

It gave Vivien false hope and she dashed any sentimentality she held for Leigh and Suzanne and plunged head first into devoting her every waking moment to Larry. A cruel thing for Larry to encourage; he was in love with Joan Plowright and had made up his mind to leave Vivien.

At the beginning of November 1957, Vivien had travelled to Glasgow to join Larry, who was touring with *The Entertainer*, which had, at the time, transferred to the Palace Theatre in the West End and was undertaking a national tour before returning to the Palace. It was her birthday – had he forgotten? Maybe not, as nobody wanted her there. Everyone in the company felt uncomfortable and pitied her naivety in thinking Larry was longing for her presence. They had a celebratory dinner at a hotel and its menu was formed of dishes named in her honour, which did not flatter her at all. If she did not know of the affair – Joan was absent – at least her instincts gathered something was not right and she showed it in her dismissal of the birthday tribute. Of course, everyone else knew and accepted Larry and Joan as lovers. It was something deeper than a theatrical flirtation; there was nothing clandestine and nothing to expose. Vivien had walked straight into their lives, lived out in the open.

A month later, Vivien's life continued to transition into phases beyond her control. She stepped into the role of mother of the bride but everyone knew, by right, it belonged to Gertrude. On the eve of Suzanne's wedding, Vivien wrote her daughter an affectionate letter, telling her how much she loved her and hoped she would depend on her if she ever needed help. Suzanne only ever viewed Vivien as a part-time mother – the kindest way to describe her parenting – and recalled she visited her at school in Switzerland three times a year.[19] The critic, Beverley Baxter, once wrote that Vivien lacked the warmth of normal womanhood: she had achieved her highest womanhood in the theatre.[20]

Suzanne had married Robin Farrington at Holy Trinity Brompton on 6 December 1957. Vivien and Leigh departed together to host a reception at the Hyde Park Hotel. Larry was left playing gooseberry among the divorced couple and their daughter, and he remained in the background, disappearing into the scenery as only he could. There, under the central figure of Christ Enthroned, was a farcical scene: Leigh the devoted ex-husband, Vivien the soon-to-be divorcée, and Larry the adulterer.

Church, however, had always been a source of high drama for Vivien; in Sanremo, as a schoolgirl, she had scattered rose petals beneath the feet of the monks and received the sacrament in Latin. As a child in India, her Hindu governess warned her of the evil deceptions of a religion in which everything was mysterious and dramatic. One day, she was led by her governess to a Hindu temple and while she stood frightened and overwhelmed, the guru appeared and took her by the hand. 'Bachcha,' the guru said, gaining her trust. Then, with terror in his voice, he continued, 'I saw high flames and you were struggling among them.'[21]

⋘⋙

At Notley, the spring bulbs sprouted from beneath the cold ground, and she waited for Larry's return. There was news from New York which put the final nail in the proverbial coffin of their lives together. Larry had adapted *Macbeth* for the screen, worked on the logistics and budget, and travelled to Scotland with his son to scout locations the summer before. Now, it seemed, there would be no *Macbeth*; Mike Todd, who had verbally agreed to finance the picture, had been killed in a plane crash on 22 March 1958.

The previous year, Vivien and Larry had attended Todd's party to celebrate the premiere of *Around the World in 80 Days* at Charing Cross amusement park. It had cost £200,000 and, as the rain pelted from the heavens, their spirits were lifted by a brass band playing *Rule, Britannia!* It was an excessive display of silliness and wealth; in Todd's world, the two might have been interchangeable. Vivien had slipped on a see-through Mackintosh and rode on the carousel, side-saddle, with a cigarette in her hand.

'Poor Mike Todd,'[22] Larry said after hearing the news of his death.

There were no other investors, nobody seemed enthusiastic about the Oliviers appearing together on screen. His time had been wasted and his pride hurt, though he wistfully confided he was grateful for his film opportunities thus far. Vivien was equally upset; she placed all her hopes in reviving their partnership in whatever medium it would thrive. No longer tangible, the dream was shattered. To compensate for the loss, he gave her a ruby ring with an arrow piercing through it.

At a turning point in her career, Vivien was performing as Paola in *Duel of Angels*, Christopher Fry's English translation of Jean Giraudoux's French play, *Pour Lucrèce*, inspired by the story of Lucretia, the virtuous Roman housewife who was raped and driven to suicide. After touring for six weeks, the play opened at the Apollo Theatre in London. The reviews were favourable and Larry, whose production company co-produced the play, agreed she had become an actress of the first rank.[23]

For the first time, Vivien played a character whom she disliked. Set in a provincial French town, Paola exploits the sexual weaknesses in men and is disturbed by the strict moral code of her contemporary, Lucille, so she drugs her and has her taken to the bedroom of Count Marcellus. Lucille, believing she had been raped, appeals to her husband to restore her honour but he declares her tainted and she kills herself. '[Paola] stands for paganism against purity, vice against virtue. As so often, the Devil has the best tunes,' *The Sketch* reported.[24]

The part of Lucille was played by Claire Bloom, whose character wore contrasting white Dior gowns to Paola's red and loathed anyone who committed adultery. As Paola dominated Lucille, Vivien would also dominate Bloom's subconscious. Bloom wanted to imitate Vivien as a woman: she longed to have her spontaneity, to dress like her, to possess her social manners, and to manage a house like her.[25] Years previously, Bloom had been privy to the orderliness with which Notley was run and, although she had had an affair with Larry during the filming of *Richard III*, she had not yet encountered Vivien, who knew of the dalliance but bore her no resentment. Now, Bloom witnessed the same control over Vivien's acting and each night she gave precisely the same performance. On the stage, nothing was left to chance.

Then, Vivien seemed to lose control or perhaps she had absolute control, depending on how one viewed the situation. Manuel Puig, the Argentine author and playwright, visited her backstage to offer his congratulations and pitch his screenplay, *Ball Cancelled*, written especially for her, but she was not interested. Puig detected her strange mood and how she babbled incoherently, and he politely rejected her sexual advances.[26]

At home, Vivien bombarded Bloom with telephone calls. 'Would you come over at once?' she cried down the phone to Bloom, having cancelled a performance. She claimed to be alone and suicidal and had tried to drown herself in the bath. Responding to the distressed call, Bloom took a taxi to Eaton Square and found a party in full swing, with Vivien, intoxicated and her face swollen from crying, surrounded by equally drunk guests and a doctor trying to coax her into the bedroom for a sedative injection.[27]

Unsurprisingly, Bloom was disturbed by the scene and cast her mind back to her affair with Larry and his complaints about Vivien's instability. A short time later, Vivien behaved in a similar erratic manner with Jeanne Moreau, who visited Notley and offhandedly spoke of appearing in a play with Larry. 'Oh, you speak English well enough do you, to play with Larry? And you think you look young enough to play the part, do you?'[28] Vivien asked Moreau, jealous of her interest in acting with him.

What had driven Vivien to behave as she did? News came from Larry that he was extending the run of *The Entertainer* in New York and it upset her greatly. She knew there was nothing to entice him home. There were rumours that she was sleeping with her leading man, Peter Wyngarde, and like his predecessor Peter Finch, he grappled with her mood swings and unpredictable behaviour. It was claimed that Wyngarde found her running around the garden naked and later sobbing on the bathroom floor.[29] Lovers or not, Vivien needed the flattery of a handsome man during a time when Larry had more or less abandoned her.

That spring, the international press wrote of an impending divorce between Vivien and Larry and surmised there were two women in his life – Susan Strasberg and Joan Plowright – 'one of whom should take the place now occupied by Vivien Leigh'.[30]

'I love my husband and he loves me,' Vivien stated. 'He loves me. We are a happy couple. My married life is not clouded by any doubts or dissent.'[31]

In her mind, their marriage was not over, as neither had made the first move to leave for good. Yes, there would be affairs and poorly executed plans to run away – as she had done with Peter Finch – but she viewed it as respite; a break from the monotony of their domestic lives. When they were working together, they were at their greatest and she felt invincible with Larry by her side. She did not know that Larry, or rather Laurence Olivier Productions, considered her a liability and old fashioned – a one-trick pony of the traditional theatre. Somehow, she did not know how to lure him back to her. She saw them moving in different directions for the sake of their art but, like a murmuration, they were always in sync. How could she meet him on his new artistic plane?

During the initial run of *The Entertainer* in London in 1957, she had befriended John Osborne and invited him to lunch and dinner and together they went to the cinema. Of course, at the time of their meetings, he knew of Larry's affair with Dorothy Tutin and observed it as a midlife crisis on Larry's behalf. 'Separate bedrooms, dear heart,'[32] Larry told Osborne before he and Vivien accepted an invitation to stay with him in Kent.

There would be no judgement between the playwright and the actor. Osborne had no empathy for women and was known for his mistreatment of his wives and lovers, stemming from his hatred of his mother. He also loathed everything Vivien seemed to stand for and yet he was falling into a murky pool of self-doubt which washed away his bravado. Where did he stand with her? His coarse language did not shock her, nor did his angry monologues about social injustices – under such circumstances, she closed her eyes and laughed, dragging on a cigarette and expelling the smoke for dramatic effect. She made him question his feelings towards her, as the nature of their encounters confused him.

In Vivien, Osborne found a sympathetic companion who taught him about fine dining and how to read wine lists,[33] guiding him in a way he had expected Larry to. Was this a maternal instinct in Vivien or was she merely treating him like a young gigolo? Osborne leaned towards the latter and wondered if she expected him to consummate their friendship; perhaps she had wanted him as a lover. The ambiguity clouded his judgement and he began to pull away from her kindness. She wanted to be neither mother nor lover: she wanted to feel part of Larry's new world and Osborne fulfilled those needs for a time. She had dabbled in espionage twenty years before, as Madeleine Goddard in *Dark Journey*, playing a spy masquerading as a couturier who transmitted intelligence in her garments to uncover the chief of the German secret service. The *Evening Standard* had hailed her as 'now an actress, not just a decoration'.

At the beginning of summer, Larry returned home to the grave news that his brother, Dickie, had terminal cancer and it was agreed between Larry and Dickie's wife, Hester, to spare him the truth of his prognosis. Larry, however, would eventually break the news to him. So, Larry, Dickie and Hester went to Spain before the inevitable happened, leaving Vivien behind at Notley.

In Larry's absence, Vivien fell into one of her 'dangerous moods'[34] and her weekend guests, including Peter Finch's mother, deemed her beyond help. After a picnic by the river, she alarmed everyone by screaming frantically as a wasp circled her, and she fought with her mother.[35] A telegram reached Larry in Spain, imploring him to come home to his wife. He begrudgingly left his dying brother and went to Notley, finding Vivien's mother and father attempting to parent their middle-aged daughter, who had scrubbed the walls and floors in preparation for his homecoming. No matter how much Vivien scrubbed, she was not satisfied and repeated the process. Two psychiatrists and two doctors came to the house and tried to manage the episode which had to run its course. Only when depression set in – the crashing low as it were – could the situation be controlled.

Two weeks into the episode, Vivien and her mother went to San Vigilio. The tranquillity of Lake Garda did nothing to improve her mood and she became confrontational, throwing a glass of water in Gertrude's face at 2.30 in the morning. The balmy weather enhanced her irritability and her hair frizzed in the heat and stuck to her clammy face, which had become a garish mask of heavy makeup.[36] A day or so later, she went for a drive and the car broke down; she encountered a passing fisherman who drove her to the Locanda Hotel and accepted her invitation to come in for a drink and to dance. The seemingly innocent gesture was misunderstood by the management and led to Vivien being evicted and banned from the hotel. She refused to leave and when, two days later, the police came to remove her, she bit two fingers of one of them.[37]

To distance himself from Vivien's mania, Larry departed Notley and stayed with friends, feeling like 'the most grasping scrounger that ever was'.[38] In a bid to avoid Vivien, Larry left for Europe. There was no logic to his wanderings and he acted on impulse, having remembered an old car he had abandoned in Florence and he set off to retrieve it, then drove to Portofino before making his way to Paris. From Avenue Marceau, he wrote Vivien a long letter of twenty-three pages, an exorcism of his thoughts and feelings, laying bare his intentions for the future. His attachment to her, like a Dybbuk spirit, had caused havoc before dying, having achieved its mission on earth. But what was its goal? Passion, abandonment, madness? In the end, he asked her for a divorce. Shrouded in his long-winded letter were fibs to settle her concerns: there was nobody else in his life; he had simply grown apart from her and wanted his freedom.

Naturally, Larry's request for a divorce stunned Vivien and she had an emotional response to it. She went to stay with Leigh at his country house in Zeals, Wiltshire. Leigh did not overlook the irony and recognised the karmic cycle at work: Larry was doing to Vivien what she had done to him over twenty years before. Rather than gloat, Leigh supported her as best he could and advised her to stop tormenting herself by trying to save her marriage.

When Vivien finally spoke to Larry on the telephone, she knew she was talking to a stranger. 'When I was a little girl and I was going to a party my mother always said, "Now do what the host wants, to please him,"'[39] she recalled, perhaps taking strength from Gertrude's philosophy and bending to the will of others.

'When can I do what I want?' Little Vivien asked.

'Not doing what you want is good manners,'[40] Gertrude replied.

Regardless of her mother's advice, she had made the same plea to Leigh Holman all those years ago; however, unlike Larry, she did not stoop to cowardice by telling lies. The impulsive way in which she spoke her mind alarmed people but at least they knew where they stood.

In terms of her divorce from Leigh, it had been a lengthy process with the power solely in his hands. Leigh wanted Vivien to wait for three years before making up her mind and, in those three years, he believed she would come home. She reiterated her longing for a divorce and promised it was not to hurt him; in fact, staying with him would have been crueller than parting. 'Complacency is a fatal state, though a very pleasant one, if you can remain in it. I never can,'[41] she had said. Two Scorpios – Leigh and Vivien's birthdays were two days apart – they were headstrong and quick to react when crossed. Leigh demonstrated his 'revenge' (she once called him a villain) by withholding her freedom. Or so she thought. Then, fame pulled her closer to Larry and they were isolated from their peers in America and viewed Leigh, albeit briefly, as the antagonist in their story. For Leigh's birthday on 3 November, the first since she had walked out, she sent him a book and asked him not to write to her. For her birthday, on 5 November, Leigh ignored her request and sent her a ring. Reciprocity, if not yet on equal footing.

Somehow, through tokens of friendship, Vivien and Leigh resolved their different points of view. They were still a family in the traditional sense of the word: they both belonged to the Catholic church and were not supposed to believe in divorce. Marriage was lifelong; they were married in a church, and spiritually, she would always be Leigh's wife. That would have been a lyrical way of looking at things. As the matter stood, their love became platonic and the friendship between the former spouses was deeper than any marital contract.

On Vivien's forty-fifth birthday, Larry took her to dinner and repeated his wish for a divorce and she did not resist, though she was screaming inside. Almost two decades earlier, they had provoked something awe-inspiring when they were together, doing ordinary things, and not saying very much at all. 'As I looked at Larry and Vivien across the tea table, I reflected that it isn't often in this lifetime that one comes across two people who have everything – youth, good looks, health, success, love,'[42] the reporter, Radie Harris, wrote in 1940.

Now they were strained and Vivien must have felt Larry had invited her under false pretences. Her birthday outing was used to argue his case for a divorce, to serve his motives, and doing it in public was a cowardly approach to a private matter. He offered her a new Rolls-Royce Silver Cloud, a parting gift even if he did not say so. An elaborate gesture when she only really loved two things: flowers and scent.[43] As with Leigh, she hoped Larry was extending the hand of friendship and would grow to love her in a different way. She wanted them to be close, always. Serendipity, after all, was listed among her interests: 'the gift of finding valuable or agreeable things not sought for'.[44]

For the time being, Larry found no solace in having a different relationship with Vivien and he bided his time until he could break free. Circumstances would call him back to Notley: at the end of November,

Dickie succumbed to leukaemia and was buried at sea. After the funeral, Vivien and Larry went home together and later that evening, she burst into his bedroom – they had been sleeping separately – and demanded sex. She was on a high and there had been no comedown except for moments when she had appeared reasonable and calm which he knew to be an act. Humiliation seemed to be her vice and, in recent days, she had asked him, in front of his colleagues, 'Larry, why don't you fuck me any more?'[45] However, that night, after the funeral, a furious row erupted and he stormed out, slamming the door behind him. He drove to London for business obligations and spent the evening with Joan; it was to be their last for six months, as they were busy with commitments and he would soon leave for Hollywood to film *Spartacus*.

Nobody, least of all Vivien, took their separation seriously and Noël Coward predicted Larry would go back to her. Vivien herself might have believed it to be true; they had always been good at putting on a united front – 'the show', as it were. A few months before, when he had hated her most, he had managed to kiss her for the reporters who came to photograph a dress rehearsal for *Night of 100 Stars*. They had both been dressed as clowns.

The milestones that were to come were marked without Larry, which Vivien felt was symbolic of his desertion of her. Her first grandson, Neville Leigh Farrington, was born in early December. At the age of 45, she was a grandmother; a transition that often marks a watershed moment in a woman's life. Not so for Vivien: her relatives were treated like background players, always supportive but never meddling. Only later would she call herself a bitch for how she had treated Leigh and Suzanne. The occasion brought the unconventional family together: Leigh and Vivien, and their descendants. Larry had, incidentally, flown to New York on that same day without a backward glance in Vivien's direction. The following evening, Vivien and Leigh gave a party in honour of Gertrude's seventieth birthday. Larry's absence was hurtful; his silence, deafening.

They spent the festive season apart with Larry in America and Vivien going to Geneva to see Noël Coward, who squired her around and did his best to keep her spirits lifted. She was a tiresome companion: her two polar opposites were interchangeable and the manic side was heightened from heavy drinking, then came the melancholic

lows from her troubles with Larry. In private, she looked up Peter
and gave him a call; she was free of Larry and wanted to be with him.
Did he want her too? Peter declined her offer and his rejection sent
her into a deep depression. 'I need a man in my life,' she said. 'To be
alone is nothing.'[46]

With Vivien safely out of sight, Coward scribbled in his diary
– he knew she was unhappy inside but he blamed the predicament
entirely on her.[47] Only a few days earlier, they had argued in the
back of a car; she had slapped him and he had responded by hitting
her back. He observed that women of her temperament, 'looks and
exigence, can raise too much hell for themselves and everyone near
them'.[48] Furthermore, he praised Larry for managing to break away
– 'good luck to him'[49] – and was exhausted from Vivien's behaviour
and wanted her to recover, for everyone's sake. On New Year's Eve,
they played Twenty Questions, which gave her twenty reasons to
talk about Larry.

There was no antidote for her despair; the longer Larry stayed
away, the more she believed he would return to her. She waited for
the phone to ring on her personal line (Sloane 1955),[50] hoping to hear
an operator's voice on the line, asking if she would accept his international call. Yes, she would. It was a pipe dream on her behalf: there
was only silence and in that rhetorical silence she lost part of her
identity. One day he stopped phoning and writing, and it seemed, to
her, that he had disappeared. There could be no more delusions: he
was not coming home.

Vivian Mary Hartley in India. (Courtesy of Vivien Leigh Circle)

Mrs Leigh Holman, the expectant mother, 1933. (Courtesy of Jonathan and Victoria Aitken)

Vivien on the day of signing her contract for *Gone with the Wind*, 1939. (Courtesy of the Billy Rose Theatre Division, New York Public Library)

Vivien, during the filming of *Caesar and Cleopatra*, 1944. (Courtesy of Gina Guandalini)

Vivien and Larry at the races, 1948. (Courtesy of Gina Guandalini)

Vivien in Alexandria during her tour of North Africa to entertain the troops in 1943. (Courtesy of BNF, Gallica)

Cairo, 1943. (Courtesy of BNF, Gallica)

Vivien performing a skit in North Africa, 1943. (Courtesy of Eric Sanniez)

Hollywood glamour, 1941.
(Courtesy of the Billy Rose
Theatre Division, New
York Public Library)

Angus McBean studio portrait,
1949. (Courtesy of Harvard Theatre
Collection, Houghton Library, Harvard
University)

Sketch of Vivien by René Bouché, 1959. (Courtesy of The Estate of Denise Bouché)

Jill Esmond, 1932. (Courtesy of Picture Play magazine)

Vivien at an official function in Australia, 1948. (Courtesy of Shiroma Perera-Nathan)

Happier times for the Oliviers. (Courtesy of Queensland State, Library of Queensland)

A farewell at Euston
Station, 1948.
(Courtesy of Shiroma
Perera-Nathan)

Presented with pineapples at
Archerfield Aerodrome, 1948.
(Courtesy of Queensland
State, Library of Queensland)

Archerfield Aerodrome, 1948.
(Courtesy of Queensland
State, Library of Queensland)

Speaking at a Food for Britain rally, 1948.
(Courtesy of Shiroma Perera-Nathan)

Vivien en route to Surfers Paradise, 1948.
(Courtesy of Queensland State, Library of
Queensland)

Larry returning to his suite at Surfers Paradise, 1948. (Courtesy of Queensland State, Library of Queensland)

Picnic, Australia 1948. (Courtesy of Shiroma Perera-Nathan)

Drinking wine in Australia, 1948. (Courtesy of Shiroma Perera-Nathan)

Sydney, 1948. (Courtesy of Shiroma Perera-Nathan)

Vivien with Leigh Holman, Peter Finch and Larry. (Courtesy of Eric Sanniez)

Vivien and Larry with Suzanne in Hollywood, 1950. (Courtesy of Warner Bros)

Vivien and Larry
towards the end
of their marriage.
(Courtesy of Gina
Guandalini)

Vivien, Leigh and
Suzanne on the
infamous holiday of
1957. (Courtesy of
Greta Ritchie)

This page and opposite: Vivien, Leigh and Suzanne on the infamous holiday of 1957. (All courtesy of Greta Ritchie)

Below: Vivien and Larry on a train in Maribor, 1957. (Courtesy of Gina Guandalini)

An animated Vivien in 1961.
(Courtesy of Greta Ritchie)

Chapter Ten

'In the meantime, let me be that I am, and seek not to
alter me'

Much Ado About Nothing, William Shakespeare

1960

In times of crisis, Vivien and Larry were separated by water and, in the
past, he had crossed oceans and seas to rescue her. She was drawn to
water, still water like lakes and streams, and was afraid of the sea, the
ever-changing, restless currents that called to her, 'Come in, come in.'[1]

They were on opposite sides of the Atlantic: she was in New York
for *Duel of Angels* and he was in London, starring in *Rhinoceros* and
infatuated with his leading lady, Joan Plowright. Vivien's SOS was
discarded, as were the appeals from her friends and, finally, Suzanne's,
asking him to reconsider his plan to divorce her mother. When Vivien
was going to leave Leigh, sensible friends had implored her to 'think
of the child' and now the abandoned child begged her stepfather to
think of the woman who had closed the nursery door without a backward glance. Their warnings were meaningless, Larry had heard them
all before: Vivien would refuse treatment if he did not concede, and,
worse still, take her own life.

The past year had been a stretch of nothingness: the abyss of
his departure and her run in Noël Coward's *Look After Lulu!* in
London enhanced her loneliness and the inability to connect with

her surroundings. 'I hated doing it, although it was a big success. I did it because it was expedient to do a play at the time,'[2] she said of Coward's farce. All the laughs were reserved for the stage and when the curtain fell, misery prevailed. Once, Larry came to her dressing room and left in tears and she wailed like a keening woman, holding on to his coat and refusing to let him go, and he dragged her down the stairs with him.[3]

Vivien's emotions were channelled in desperate letters that were sent to Larry as she experienced the seven stages of grief – shock, denial, anger, bargaining, depression, hope and acceptance – but not quite. She could accept Larry had walked out on her but she could not foresee a future without him. Honesty was a virtue of integrity, but it was also a means to be cruel. Larry sent her a letter telling her it was time to drop the legend and she ignored his crude description and went to Stratford, where he was performing in *Coriolanus*, and sat beside him at a reception. Then, he delivered the damning news and asked her not to come to see him again.

The coldness startled her: how could he forget those days at Shepperton Studios, in 1937, when they had filmed *21 Days* and promised to stay together forever? Despite the grave consequences they had faced at the time, he had still burst into her dressing room and kissed off her makeup. They had laughed so much during the takes that production ran over budget and the final edit was a dismal job.

To fill the echoing void, Vivien took up with Jack Merivale, the unsuspecting victim of her outburst in 1940 when she had warned him, 'Don't you try to come between us. We've been together for years. Nobody's coming between us. Don't you try!' Jack, four years her junior, was the stepson of Gladys Cooper and existed on the fringes of repertory theatre and played bit parts in British pictures. He joined the cast of *Duel of Angels* in New York and had grown a beard for the part of Armand and she was impressed by his efforts. It was the little things that pleased her. When Jack mentioned their past encounter in 1940, she said, 'Perhaps I had some premonition that you were going to come between us. Look at us now.'[4]

Around that time, she had her birth chart analysed and the astrologer warned she would be lonely. 'Look how right that turned out to be,'[5] she said, upon reflection. In that sense, Jack proved to be a worthy distraction. He was a shadowy figure, in the beginning, and was always in the background keeping tabs on her drinking – he would take glasses of alcohol from her hand and pour them down the sink[6] – her spending and her mood swings.

They toured America with the play, and in Hollywood she attended a party given by director George Cukor in her honour, with fountains and bands and the swimming pool illuminated by lanterns. 'Oh, darling, can you really afford this?' she asked Cukor, taking in the splendour. Hours later, she sensed the guests were outstaying their welcome and knowing he had to work the next day, she said, 'Let me tell them all to fuck off now!'[7]

Onward, they went to San Francisco, her favourite American city because she could see the water from everywhere. Jack entertained her with excursions to dolphin shows and deep-sea fishing at the Bay. Later, he gave her a pendant of St Genesius, the patron saint of actors, clowns and those who have been tortured. One day, in Connecticut, she asked him, 'When are we going to make love properly?'[8] And that was that. She phoned Larry, sobbing, telling him she had fallen in love with Jack. Or that was Larry's recollection, to ease his guilt, while his attention was spent elsewhere.

At the time, Jack knew she was ready to drop him if Larry wanted her to and he also knew that Larry would not ask her to. Had she wanted to make her estranged husband jealous? It did not work and Larry wrote to Jack, asking if there could be a chance of a serious union between them. Reading between the lines, he wanted to know if Jack would take her off his hands. Soon after, Larry received a letter from Jack, stating that he and Vivien were happy together. Where was Vivien while the men in her life were bartering over their duty to her?

Trapped by the legend of her own making, there was something of the Cumaean Sibyl in Vivien's suffering. As with Sibyl and Apollo, she had decided to love Larry after the grains of sand had run out and that was when he started to hate her. 'I think it helps people to retain a sense of proportion to see performed the experiences of others whose troubles are far greater than their own,' she said. 'Moreover, the Greek tragedies are largely the reflections of troubled times strikingly analogous to our own.'[9]

In the spring of 1960, she was living at Hampshire House, a high-rise on the southern edge of Central Park which had a small garden with a fountain. Inside the Art Deco tower, she fell into the depths of depression, the despair confined to the bruised tones of black and turquoise rooms with plaster mouldings and glass blocks. The stagnancy followed her to the Helen Hayes Theatre and the compact venue spread over two levels made her feel cornered by the faceless audience. She exerted her control, or attempted to, by demanding the entire front row seating be removed; she did not want the public to see her up close.

Overcome by darkness, Vivien honed in on her co-star, Mary Ure, the beautiful wife of John Osborne, whose sweetness[10] disguised her emotional fragility. When Vivien was manic, she targeted one person in particular and made their lives hell. Ure, who was in a sadomasochistic marriage with Osborne, handled it graciously, but it was still disturbing to witness, and endure. The first warning sign had been an increase in Vivien's appetite and she had begun to devour two large breakfasts every morning. As a result, she had gained weight and struggled to fit into her Dior costumes; the stage manager had to pull the dress together while her dresser fastened the hooks and eyes. Nevertheless, there was the curtain call and applause, the two sure things in her life that would always come, and the audience was oblivious to the truth. The critics wrote, 'Seldom have physical beauty and superb acting been so exquisitely blended.'[11]

From across the Atlantic, Larry's letter fell into Vivien's hands and its instructions were simple: he wanted a divorce. She went to her car and wept before being driven to a doctor, who prescribed Valium to calm her nerves. Later that night, and under the influence of tranquillisers and booze, she made up her mind to expose Larry's wrongdoings, perhaps in an attempt to shame him into coming home. That's when she appeared on American television, looking pale and vulnerable, and telling her side of the story. An eruption in America, followed by an aftershock, reached London. The headlines were much the same: 'Lady Olivier wishes to say that Sir Laurence has asked her for a divorce in order to marry Miss Joan Plowright. She will naturally do whatever he wishes.'[12]

Vivien would claim she had no recollection of making the press statement and it was true: she was going through a manic episode and endured a course of ECT; the burns were still visible during a performance of *Duel of Angels*. Her doctor in London, Dr Conachy, described the amnesia as a 'sudden onset ... within twenty-four-hours there is marked elevation of mood and general activity. She rapidly loses her natural restraint and normal reserve, talks freely, and during this period loses judgement, reasoning power and insight.'[13]

'Give me the right to have some secrets,'[14] Vivien snapped to the reporters who swarmed around her. Having opened Pandora's Box, it was too late to repair the damage she had done. Or had she? She was merely professing the truth, but at what cost? The press gathered outside Larry's flat in London and Joan left *Rhinoceros* and went into hiding. Collusion, the legal term, might have been suspected and, if so, a divorce would not be granted.

In survival mode, Larry climbed into a life raft and headed for the horizon while Vivien drowned in a metaphorical sea. Like the water's memory, she was trying to go back to from where they came, but the tides were pulling them further apart. He ignored her pleas for forgiveness, and help. 'No, I'm sorry. I can't pull you out. If I pull you out, you'll pull me in.'[15]

⁂

During the early days of their marriage, Vivien had travelled to the ends of the earth to be with Larry. An exaggeration; however, it was wartime and he had been training with the Fleet Air Arm at Worthy Down, Hampshire. She was touring Scotland as Jennifer Dubedat in *The Doctor's Dilemma*, its theme of tuberculosis hitting close to home but during the war, everyone walked a fine line between life and death. Her leading man, Cyril Cusack, was an alcoholic and began drinking heavily during its run; one night he began to recite dialogue from *The Playboy of the Western World* and violently assaulted her on stage.

From her post in the north, she travelled south in rickety trains during the blackout; the windows were shrouded in sheets and she read Charles Dickens under a dim blue light. After hours and hours of stopping and starting and waiting for signals to proceed, she was met by Larry in his Invicta car and off they went, speeding through the countryside on his rationed petrol.

At Headlands, his rented bungalow in School Lane, she cooked and cleaned, and unrolled her antique Kashan prayer rug from their London house (bombed during the Blitz) and hung art on the walls. She had spurts of simplicity, such as driving the car and finding shrubs and roses, and taking cuttings to propagate for her own garden and carrying bags of thorns to friends to plant in theirs. The weekend of domesticity over, she returned to the theatre and he to the guise of lieutenant despite his dubious skills as a pilot and near misses in the sky. Rumour had it he borrowed a Swordfish plane to take her out to dinner, but that might have sprung from the Hollywood gossip columns so far removed from their reality at home where they dug a victory garden and she wore thick gardening gloves and he slung a spade over his shoulder.

She had a purpose with her play and he was jealous of his colleagues at the base, earning their stripes and taking off in their flying machines, destined for a hero's homecoming or a valiant death. Depressed, he felt useless at not seeing action and being given mundane tasks such as packing parachutes and talking to the Boy Scouts. He knew he was no good at being himself. Perhaps it marred his memories from those days, of collecting Vivien from Winchester station and the car's soft top and rickety windows leaking during a downpour on their Sunday drives. She thought it was romantic but he considered it an inconvenience. It was a relief when the Ministry of Information sent for him and appointed him the actor patriot, drafting him into *The Demi-Paradise* and *Henry V.* Much of the latter was filmed in neutral Ireland.

Before Larry went to Ireland, Vivien left for a three-month tour with the Entertainments National Service Association (ENSA) to entertain the troops in North Africa. In the deathly heat, she recited verses to the wounded in makeshift hospitals and on stages before audiences of 8,000 men. Her hair curling from the humidity and her nose sunburnt, she charmed the Allied soldiers who watched the mirage amid the sand dunes. One soldier said, 'Never forget the thing that caught my eye was the lovely way she walked – wonderfully slim and elegant.'[16]

Soon, the conditions began to tell on her, the initial three-month separation was extended by three weeks and she missed him terribly. Their last long separation was a lively affair, taking place during *Gone with the Wind* and his performing on Broadway in *No Time for Comedy* when she sent him a pair of her knickers in the post and he returned the favour by posting a carnation which he had worn in his underpants. His letters reached her on the set in Culver City, where she sat encased in corsets and stays, weeping at his prose and frustrated by the distance between them. When they did meet, incognito in Kansas City, they locked themselves in their hotel room and she gleefully recounted to her colleagues, in explicit terms, what happened over the course of the weekend. Now he wrote to her of the logistical difficulties of staging a battle scene in *Henry V* in Ireland. Meanwhile, she was overwhelmed by the dry desert air and young men in army fatigues.

In Cairo, she was surprised by the banquets and parties at sandstone villas and in nightclubs, as if the war did not exist there. At Shepheard's Hotel, she kept the reporters waiting in a room as hot as a Turkish bath, its heat contained by the stained-glass windows and Persian carpets. She walked in and meekly asked for their forgiveness. 'The Cairo stores are so beautiful, I couldn't leave,'[17] she explained. She told them Larry loved the trees in Cairo, talking as if he was lingering in the next room.

In the stores, one of the assistants called her 'Miss' and she flew into a rage. 'Don't you know I'm Laurence Olivier's wife?' she said in French.

'Yes, Madame, I'd forgotten. Excuse me. I admire your husband,' the assistant replied.

'I admire my husband more than you do. He is a wonderful man whom I love very much.'[18]

Her longing for him had reached its crescendo and she felt stifled to express herself due to the wartime censors and unreliable postal service. In a brief letter, she told him she called out 'Baba' in the day and night, hoping he would hear her and reciprocate their mutual nickname, by calling for her too. Somehow, they would meet on an astral plane. He promised her a passionate reunion.

⫸

At the beginning of June 1960, Vivien was in London and so was Larry – a rarity owing to his avoidant behaviour over the past two years. She longed to see him in the flesh and he was advised by his solicitor to refuse any form of contact, even written. Still, the letters, pages and pages of her stream of consciousness, reached him.

Dr Conachy called it a 'pathological and an almost obsessional devotion'[19] to Larry and warned her of an oncoming manic-depressive psychosis. In all of the psychoanalysis and medical reports, nobody considered the lack of closure she felt and the tormented state of mind she was in. It was as if Larry had erased her from his life and each time she asked for a straight answer from him, her simple request was denied or met with hostility and she was portrayed as unreasonable. 'I can't talk yet. I must think. I really must rest. I love Larry but we can't go on like this,'[20] she told reporters, the only ones seemingly listening to her.

Five treatments of ECT were administered, the procedure was far more humane in a private clinic in Harley Street than her first experience with it in 1953. Sedated, she then opened her eyes to the unfamiliarity all around her and felt a burning headache, the only physical feeling she could detect at that moment. Memory, at least for a brief time, was lost. It was like a scene in her 1940 picture, *Waterloo Bridge*, when her character, Myra, walks through a sea of strangers – servicemen – who, all dressed alike, cannot be distinguished one from the other, but she looks up and sees her dead lover, Roy, walking towards her; her eyes register him immediately. In the haze, Larry stood out and Vivien's singular thought would always centre on him.

She was meant to be with him, and vice versa, and no sensible argument could persuade her otherwise. Their souls were aligned and sooner or later, destiny would have brought them together. As children, they had shared a mutual friend, Bridget Boland, who played with Larry and his siblings in St George's Square, a private communal park around the corner from Lupus Street, where Larry first lived as a boy. Bridget attended the Convent of the Sacred Heart in Roehampton and went home at the weekends and for the school holidays. 'I wonder what would have happened if I had ever asked

[Vivien] home in the holidays,'[21] Bridget wrote in her memoirs. Maybe Vivien, with her peach complexion and shingled hair, shorn by the nuns and affixed to the Christ Child, would have smiled at Larry in passing, as he retrieved a lost ball from the square. Alas, she remained at school when everyone went home.

She never had a sense of home – of permanency – until she had eloped with Larry and built their lives together out of hurt, betrayal and chaos, first at Durham Cottage and then at Notley Abbey. It was, therefore, a cruel thing when Notley was sold in the spring of 1960, and she felt it was sacrilegious to pack up what was left of her things, much of the contents being sold with the house. Larry did not want to keep their wedding gifts, such as an inscribed goblet from Katharine Hepburn, or, in fact, many of the things they had purchased together. They were waiting in boxes for her at Eaton Square and she inspected them upon her arrival from New York. What was there to salvage from the ruins? China plates, photo albums, her 3-D stereoscopic slides, a few sticks of furniture, and Larry's wedding present to her, Jack Butler Yeats's painting, *A Farewell to Mayo*.

Attempting to feel close to him, she visited Notley and its new owners, whose décor she openly criticised, and listened to their plans to install a swimming pool; her rose garden turned into a watery grave. A walk in the garden, among the flowerbeds she and Larry had planted, was reminiscent of Ophelia's mad scene in *Hamlet*:

There's rosemary, that's for remembrance. Pray you, love, remember. And there is pansies, that's for thoughts ...
   There's fennel for you, and columbines. There's rue for you, and here's some for me. We may call it herb of grace o' Sundays. O, you must wear your rue with a difference! There's a daisy. I would give you some violets.[22]

Two days before Vivien left for New York, Larry agreed to visit her at Eaton Square and entered through the servants' door to avoid the press. She pleaded her case: divorce was not the answer but, like a stranger exposed to unrelatable pain, he remained unmoved. Yes, to her he looked like a stranger: his ageing face, ordinary spectacles and unfashionable clothes. It was her love that made him special:

her passion reflected on to him and he lit up rooms. Somehow, she saw past the physical shell and tried to touch his soul, and she hoped, before it was too late, he could look past the singe marks on her temples, her swollen face and her desperation to find his Vivling; his beloved. He kept his distance, perhaps afraid of getting too close to her, should her spark ignite their twin flame.

In the past, he had compared their love to religion; in the present day he could not tolerate her in any form. 'I can't tell you why I stayed with her so many years,' he wrote, later, in his memoirs. 'I did. I didn't know what else to do, but to stay along and suffer. I couldn't have been in love with her all of the time, possibly.'

Her own scars were evident and she romanticised her suffering; it was not so much the facts that were important but the recall. 'We were so young,' she said of the past. 'I mean all of us were so young. Like those who went to the war and did not come back. I trusted everyone and I imagined, like the very young always do, that everything lasts forever.'[23]

On the aeroplane to New York, she wrote Larry a letter, assuring him that Dr Conachy's treatment had restored her to her old self, the woman he loved – after twenty-five years of loving each other, it would be reckless to throw it all away. How could he forget the intensity of their affair and magnetic pull to one another – how they would take off in her two-seater car with the wire wheels and go to country inns and check in as Mr and Mrs Kerr? On a motoring trip to the Continent, they went to an Austrian forest and stripped off to bathe in the lake and took nude photos of each other: Larry wading into the water and Vivien, in profile, standing next to a rock with the pine trees in the distance. Two pagans, ruled by the elemental forces of passion and totally absorbed in each other. She kept those photos in an envelope in the cabinet next to her bed; she still did. In candid photos, taken by others, he could not take his eyes off her and now he waxed lyrical about watching Joan sleep. 'I don't remember sleeping, ever; only every precious moment that we spent together,'[24] Vivien said of those days.

She moved through the clouds, further away from him; the distance only strengthened her determination to keep him. Fighting to win, she could not lose and would not lose.[25] Those close to her claimed she had never lost in her life but that was not true: the person she was, was being governed by mental illness and the instability drove Larry away. But Larry had his own demons – his ego, which took control of his moods and actions and also made him impossible to reason with. Jealousy would destroy his relationships. Did he care? He would stop at nothing to practise his craft. His behaviour was his 'genius' and was tolerated, even celebrated, yet Vivien was deemed 'mad'. Manic-depressive psychosis was Dr Conachy's diagnosis and, privately, Larry considered her to be suffering from undiagnosed schizophrenia.[26] Unfortunately for her, Larry's letter from his solicitor reached her before she sent her plea to him. His decision was final and he repeated his familiar cry: he wanted to part ways with her and marry Joan.

So, it would be a divorce and when it came, everyone thought she would fall apart. She went to the hearing in London, six months later, on 2 December 1960, and held on to her fantasy that he would call it off. He was absent; he was in New York, performing on Broadway, and Vivien cited Joan as the co-respondent in the petition. She sat with her head in her hands, weeping openly, as the decree nisi was granted. Their union was dissolved in twenty-eight minutes.

Twenty years earlier, Leigh had attended their divorce hearing alone, dressed in his naval uniform – he was a voluntary sub-lieutenant – and had listened to Mr Justice Hodson grant a decree nisi on account of Vivien's adultery with Larry and give him custody of Suzanne. For two years, Leigh had coped as best he could, by holding on to their marriage, telling her and others that he would never let her go. Finally, he had consented to her wishes. 'I do so hope you will not have a very unpleasant time at the divorce thing,'[27] she had written to him from Hollywood.

After the hearing, Leigh had returned to his rooms at the Bath Club in Dover Street. The house in Little Stanhope Street had been rented out after Suzanne's evacuation to Canada. Maybe in Vivien's absence, Leigh's love for her had grown and, in his mind, become unrequited. As a newly-wed, she told her friends she had married him because she found him intelligent but, as a husband, he was dull and restrictive. She had wanted him to be passionate and spontaneous and to live in the moment, the way she did. His restraint should not have surprised her; she knew who he was: quiet, reserved, and with a strong sense of duty to his profession and his family. In the beginning, she pursued him and knitted him a sweater, and wrote him chatty letters, letting him know he could *have* her anytime. Marriage would be the answer to temptation, he thought, and he proposed to her in the car driving from Devon to London.

When Vivien and Leigh first married, they had lived in a tiny apartment at Eyre Court in Finchley Road. As a young bride, she had negotiated her place in the confined space, presided over by a house-keeper. Nobody expected her to cook and clean but Leigh had wanted a traditional wife who would always be by his side and waiting for him to come home. She complained to a friend that she had aged fifty years from writing shopping lists, planning meals and delegating tasks to the housekeeper. After they moved to Little Stanhope Street with their new baby, and she was forging a career which came with a social life, he had sat on the stairs while she entertained in the drawing room, waiting for the party to be over so peace could be restored.

So much had happened in that house: the walls harbouring past memories of her parties; her lovers coming to take her for dinner while he worked late at his chambers; and her breaking the news to him that she was leaving. A year after their divorce, the house at Little Stanhope Street was bombed by the Luftwaffe.[28] There was nothing left except a hole in the ground and the souvenirs from their life smoking in the embers.

Six months after Vivien and Larry's respective divorces from their spouses, they married in secret on 30 August 1940. They decided on Santa Barbara, at the San Ysidro Ranch owned by Ronald and Benita Colman, and drove from Los Angeles in the evening with their witnesses, Garson Kanin and Katharine Hepburn, in the back seat. Larry took a wrong turn and Vivien scolded him; they fought all the way there, their scrapping punctuated with risqué comments.

A few minutes after midnight, as the old night slipped into a new day, Vivien and Larry stood on the porch under the waning crescent moon and were married by a police court judge who skipped over the vows to cut straight to the 'I do's'. Vivien complained he omitted her best lines; she wanted to say, 'Love, honour *and* obey'. At the end, the judge shouted, 'Bingo!' She would have three wedding rings from

Larry, losing the first in a cinema, with the final being a celestial band inscribed, *Laurence Olivier Vivien Eternally*. They honeymooned on a schooner, sailing around Catalina Island and docking at Lover's Cove.

'I don't suppose there ever was a couple so much in love,' he said.

'Our love affair has been simply the most divine fairy tale, hasn't it?'[29] she replied.

Two days after the divorce hearing in December 1960, Larry wrote to her in his old familiar way and addressed her as 'darling' and called her 'Vivling', the nickname Leigh had given her. He thanked her for making the sacrifice so he could marry Joan and implored her to find her own happiness without him. The letter, effeminate in its tone, was a sign of his discomfort.

Six months later, on 17 March 1961, Larry would marry Joan in Connecticut in a quiet ceremony to escape reporters, as he had done with Vivien in 1940. As the fates would have it, she was filming *The Roman Spring of Mrs Stone* at Pinewood Studios, the film adaptation of Tennessee Williams's novella of the same title. Her character, Karen Stone, is an ageing actress who abandons her career and loses her husband, her only protector, and she begins a new life adrift in Rome, seeking solace from a young gigolo played by Warren Beatty.

The last to know of the news, Vivien was ambushed by flashbulbs and voices, each intrusive question was a dagger to her heart:

'Miss Leigh, what do you think about what happened today?'
Flash.
'Did you know about the marriage before?'
Flash.
'You know it happened this morning.'
Flash.
'Do you have anything to say?'
Flash.

She stopped, piqued by their statement. What happened this morning? Time stood still as she awaited their answer. 'They got married this morning.'[30]

What must have raced through Vivien's mind at that moment? She remained composed, stiffening her body to contain her emotion. A baby boy was born to Larry and Joan, a year and a day after the divorce hearing. Sinister notes arrived through Vivien's letterbox, with newspaper clippings of Larry and Joan and the news of their newborn son. 'Jealous?' one poison-pen letter asked. He had always wanted a daughter – the last baby Vivien had lost was a girl – and two would follow with Joan.

So, his life had come full circle and he had become a father again; he had just become a father when he left his first wife to be with Vivien. It was impossible to claw back what she had lost and perhaps as a sort of gratification to see what made him happy, she asked to meet Joan, and then his children. Larry refused, as Vivien's psychiatrist advised him against it. It would be hard to stop, once started.

'You can reach a point,' Larry said, 'where it's like a life raft that can hold only so many. You cast away the hand grasping it. You let it go … Then you go on living and there you are, with it, knowing what has happened, remembering its details. Yet what else is there to do?'[31]

Chapter Eleven

'There is nothing left remarkable beneath the visiting moon'

Antony and Cleopatra, William Shakespeare

❧◦❡◦❧

1961–1962

'You must understand that this is a moment of transition for me. A breathing space. I am trying to refill the reservoir. Every woman has to do that at some stage in her life … All I do know is that I want to lose myself in work,'[1] Vivien said. She could go anywhere she wanted, to the places she and Larry had been together, everywhere except the place they once called home.

In an attempt to go forward, she went backwards and supported by the British Council, she led the Old Vic Company on an eight-month tour of Australia, New Zealand, Mexico and Latin America, performing in *Duel of Angels*, *Twelfth Night* and *The Lady of the Camellias*, directed by Robert Helpmann. A courageous undertaking lasting from July 1961 until May 1962, she knew it would be compared to the tour of 1948. Maybe part of her wanted to relive those glittering moments when she and Larry, in the eyes of the public, were invincible. 'It is Viv and Larry no more,' a newspaper reported, diminishing her worth. 'It's just Viv now.'[2]

As the Qantas flight prepared to land at Sydney Kingsford Smith airport on 6 July 1961, Vivien must have recalled her arrival in

Fremantle on 15 March 1948. The scorched fields surrounding the runway contrasted with her first visit and the memory of a 'strange and wonderful perfume'[3] from the gum trees 60 miles from the shore. Back then, she and Larry had waved to thousands of people lining Victoria Quay, and newspapers spoke of her girlish beauty and the magic she possessed. They had showered her with flowers and she had pinned frangipani to her lapel.[4] A star-struck reporter wrote, 'Her beauty is as soft as gossamer. She is a fairy thing, laughing, twinkling, gay. Olivier is a man of lights and shadows.'[5]

On the airport runway now, the news cameras were there to capture Vivien's swift walk from the plane to the airport lounge. Jack Merivale, who had the dual role as her protector[6] and leading man, followed several paces behind, carrying the hand luggage. They had played 'Spill and Spell'[7] to pass the time on the long flight; she was careful to choose games where Jack won, as he did not like to lose.[8] It was his only competitive streak; he was, otherwise, a dispassionate man.

In the airport lounge, Vivien sat by the window and the daylight emphasised every aged and fatigued line on her face. A news camera was pointed at her, capturing her heavy makeup and tired eyes ringed with Kohl liner, concealed by a wide-brimmed hat. The reporters crouched forward, scribbling as she spoke with little enthusiasm, her voice deepened by fatigue and smoking – startling to those who had been enchanted by her lilting tones in 1948. Before her arrival, the cinemas screened *Gone with the Wind* and critics described her younger self as 'piquant, pert, and pretty'.[9] Now they wrote, 'Miss Leigh, 47, was tired. She showed it.'[10]

So, there it was once more: the present woman was marred by her past self and the exhaustion of living up to the public's expectations. A year earlier, she had attended the reunion of *Gone with the Wind* in Atlanta to mark the centenary of the American Civil War. She drank mint juleps and wore a ballgown reminiscent of Scarlett O'Hara and framed her face with kiss curls, but she was in a bad way as she toured the Cyclorama of Gettysburg. She would never forget the three-day celebrations in December 1939, when the picture premiered in Atlanta to frenzied crowds who lined the streets to catch a glimpse of her as the motorcade made its way to Peachtree Street. 'Ladies and Gentlemen,' Vivien had said to the public, some of whom waved Confederate flags and wore Antebellum costumes, 'I've spent quite a good deal of my time on Peachtree Street this year. And now that I'm here it feels just as if I were coming home.'[11]

Nothing could distract her: her mind was on Larry and his new life with Joan Plowright. Why could she not cast him aside, to exorcise herself of him, as he had done? Maybe she did not want to. She was still Lady Olivier; her luggage carried the monogram VLO, and she was addressed as such in formal settings.

To the onlooker, only the star existed: fame was a good friend and a cruel master. What was the point of trying to change direction, acting-wise, when everything pulled her back to the past? Nostalgia seemed to be the selling point when it came to her audience. Whether she liked it or not, she had enormous star quality but a chequered career.[12] She wanted the audiences to accept her for who she was at that moment: a seasoned actress secure in her singular identity and not the product of a famous marriage. It was the mantra she told herself, to justify the professional rut she was in. 'The theatre in London is flourishing,' she said, optimistic the public would support the tour. 'So, I imagine some people leave their homes to go to the theatre – thank goodness.'[13]

More than forty years earlier, Vivien had found herself far from home and using the camaraderie of others to fill a void. That cold spring day in 1920, Vivien and Gertrude stood in the ballroom of the former mansion which housed the Convent of the Sacred Heart. The high ceilings and long passageways had been stripped of their splendour and painted a sterile white. Pleasure into piety, with startling murals of Christ in all of his incarnations, from a halo in the heavens to a thorned crown on the crucifix. Vivien kissed her mother goodbye and was led by the Rev. Mother General to the Nazareth Dormitory. She changed from her town clothes into the convent uniform: a white blouse with a starched collar and a linsey-woolsey pinafore, rigid and shapeless. The first girl who greeted her was an

Australian,[14] and the rest gathered around her, studying her heart-shaped face and chestnut curls.

A sense of displacement washed over Vivien and she later compared the feeling to that of Blanche DuBois, at the beginning of *A Streetcar Named Desire*, when she finds herself lost and bewildered in New Orleans. In hindsight, every emotional upheaval would connect Vivien to Scarlett and Blanche; she had given them life, after all. The exterior of the convent with its columns and evergreen gardens and a tunnel leading from Roehampton Lane – a schoolgirl had darted out and been killed by a motorcar the year before – had echoes of Tara and Belle Reeve, the characters' beloved plantations in the American south.

In time, Vivien transitioned from the older girls' pet to their queen bee – a natural leader with beauty and vibrancy – and they did not begrudge her that status. They loved her, as, to their mind, she was delicate and it inspired in them a need to protect her. She was not yet of an age where girls were fair game to be ridiculed and their sparks of individuality extinguished. Loneliness always loomed in the shadows; the girls went home during the holidays and she remained behind, sleeping alone in her cold bed in an empty dormitory with hot compresses on her chest to warm her weak lungs. Amid the feminine kinship, she learnt to fit in: to be something to everybody.

At school, Vivien played the part of Mustardseed in *A Midsummer Night's Dream* and recited a total of five lines. Then, wearing a peacock-coloured shawl sent from India, she acted as Miranda in *The Tempest*, the dialogue heavily censored for its juvenile audience. 'Shakespeare is like bathing in the sea – one swims where one wants,'[15] she later said, when her star was firmly established. For now, at school in Roehampton, she was a bright light around which the other girls would orbit: 'Most sure the goddess/ On whom these airs attend!'[16]

Those two outings on the stage made her stage-struck and a year or so later, she saw George Robey in *Round in Fifty* at the Hippodrome and returned to see it sixteen times, collecting a dozen autographs from him. Robey became her idol for years to come: she was always prone to hero worship. At age 11, she saw him at a hotel restaurant in the Lake District, eating bacon and eggs, and overcome by emotion, all she could mumble was, 'I adore you.'[17]

The nomadic life carried her far from her birthplace of India, and in 1928, from Roehampton to Europe and beyond. The common link was the Sacred Heart, and the friendships she formed, sometimes fleeting, were mere footnotes in the story of her life. In her jotters, from place to place, she kept score of the letters she received and transcribed W.B. Yeats's poems, one being *The Pity of Love*:

A pity beyond all telling
Is hid in the heart of love:
The folk who are buying and selling,
The clouds on their journey above,
The cold wet winds ever blowing,
And the shadowy hazel grove
Where mouse-grey waters are flowing,
Threaten the head that I love.

'The folk who are buying and selling', so poignant were those words that they resonated with Vivien's thespian way of life. The first stop of the 1961 tour was in Melbourne, a place of conflicted memories for Vivien from her time spent there with Larry. If Larry thought she was lost to him on the 1948 tour, then she had been oblivious to any discord. She had loved him all the more and felt a swell of pride when they were announced as Sir Laurence and Lady Olivier and thundering applause surrounded them like a forcefield.

At that moment, in 1948, it seemed incomprehensible that Vivien wanted Larry to reject his knighthood. She worried that, if they became too important and moved too far beyond their artistic world, there would be an imbalance of power. Later, he would find their pseudo-aristocratic world oppressive and hated her formal dinners, imported wine lists and games on the lawn. All he craved was the mundane task of reading his newspaper at the breakfast table and the anonymity of taking the train to London.

At the Empire Youth Rally at the town hall, Larry gave a speech to the Australian children:

Our chief blessing is that we are a family. We are happy to have a family to talk to. While we are in the family we have friendly hands to touch, and when we feel we need to there are the paternal knees upon which we can climb for comfort.[18]

Back then, Vivien and Larry were still a family of two – their respective children, reduced to visitors in their lives, did not count – and being a twosome meant one way in and one way out; there were no additional influences in their small circle. Nothing could sink the ship. Every high and low was experienced together and the jubilation of their admirers gave them a false sense of security that not only were they bigger than life but they were somehow responsible for setting an example. For carrying the sacred torch of the British theatre. A promise that, though they may bicker, the external admiration would bind them together. He fulfilled that oath in Melbourne, just as she was losing her grip on herself. Her slight depression and emotional outbursts, which conspired to make her insecure and clingy, pointed to a deeper malice which he ignored for the time being.

On another occasion, Vivien and Larry attended a press reception at Menzies Hotel which sixty people gate-crashed to catch a glimpse of them in the flesh. The smitten look in Vivien's eyes – or was it anxiety – as she gazed at Larry made the reporters' questioning easy. Larry said Vivien was his favourite actress and when questioned about her favourite actor, she said, 'Why Sir Laurence Olivier, of course!'[19]

In 1961, the mood in Melbourne had changed and on the opening night of *Duel of Angels*, Vivien found the public hostile. The women were more interested in having their gowns photographed and were swathed in white fox furs, which she thought resembled a pack of huskies. Her production was merely an opportunity for the city's socialites to be seen, not to revel in the artistry of the theatre. They claimed they could not hear her and she went on television to criticise audiences for coming in late at every interval and for being undemonstrative. After six weeks, the company had outstayed its welcome. 'True monsters!'[20] Vivien called them. How dare society advance and its tastes for art change when she remained in the past, upholding the reputation that was so precious to her in 1948.

It was a bad start: the British Council assumed Vivien would be the star attraction she had been in 1948, but they did not foresee the challenges ahead. To them, or perhaps to herself, she was no longer special: time should have stopped to let her catch up. The Australians wanted Larry and Jack Merivale was a poor substitute, both in talent and charisma. Even the rehearsals lacked the romanticism of 1948 when they had rehearsed in the ship's ballroom, with later rehearsals taking place at the Finsbury Park Empire, a former variety theatre in north London.

In Brisbane, Vivien found the heat oppressive, especially in her *The Lady of the Camellias* costumes with her body swaddled in boned corsets and crinolines. On days off, she hosted a barbecue on the beach for the company and visited tropical gardens known as the Oasis. It was an attempt to recreate the camaraderie of the first tour when, every Sunday, she and Larry had arranged picnics and outings for their colleagues. She and Jack rented a bungalow on Orpheus Island in the Great Barrier Reef, a place she dreamt of visiting: 'I believe it is absolutely marvellous and it would be a complete break in routine.'[21] There, she could relax for twelve days and it relieved her from the pressure of the tour and the startling fact it was losing money. A blow to her pride, no doubt.

On the last tour, Vivien and Larry had gone to Brisbane to steal a few precious days together. Or so they had hoped. At Archerfield airport, a crowd of 500 fans and reporters waited to greet them. 'Here is your first gift from Queensland,'[22] a young woman said as she presented Larry with two pineapples, one for him and the other for Vivien. Within minutes of arriving, Vivien and Larry got into a waiting car and drove south to Surfers Paradise. To their horror, they found 200 people outside the hotel awaiting their arrival. After twenty-four hours of their fans' vigil outside their hotel, they fled and hid in a private house by the river on Cannes Avenue. A week later, they returned to Archerfield and avoided the crowd by hiding in the aircraft hangar until their flight was ready. One disgruntled fan told the reporters, 'We are really very kindly people, and I should like to assure Sir Laurence and Lady Olivier that we do not bite or attack strangers, even if we are so rude as to stare at them.'[23]

Now, in Sydney, Vivien experienced a mild episode and it was partly due to Jack's constant presence and fussing over her. Or was it also due to her memory playing tricks on her? She recognised the significance of Sydney: it was where she had first met Peter Finch and where Larry had convinced him to go to London. In other words, it had changed the course of her marriage, but she was a believer in fate.

As for Jack, Vivien might have felt his controlling, albeit well-meaning, influence too much to bear and she lashed out at him. It was Jack's kindness which had attracted her to him, for, materially speaking, he could not offer her financial stability nor the life she had led with Larry. There were shades of her last screen character, Karen Stone, in *The Roman Spring of Mrs Stone*, who relied on Paolo, her young gigolo, for emotional and sexual fulfilment. The two were interconnected, as far as she was concerned. During the tour, the picture opened to mostly negative reviews but her performance was singled out as visually pleasing and Tennessee Williams compared it to a poem.[24] *The New York Times* agreed, 'her torrents of grief are as liquid as though they came from a heart truly crushed.'

In Vivien's defence, she did not care for Jack's status or lack of, as it were, and she only judged people on whether or not they were 'proper' – proper meaning their strength of character. As mania gripped her, she missed the toxicity of what her dynamic with Larry had become and goaded Jack into being her sparring partner but failed to make him reciprocate her verbal abuse. As with Larry, he stood firm, waiting for the storm to pass, but unlike Larry who found comfort in Joan, he promised to never leave her.

Months prior, Vivien had told Jack she loved him and thanked God for him, yet now the dark clouds were gathering and impulsivity followed. She studied the map of Australia for a place to relax, preparing to 'go native'[25] and live in a hut if she had to. 'I don't care how isolated the island is. I'll get there somehow,' she said. 'But it must be off the tourist routes, be good for swimming and it must have a sandy beach, not coral.'[26] In the late 1950s, she had spoken of buying a house in Lake Garda and, later, she wanted to build a holiday home in Corfu.

In that frame of mind, she accepted an invitation from Mr and Mrs John Thompson to stay at their house 200 miles from Sydney and Jack protested it would be impossible, as she had a performance the following day. 'I said we would go and we will,'[27] she said, warning him if he did not want to go, she would go alone. He followed her to the car, which she insisted on driving herself.

They drove in silence until Jack noticed the Sydney Harbour Bridge and advised her to turn around, as they were going in the wrong direction. Vivien violently turned the car around and they continued for another 100 miles in silence until the tyre suffered a puncture on the red dirt road. Not a word was exchanged as Jack changed the tyre and Vivien stood behind him, swatting flies with a roadmap. They proceeded on their journey and came across a small town with a pub and Jack said, 'We really must have a drink.'[28] She agreed, even though she was still not speaking to him.

Finally, they arrived at their destination to learn that their hosts were throwing a party in Vivien's honour at the country club. Come and meet Scarlett O'Hara, the invitation promised. 'I really must have a lie down,'[29] Vivien said, leaving the room. An hour later, Jack tried to wake her, to prompt her to dress for the party. 'It's my Sunday,'[30] she answered sleepily and agreed to join him later. She did not show up, and Jack and Mr Thompson, who went to the party, learnt that one of the guests had gone to the Thompsons' front lawn and shot himself in the head. Vivien slept through the fatal gunshot and the commotion.

The following morning, Vivien and Jack left for their 200-mile drive back to Sydney. On the way, they stopped in the mountains to have a picnic and it was there, in Jack's words, they made up.[31]

What had provoked her bad temper and mood swings towards him? Jack claimed she struggled with her mental health on the tour, understandably given it was being sold on her name alone. Had she wanted Jack to become a star like Larry and to share the burden of her celebrity? Did she resent that he was not a strong masculine presence in her life, the way Peter Finch, 'a proper man',[32] had been? 'You are going to have such a wonderful success. I know it,'[33] she wrote to Jack before their opening night in *Duel of Angels* in Melbourne. Since Melbourne, the Australian press, in their scant reviews, had described his talent as poor and a hindrance to her stage presence.

Ironically, her performance in *The School for Scandal* in Sydney in 1948 was reviewed badly: 'Vivien Leigh was a disappointment. She is not top-ranking Old Vic calibre. Without the aid of all the science of Hollywood, Miss Leigh is just another ingenue.'[34] However, the adoration away from the stage had continued and Romano's restaurant manager, Tony Clerici, invented a dish called Oysters Olivier for her. The recipe was thus: oysters on the shell with a few drops of vinegar, a speck of chopped garlic, chopped parsley, chopped celery and salt and pepper to flavour, cooked on a bed of coarse salt and browned under the griller.[35] And at the Killara Camellia Show, she had been mobbed by fans who wrecked displays and broke through police barriers to get to her. 'It's the price of fame,'[36] she said at the time.

In December 1961, the Old Vic Company moved to Adelaide and Vivien was all too aware of the tour's failure, having been informed it would not advance to Russia and the Far East as she had hoped. A quick change of itinerary was made and they were told they would close in Latin America in May 1962.

Perhaps it felt odd to be thinking of the future when so much was connected to the past. In 1948, 300 people had waited outside the town hall in Adelaide as Vivien and Larry entered and 1,000 more had gathered to watch them leave, creating a traffic jam along King William Street. On the eve of the tickets going on sale, fans had camped in the street and some recited speeches from *Richard III* by torchlight to pass the time. Vivien and Larry made a surprise visit to thank them for their kindness.

When the tour progressed to Perth in January 1962, before heading to New Zealand, Vivien knew they were only marking time. The young members of the company were kind to her and respected her, as they should, but how could anything compare to the past?

Indeed, it was romantic to think of Vivien and Larry swimming with the black swans at Scarborough Beach and attending a performance of *Oedipus Rex* at the University of Western Australia's sunken garden before going on a drive and picnicking at Mundaring. As in Adelaide, they had greeted their fans who slept outside to secure the coveted tickets.

'We have just come to say "Good Evening" to all you brave people,' Vivien said.

'When are you going to get some sleep?' Larry asked. The crowd responded with laughter. 'Anyhow, you can sleep during the show,' he added.

'Gee, you're beautiful,' a young man said to Vivien.

'Am I?'[37] she asked.

As in 1948, the present tour left Australia for New Zealand's North Island and she was once more reacquainted with the past. Sir Ernest Davis, a brewery baron and former mayor of Auckland, had made his presence known on the last tour when he had put his chauffeur-driven Rolls-Royce at Vivien and Larry's disposal and sent flowers to their suite at the Grand Hotel. 'If I was forty years younger I'd be chasing after her,'[38] Sir Ernest said after their first meeting.

Now in his ninetieth year and widowed from his opera singer wife, Sir Ernest's passion for Vivien was reignited. He took her sailing on his yacht, *Moerewa*, around the Hauraki Gulf and proposed marriage on several occasions. Flattered as she was, she gently turned Sir Ernest down and continued to enjoy his hospitality, even if it had made Jack jealous. His admiration was a contrast to the public's scrutiny, for she had dared to age and get divorced and that was unforgivable to those who recalled the 1948 posters advertising the tour as 'Sir Laurence Olivier's Crown Jewel of the Old Vic Company'.[39] Did her mind wander to Larry as she and her admirer drifted out to sea? Although Vivien did not know, in 1961, Larry had begun an affair with Sarah Miles, his 19-year-old co-star in *Term of Trial*, who idolised him as Heathcliff in *Wuthering Heights*. As Miles made up for a scene, Larry compared her eyes to Vivien's, whom, he confided to her, was 'a schizophrenic, manic-depressive maniac'.[40]

As far as Sir Ernest was concerned, he did not see the passage of time or the sadness that still consumed her. She laughed when he repeatedly told her the physical side of marriage did not matter to him,[41] and he was charmed when she gave him a ring and a party for his ninetieth birthday. Perhaps the men in her life, one in her present and the other in her mind, were not dissimilar: they each needed a younger woman. Women who were otherwise unattainable in their everyday lives.

If Larry had felt something was amiss in Australia, then Vivien might have felt their dynamic shifting in New Zealand. There were still sparks of romance when they first arrived in Christchurch and checked into the United Services Hotel, where they were amused to find a room with two single beds which they pushed together to form a double. By the time they reached Wellington, Larry was consuming painkillers and using a crutch during *Richard III*, and Vivien resented his complaining about the pain in his knee and being indisposed. He had an operation and was ordered to rest. Bored, Vivien had worn a black dress slit to the waist and flirted with the young men in the company; the provocation did not go unnoticed. On the closing night, she curtseyed in her Lady Teazle costume, and said, 'Farewell Wellington! Farewell New Zealand! Farewell Australasia!'[42] Larry, who was bed-bound, heard the news and was so proud he wept.

Although to the press it seemed Vivien and Larry had left New Zealand in glory and their tour was a financial success, in truth, the ship had sailed from Wellington under gloomy skies and the rain pelted down as the company bid farewell to the few fans who came to see them off. In hindsight, some might have argued that the ship to England was carrying them to their doom. In Sydney, Larry had received a telegram from the board of the Old Vic, terminating his directorship due to structural changes. He confided only in Vivien, who shouldered the burden of his secret and shared his pain. Halfway into their crossing, he broke the news to the company. 'Sacked, old boy, sacked,' he said, flippantly. 'Left without a job.'[43]

In March 1962, Vivien and the company departed New Zealand and a similar apprehension awaited her in Mexico City, as her arrival preceded President John F. Kennedy and the First Lady's State visit. Her mental health was deteriorating and the company recognised the first signs of trouble. All too aware of the manifestations but helpless to stop it, she was 'so ashamed' of her illness and 'tried to keep it quiet'.[44] So, when they saw her removing her jewellery and setting it on the table, they began to remove their jewellery to mimic her actions and offer support.

In the Notley days, she would go around the greenhouses in a hectic way and take the long way back from anywhere. People, who were unaware of her illness, thought she was being difficult but she could not help from sabotaging herself and others. The young people in the company, like so many who loved her, could differentiate between the two personalities – the mania made her hostile and mischievous[45] – and knew the illness was not a reflection of who she was. When she was well, she was always thinking of gifts for the cast and crew and familiarising herself with the stagehands and dressers. Nobody could fault her consideration towards others, but it was all too fleeting.

Moreover, there was no nostalgia steeped within the theatres and locations of Mexico City and the cities of Latin America. She was in an entirely new place, one she and Larry had never been. The reception was warmer and, as always, socialites flocked to see her and wore the latest Parisian designs, making Vivien's last season Balmain look dated. 'What the hell do they expect, I've been gone for a year,'[46] she responded to their criticism.

Everywhere she went, she was greeted with enthusiasm even if many did not understand the language. However, in Santiago the audiences were formed of intellectuals and they were fluent in *Twelfth Night* and *The Lady of the Camellias*, if not in English, and detected when a scene had been changed. They understood her emotions and, in many ways, it was not acting on her behalf. 'Never on the stage before have I heard such sounds of utter human heartbreak as are torn out of her when the full realisation of her loss sweeps over her, it is acting of the highest order,' *Theatre World* wrote. It was enough for audiences to see her on the enormous stages in opera houses with an apron stretching for what seemed to be miles. Her voice struggled to fill the space; nevertheless, serious theatre-goers were charmed by her speeches given in Spanish and Portuguese, which she practised on a small tape recorder. Behind the scenes, she was slipping into a high, provoked by exhaustion and the heat, and perhaps the inability to tether her thoughts to familiarity.

In Peru, she gave an interview and her mind was on Larry when she was asked about the artistic merit of the cinema. Larry's screen acting, she said, was among the 'true works of art'.[47] Unlike her lament for their love, Larry did not speak kindly of his former wife and he told his mistress, Sarah Miles, that Vivien possessed a dark energy; she was a witch.[48] Spoken, in his case, like the true son of a parson.

She was in familiar territory when the press, so enamoured by her, wrote favourable reports on her beauty and charm:

> I ... entered the dressing room and saw the eyes of Vivien Leigh, those wonderful eyes of the changing and always the young colour of the sea and, like the sea, capable of reflecting both the golden light of noon, and the glow of the most terrible skies. She was a spontaneous and

charming woman, an authentic lady of the theatre, in all the aristocratic and traditional meaning of those words.[49]

The engagements in Buenos Aires coincided with a military coup
orchestrated by General Raúl Poggi and fighting broke out in the
streets; the sound of gunshots often interrupted the performance
inside the theatre. Vivien's nerves were on edge and the instability of
the overthrown government and the violence around her tested her
resilience. Despite the dangerous surroundings, she fell for the charms
of several local men and agreed to go to a party with them. Jack
followed from a safe distance, ensuring she did not come to harm.
However, back at the hotel, she lashed out at him for behaving like
her jailer and she lifted a brass clock he had given her and hurled it
from the hotel window. 'That's the worst thing you've ever done,'
Jack said.[50]

As with Larry, when she was experiencing psychosis, she despised
Jack and verbally and physically attacked him.[51] Some of Vivien's
friends felt he was not a good match for her and she let him know it.
Others marvelled at his patience and ability to care for her but it must
have been daunting to be far from home, for one year, with someone
so unpredictable. Jack tolerated her keeping Larry's love letters in her
bedside cabinet and his photograph next to her bed. Had he saved
her from hopelessness after her divorce from Larry? Or had Vivien
given him a purpose in a world where he worked sporadically and was
at odds with modern society? He remained stuck in the Edwardian
world of his mother, the famous stage actress Viva Birkett who had
died when he was 16. His dislike of contemporary literature, art and
music might have satisfied Vivien's ego, as to the outside world, she
projected an image of a well-bred woman from a bygone era and he
was content to play the part of her liveried footman.

In May, Vivien went to Rio de Janeiro, where she gave her cus-
tomary interviews and met the actress, Maria Fernanda, the daughter
of the poet, Cecília Meireles, who was performing in a local production of *A Streetcar Named Desire*. A press conference was held
for three interpreters of Blanche DuBois: Vivien, Maria Fernanda,
and Henriette Morineau, a French-Brazilian actress who had also
played the part on stage. Vivien wore a headscarf and refused to be

filmed, explaining she was not properly made up for the screen but she accepted a bouquet of flowers from Fernanda's 5-year-old son. Throughout the interview, Vivien noticed that Fernanda was sad and she asked why, and Fernanda confided that her mother was hospitalised with terminal cancer.

In the following days, Vivien visited Cecília Meireles and brought her flowers and waited by her bedside until she woke up. They struck up a friendship and Meireles, touched by Vivien's kindness, was inspired to write the poem, *Vivien Leigh in the Sunset*, in which she described her beauty as being similar to roses; the variation of her emotions as different as each petal.[52]

In a way, the poem affirmed Vivien's evolution from an actress in the shadow of the Oliviers at the beginning of the tour, to a singular actress in her own right. The tour concluded on 25 May 1962 and Vivien flew home to London via New York. The tour, although a financial failure, ended on a high in Latin America and would encourage her next move. If Larry could reinvent himself in a new genre of the theatre, then so could she. She announced she would be starring as an exiled Russian Grand Duchess in *Tovarich*, a Broadway musical. 'Such a thing would never have happened,' she said, 'had I not been in the Antipodes and therefore upside down.'[53]

Chapter Twelve

'What's past is prologue'

The Tempest, William Shakespeare

❧◦❦◦☙

1963–1964

The seasons of Vivien's life, like the acts of a play, had come full circle. She found herself bound to a stretcher with a piece of fabric covering her face as her body was transported from the ambulance to the aeroplane, departing from New York to London. It was reminiscent of Ceylon and Hollywood ten years before, in 1953, but perhaps much worse: her breakdown had happened live on stage in front of a Broadway audience who believed they were in on the act:[1]

> O for a Muse of fire, that would ascend
> The brightest heaven of invention,
> A kingdom for a stage.[2]

As the plane took off into the sky, she awoke and caused a scene, and was restrained by her nurse. At Heathrow, she was carried from the plane on a stretcher and covered with a fur coat to fend off the early morning chill. She had the usual conflicting feelings of forgetfulness and paranoia which preceded a breakdown, of losing her ability to recall recent events but still feeling as if some invisible force was plotting against her. And knowing she had behaved badly and hurt others and the pressing matter of finding them to apologise. For months she had existed on nervous energy and, finally, in September 1963, it reached its breaking point. Before a sedative injection was administered in New York, she asked, 'Does Larry know?'[3]

Naturally, Larry was not far from her mind as she prepared for *Tovarich*, a musical that would challenge her as an actress, for she could not sing and it terrified her. She loved music, but she was not a musician: she joked she had given up the violin aged 6 because it hurt her fingers.[4] Her part was that of Tatiana, an exiled Russian grand duchess who ekes out a living as a maid in Paris. It seemed like a good idea at the time and she impulsively accepted while touring with the Old Vic, having auditioned for Abel Farbman who flew to New Zealand to hear her sing. 'If I've made up my mind to do something, I can't be persuaded out of it,' she said. 'I just plunge ahead without thinking. That's my trouble. Every so often I bump into stone walls and have to pick myself up and climb over them.'[5]

Then reality set in, as Leigh Holman had suspected it would, when she confided in him the day before she left for New York on 12 November 1962. She was worried, which Leigh assured her was normal and he commended her bravery for venturing into the unknown. His praise restored her confidence and she began to relish the challenge of a musical.

Adopting a sense of bravado, Vivien said, 'So what? Sounds like it will be fun,'[6] to Jean-Pierre Aumont, her leading man who was to play the part of Mikail, when he doubted their musical abilities. She had sung Ophelia's bawdy songs on stage in *Hamlet*, but the mad scene was a musical interlude; a relief from the tragedy of the plot. Aumont visited her at home and observed her lying on a chaise longue and reading the script. Her mood, like a sundial, changed with the elements.

Maybe Aumont told her about the first time he had seen her in 1936 or 1937, dining in Soho with Leigh and making eyes at Larry, who was across the room with Jill and pretending his paramour did not exist. 'That young woman and that man sitting at the other table are madly in love with each other,'[7] Aumont told his companion. She was, to Aumont's mind, 'pursuing some interior dream'[8] with Larry; the danger of catching his eye and the pretence crumbling thrilled her more than any first night could.

In Vivien's dream world, she and Larry would be sitting across the table in Sardi's, circa 1961, when all was said and done, and the evils which had sprung up between them[9] had settled into mutual tolerance. In the same way, nostalgia lured people back to the hellish landscapes of their past. Throughout the dimly lit restaurant Cino Sardi worked the room and the famous caricatures, a silent jury behind their frames, observed the patrons. Vivien came in from the cold and sat opposite Larry and ordered a drink. He was unmoved by her presence and sat next to Joan, who remained by his side for part of the time before leaving. Vivien took no notice of Joan, whom she considered a pretender to the title of Lady Olivier. Both Larry and Joan, not yet free to marry, were performing on Broadway in separate productions, and Vivien was on her way to Atlanta for the centenary of the American Civil War – in other words, Scarlett O'Hara had been summoned. Vivien wanted to break the ice, to tell Larry and Joan that they should remain friends: she was no threat to their happiness. Why not be sophisticated about the entire thing? Wasn't that how this fantasy was to play out?[10]

Fragments of Vivien's real life and imagination were blurred and she awoke in a room at the Avenue Nursing Home in St John's Wood, unaware of how she had ended up in London or what had taken place in the Broadway Theatre only days before. The events, as they unfolded, were similar to 1953, but unlike at Netherne, she had been unconscious when she had been admitted to the clinic in St John's Wood. The area was familiar with 'lunatics', as they were cruelly known in the past, where the rich found loopholes in the law to establish clinics in private houses to take mentally ill patients who could afford to bypass the state-run asylums. As in 1953, she woke up alone: a decade before, Larry had departed for Ischia and, now, Jack remained in New York.

'Please come back with me,'[11] she had begged Jack before the doctor sedated her. In her hour of need, she asked him to marry her, promising they could do so the moment they arrived in England.

'Darling, I would marry you at absolutely any time except at present because you are really not yourself,'[12] he said.

Jack felt she was enticing him to accompany her home, only so she could mistreat him, as she often did when she was manic.[13] Once, during a fight, she goaded him, 'That's right, hit me ... hit me. Go for my eyes like that other bastard.'[14]

The room in St John's Wood was filled with wilting flowers and she sat next to her bed, in her nightgown; her clothes had been confiscated in case she tried to escape. She hallucinated and re-enacted scenes from *Gone with the Wind* for the benefit of her nurse. A decade ago, she had channelled Blanche DuBois during her mental collapse, and this time she was Scarlett O'Hara – in the words of her friend Sir John Gielgud, she lacked breadth of emotion and resorted to petulance, as opposed to the tragedienne.[15] But the strongest feelings of all were fear and loneliness, which had first stirred ten months before.

In November 1962, Vivien landed in New York and the reality of her situation soon set in. She awoke in her hotel room, paralysed by the fear of performing in a live musical. Stage fright, or 'first night nerves' as they were known, was perfectly natural and something she never overcame. 'I can't analyse my feelings before a first night. Most of the time I'm worrying about the role I play, not myself,'[16] she said. Worse still, she was alone as Jack had flown to California to shoot *The List of Adrian Messenger* and she needed their co-dependency to feel secure and to function. In letters to Jack, she told him that dining without him was loathsome and she missed him sleeping next to her. Despondency gave way to depression and anxiety, exacerbated by her schedule of rehearsals at the Broadway Theatre, singing and dancing for eight hours a day, seven days a week, for the next five weeks.

On Christmas Eve, Vivien announced she would not be participating in the play and threatened to fly home to England. Her whims, by then, were known to Aumont and he questioned her change of heart. They were both alone in New York over the festive period and he wondered if she was missing her partner, as he was missing his wife. She explained that Aumont's part was of much greater importance, an opinion undecided by her until their first full rehearsal the night before and she measured the positive response from the crew, which displeased her. Furthermore, she hated his songs and the twenty-five minutes in which she was absent from the stage, and she loathed their director, Delbert Mann.

There could be tension with her leading men, evident during her first meeting with Clark Gable who was to be Rhett Butler in *Gone with the Wind*. She showed up to a photo shoot an hour late – an honest mistake as she was given the wrong time – and overheard Gable saying, 'I couldn't make love to that dame now if she were the most beautiful woman in the world!' She crept up behind him and said, 'I quite agree, Mr Gable. If I were a man, I'd tell that Vivien Leigh to go right back to merry old England and fuck herself.'[17] They had sized each other up, or perhaps Vivien had cut him down to size.

In the New Year of 1963, Vivien and Aumont performed a three-week run at the Erlanger Theatre in Philadelphia and the audience was responsive, particularly when Vivien danced the Charleston but people had come to see Scarlett and Blanche, and not necessarily to listen to her singing show tunes. Her star quality carried the production but she felt overwhelmed by the thirty-piece orchestra and the realisation that her voice, like a prima donna's, was the main instrument. The gossip columnist, Dorothy Kilgallen, predicted Vivien's song, *I Know the Feeling*, would be a number one hit: 'Those on the inside who've heard it can't stop humming it.'[18] Much of her dread was banished by the positive reception she received.

However, Noël Coward crushed her confidence when he declared the musical was undignified and advised her not to open with it on Broadway. Coward had come to the play's opening in Philadelphia and scrutinised her singing, the bad direction, and the awful staging. A short time later, the director was fired and replaced with Peter Glenville, who ordered several musical numbers to be cut, various scenes to be rewritten, and he replaced some of the supporting cast.

The strain was beginning to tell on Vivien and by the time they reached Boston, she had convinced Glenville to cut her dialogue and rewrite it to her liking, only to regret her decision. During *Gone with the Wind*, and well into production, screenwriters came and went, the original director George Cukor was fired mid-production and replaced with Victor Fleming, and the scenes were rewritten between takes. But a lousy performance could be left on the cutting room floor, quickly forgotten and kept between the actor and director, not played out before hundreds in a darkened theatre. Aumont tried to appease her concerns and made suggestions which she rebuffed. 'You like this play,' she snapped. 'I detest it.'[19] Still, they continued to perform to a full house, night after night, and it broke box-office records. 'Poor people!' Vivien told Aumont. 'They're buying tickets to see one play, without suspecting that they're going to see another.'[20]

After each performance, she was highly strung and doubting her abilities and relying on Aumont to comfort her. He knew the success hinged on her participation and so he went to her suite and, over a nightcap, offered solutions to her woes, while his own troubles bothered him. Soon, rumours began that Vivien and Aumont were having an affair, the evidence deduced from sightings of him leaving her suite, exhausted. In truth, all they ever did was drink booze and play board games bilingually.[21] The gossip reached Jack in California and he reacted with jealousy, prompting her to write to him, promising that she was being faithful and was trying to find him theatrical work in New York so they could be together. Her spirits were lifted by a letter from Larry, who sent his good wishes, and she responded by calling him, 'Darling, Darling Larry' and referring to him as 'Baba',[22] their old pet name for each other.

In March, the play transferred to the Broadway Theatre in New York for three preview performances before an official premiere. Before the first preview, Aumont lost his voice, which he attributed to his physical and emotional stress, and he agonised over the missed performance on Friday night. On Saturday afternoon, he sneaked into the matinee to watch his understudy and during the interval, Vivien spied him and said, 'How dare you make an appearance when you are dying!'[23] He explained he was not dying and had only lost his voice. 'Only a Frenchman could have the nerve … All amateurs!'[24] she snapped. They reconciled before the curtain rose on the opening night. 'The nicest thing about *Tovarich* as a musical is Vivien Leigh,' wrote *The New York Times*.

So much could be said of Vivien's behaviour before going on stage and afterwards as the real person slowly disappeared behind the cloak of bipolar disorder and the pendulum of her moods dictated the course of the evening. Off stage, she drank heavily and relied on sleeping pills, and in a heightened state she 'hurled her-self against the walls like a poor, maddened bird'.[25] *Time* wrote, 'Although her eyes seem candlelit with some private poetry of grief, she plays the regal scamp all evening.'[26] From the footlights, she cast a spell over the audiences who flocked to see her singing and dancing even if the critics thought the production itself was poor. '*Tovarich*,' wrote *Time*, 'is the largest disaster Vivien Leigh has been involved in since the burning of Atlanta.'[27] At parties, she was equally unpredictable and when she met Barbara Cook, who was performing on Broadway in *She Loves Me*, she turned her head and ignored Cook, who spoke about seeing her at the premiere of *Gone with the Wind* in Atlanta in 1939. 'She sure as hell didn't want to hear about it,'[28] Cook recalled.

As the play reached its four-hundredth performance and Vivien won a Tony Award for her portrayal of Tatiana, the exhaustion began to tell on her. Aumont claimed she lacked originality on stage and adhered to the script; she never improvised or veered from the direction she was given. Perhaps, in hindsight, he came to view this as predictable and knew where he stood each time they performed together. They transferred to the Winter Garden and the new setting made her feel disorientated within her surroundings.

One Saturday, before a matinee performance, Aumont found Vivien in her dressing room, in tears and holding photographs of her grandsons – she was now a grandmother of three – and listen-ing to the waltz from *Gone with the Wind*. When they were called to the stage, she was pale and trembling and sang her first song three times faster than its original pace. During their duet, she turned her back on Aumont and read her personal letters. A scene, in which she, as Tatiana, confessed that her jailers had raped her, escalated her mood and she became violent, hitting out at Aumont in front of the confused musicians in the pit. She went to the edge of the stage and told the audience, 'An actress has to think before answering,'[29] before walking off. The curtain fell and everyone backstage scrambled to dis-tract the audience, sending on two actors to perform a dance number from an earlier scene. In the final scene, Vivien appeared and stood in the centre of the stage, immobile, before the curtain was dropped once more.

In a way, Vivien was living out Ophelia's mad scene: she was talking nonsense and singing songs, though it took no effort on her behalf, as an actress, to convey madness. As with the fictional Ophelia, Vivien got upset and took offence easily. To Aumont and the others, she only made half sense and there was no sensible meaning behind her words, leading the audience to believe it was part of the play. Aumont, had he been cast as Queen Gertrude to her Ophelia, would not have been out of place reciting the dialogue from *Hamlet*:

> It would be good if somebody speaks with her. Otherwise, she's likely to plant dangerous ideas in evil minds. Let her come in. *[Aside]* To the sick soul of a sinner like myself, every little thing seems like the beginning of a disaster.[30]

Later that night, Aumont went to his dressing room and discovered Vivien had torn up the photographs he kept of his children. Destroying other people's property seemed to be a familiar sign of her psychosis during which she could no longer control herself or her actions. Empathy and reasoning no longer existed; she felt only hatred and contempt for others.

In 1946, years before Vivien was diagnosed and treated for manic depression, she had torn up the portraits that Philippe Halsman had taken of her for *Life* magazine. Halsman was aware of her recent bout of tuberculosis and was shocked by her pale and fragile appearance but thought her illness gave her an otherworldly appeal. She was, to his mind, an angel-like star.[31] The negatives showed her as she really was: a sick woman hovering between two worlds. He asked her to pose once more, this time with a full face of makeup, and went to her suite at the Waldorf Astoria, but the prints were not to her liking. 'These pictures are terrible and I forbid you to show them to the magazine. I know your boss, Mr Luce, personally; if you disobey me, I will destroy you,'[32] she menaced from her sickbed. A waiter knocked on the door and entered with tea and biscuits.

'Where should I put the tray, Miss Leigh?' the waiter asked.

'Could you, please, put it on the night table,'[33] she answered sweetly.

She waited until the door closed and then tore Halsman's prints into tiny pieces. Like some unworldly demon, she was determined to leave a physical mark of destruction, as if to convey the torturous regime of manic depression.

In the present day, two doctors went to Vivien's dressing room at the Winter Garden to give her a shot of morphine and the stage manager advised her to go home. 'Over my dead body,' she yelled, and she kicked and screamed and protested that she would go on stage. Jack, who had since arrived in New York and was performing in *The Importance of Being Earnest*, pinned her against the wall to prevent her from leaving.

'Put the understudy on,'[34] Jack told the stage manager before going to his own play. Throughout the evening, Vivien remained locked in her dressing room and recited her part to her maid and the two doctors.

Later, Jack took her home and she proceeded to crawl around the floor, picking imaginary dirt off the carpet.[35] Her American doctor, Dr Henry Ross, came and sedated her while Jack held her down. It was recommended she return to England for ECT with Dr Conachy. The fear of history repeating itself agitated her: she had never forgotten the scene on the flight home from America, in 1953, when Larry had ordered the nurse to enhance her dose of sedatives, and although she hadn't been able to react, she had heard every word.

'Are you coming too?' she asked Jack before the sedative took hold.

'No. It doesn't seem worthwhile to pay two airfares,'[36] he said. His frugality was misunderstood as cruelty. Meanness, in the grand scheme of things.

She would never forget Jack's response, nor how he had left her alone at her lowest point, the way Larry had done at Netherne ten years earlier.

※

In 1961, before Vivien embarked on her tour of Australia, New Zealand and Latin America, she had bought Tickerage Mill, a Queen Anne House, near Uckfield in Sussex, hidden among the restful undulations of the Downs.[37] She went there after she was thrown out of the nursing home in St John's Wood and was accompanied by a nurse.[38] At night when she could not sleep, Vivien and her nurse filled the hours by going to the local pub, the Blackboys Inn, and roaming through her private woodland and rowing on the pond.

There was a walled garden, known as the white garden owing to her having planted white flowers – her favourite, they had to have perfume – inside of which was a bust of Alice (*Adventures in Wonderland*) on top of a column. A stone bench was concealed by a crescent-moon-shaped hedge. There were woods nearby and a lake, which was a large pond, called the Lake of Reveries, framed by a weeping willow and cypress trees. A small rowing boat was tethered to a wooden jetty and she rowed past the reeds, where Nan Tuck was accused of witchcraft and tried in the pond but fled to a nearby church and was banished by the parson – in despair, hanging herself from a tree.[39] The water offered a romantic view of the seventeenth-century house with its numerous chimneys and an Oriel window around which climbers and clumps of roses were planted.

As with Notley Abbey, the new house would serve as an extension of her image as a great lady of the theatre. Jack wondered if she could afford it and a cynic might have questioned his interest in her finances but there was a dash of realism in his concerns. She was approaching 50, how much longer could she expect leading parts? How much longer could her health hold out? Her longevity was contrasted by Larry's career progression: he was appointed artistic director of the National Theatre and his wife was part of the company of actors. 'She's one of the three or four best actresses in England,'[40] Larry said of Joan Plowright.

In recent days, Larry had telephoned from Brighton to check on Vivien's health and they made small talk, which comforted her. There were only 12 miles between them and he was closer than ever. One day, he came to Tickerage Mill, unannounced, and the housekeeper let him in. Vivien was hiding in her bedroom, too nervous to go down and see him. 'Vivien, are you coming down, or am I coming up?'[41] he called up the stairs.

Vivien ran downstairs to greet him and they went outside to walk in the grounds that were transitioning from green to rust; the golden autumnal light reflected in the pond. Did she recall the words she said, over a decade before, 'In looking back on the past I realise that the memories I cherish most are not of first night successes, but of simple, everyday things: walking through our garden in the country after rain.'[42] They sat on the stone seat by the crescent-moon hedge and she, for all her inner turmoil, felt at peace in his company. It was as if he had never left her and their lives somehow continued seamlessly from Notley.

Larry's life with Joan and the children seemed to run in a straight line and perhaps only the news of Vivien's health made him detour, briefly. The visit, he claimed, was strictly business – through their respective production companies they invested in mutual projects. A phone call from Joan, who was at their family home in Royal Crescent, interrupted the meeting and he left. He had spent the entire day with Vivien and drove away with tears in his eyes.

Seeing Larry was enough, all Vivien had wanted from him was to remain friends and he could not deny the feelings of responsibility he had towards her, even if romantic love was dead. She continued to send him affectionate notes and gifts. Later, in his old age, he would say, 'The only one I ever loved was Vivien,'[43] and past memories often disturbed him. However, in 1963, there was no denying that he loved his wife and their children and the stability (or normality) they had given him.[44] But there would always be tokens from their lives together: Larry kept a miniature portrait of Vivien, and Vivien held on to his ring and wore it. It was the kind of sympathetic magic that appealed to her, the same workings of Merricat Blackwood from Shirley Jackson's *We Have Always Lived in the Castle*, a book she had recently read.

Back in 1939, when Larry did *No Time for Comedy* on Broadway, he went every Sunday to the symphony concert at Carnegie Hall and Vivien, exhausted from her incarnation of Scarlett O'Hara and blistered from the imported red dirt on the set, listened to it on the radio at home in Crescent Drive. When the applause petered out, Larry gave a few extra claps so she would hear him over the airwaves and know they were for her.[45] Maybe she continued to believe that his last thought would always be reserved for her.

Therefore, when Jack returned from New York, Vivien greeted him coldly. He claimed he had been brought over under false pretences, as he was warned she was out of control at Tickerage. She accused him of caring more about his sore back – he was receiving treatment in New York – instead of her well-being. Did she recall her marriage proposal before being sedated and how he had turned her down? Even though they would not marry, Jack honoured their unspoken vows 'in sickness and in health'.

There was further bad news: Vivien was robbed of £2,000-worth of jewellery while she was unwell, and her trusted doctor, Dr Conachy, who administered ECT at her home, died suddenly. Everything was changing rapidly and yet Jack remained steadfast. Jack was there, by her side, to pour the drinks and tend to everything, like a butler; a dismissive suggestion by most, who saw little affection between the two, and only a one-sided affair, as though he were employed in service.[46]

Yet, for all of Jack's devotion, Vivien would spend her fiftieth birthday with Leigh, who had recently turned 63, at his home in Wiltshire. As always, Leigh was a stable force in what had become a chaotic period, and Jack observed that she did not misbehave in front of him and was always in control.[47] There was talk of her retiring permanently from the stage and screen, as her doctor had advised her to withdraw from *Tovarich*, when she spoke of bringing it to London. 'I suppose it was madness for me at my age to be knocking myself out every night on stage dancing the Charleston in *Tovarich* – but I loved it,'[48] she said. She considered starring in Wolf Mankowitz's musical based on Mata Hari but the project foundered. Her romanticism for the recent past might have surprised anyone who dealt with the fallout in New York and her recovery at home. At the time, Leigh said, 'This is perhaps her last lesson in the art of how not to live.'[49]

⸎

As always, Vivien lived at a rapid pace and her decisions were often impulsive, more so, during her recovery when she went to California in the summer of 1964. 'I suppose I'm here,' she said, as she stood on the terrace of her rented property, a white and gold house on Thrasher Avenue, overlooking Los Angeles; the cityscape was shrouded in smog. 'It's hard to tell in Hollywood, whether you're here or not.'[50] Only six weeks earlier, her depression had lifted but like any catastrophe, an aftershock was on the horizon. Uneasy, she kept sitting down and standing up, and her eyes followed an invisible force around the garden.[51] She put the music from *Gone with the Wind* on her record player and tried to relax but the wailing soundtrack disturbed her. The phantoms were really there: they were red plastic flowers, violently pushed into the camellia bushes on the terrace.[52] Horrified, she began to pull them out and throw them into a container, moving around the artificial garden, stripping it bare.

She was in Los Angeles to film Stanley Kramer's adaptation of Katherine Anne Porter's novel, *Ship of Fools*. Her character, Mary Treadwell, was a middle-aged divorcée travelling to Europe and reminiscing about her past as a Virginian socialite with both fondness and horror. However, she felt her character, albeit a supporting part, was lost among the large cast, and she complained that the book was unreadable. Perhaps there was a fear of connecting to Mrs Treadwell, an embittered alcoholic hoping to recapture her youth, who slowly descends into loneliness and madness.[53] It was a danger she knew too well, as did Larry, who said, 'Vivien was too much affected by the parts she played, and if she got ill, which she certainly did, it dreadfully had a great deal to do with playing Blanche DuBois, being ill in the same way.'[54] As with Mrs Treadwell, she faced the same identity crisis that came with menopause, which, in those days, was widely misunderstood and often considered on a par with insanity.

'Stanley, I can't make it today,'[55] Vivien told Kramer; she was caught in a blind panic, knowing she was spiralling out of control and unable to stop it. She was making up before a scene, her hands were trembling and the inner turmoil of facing the lens was too much. The camera was to capture a similar scene on film, where she tells her reflection that she is no longer young. A decade earlier she had spoken of how she could not face the camera at nine o'clock in the morning,[56] nor could she stand to see her face up close during the rushes on the screen. Now, she was to violently deface her delicate features and, as if scrying, the glass would offer a glimpse of her future.

Kramer understood, he knew the risks when he invited Vivien to accept the part. He was inspired by her inability to hold on to happiness or contentment[57] and created a scene where Mrs Treadwell hears phantom music and breaks into a Charleston. Tennessee Williams shared a similar view and felt Vivien's private life and how she conducted herself off stage was closer to the unhappy heroines she played and knew, in terms of Blanche, she was not acting. As both the director and producer of the picture, Kramer was frustrated and fascinated by her talent as an actress and yet her reluctance to accept the falseness of a film set. One day, the entire set had to be changed, as she envisioned it differently.

On edge and paranoid, she directed those feelings towards her colleagues, whom she verbally abused. Noël Coward called this side of Vivien, 'a conceited little bitch'.[58] Simone Signoret, who played the Contessa, ignored Vivien's fixation with her increasing weight – in recent years, Simone had developed an alcohol addiction and was deeply unhappy in her marriage to Yves Montand – and yet, ironically, she sympathised with her. Only once did Signoret lose her composure when she asked Vivien to stop eulogising her relationship with Larry,[59] with whom she had worked on *Term of Trial*, and according to Sarah Miles, was in love with. Similarly, Vivien had a tricky relationship with Lee Marvin, whose character mistakes her for a prostitute; he was left bruised after she attacked his face with a stiletto. Marvin forgave her: he had his own demons with alcoholism which rendered him abusive in his private life. She felt the sincerity of their kindness, even if she could not reciprocate it, and wrote to Leigh to tell him of their consideration towards her.

During a short stay in Malibu, Vivien got to know Marvin and his wife, Betty, who rented a beach house a few doors down from her. Betty found Vivien's 'self-indulgent and vulgar'[60] behaviour fascinating: those who did not know her intimately were often shocked by her explicit language and crude turn of phrase. She was going through a phase of carrying her costume jewellery in her handbag; she had special costume jewellery for the beach and readily changed its theme for the Summer Olympics in downtown Los Angeles.[61]

When Jack arrived, having been delayed by commitments in England, he noticed the decline of her mental health and took her for two courses of ECT with Dr Karl von Hagan, who, during that period, was treating Clara Bow for schizophrenia. As Vivien was not one of his patients, Dr Von Hagan was reluctant to help but eventually agreed to treat her on the basis that he was a fan. Jack drove her to the doctor's office in Culver City and knowing of her terror of needles and ECT, he held her hand while the Pentothal injection was administered. When she came to, the familiar pattern of shame and guilt consumed her and she was eager to apologise to those who suffered in her wake. Manic depression, the most convincing liar that ever was, managed to warp every aspect of her reality.

'Everyone must know I'm as mad as a hatter,'[62] she said. She dreaded her return to the set but to her credit, she completed the filming. In a way, she wanted to be like Larry, who moved in secrecy[63] and rarely discussed his plans or revealed his hand to friends or colleagues. Sometimes, when she felt her mood changing, she stayed at Tickerage and avoided London, as she could not trust herself to behave properly.

'You're not! You're not mad! You have a mental condition and that's entirely different. That can be coped with,'[64] Jack reassured her, desperate for her to believe it was not her fault. It was the intimate side that few witnessed: he did his best to shield her from harm, weathered her abuse and understood that her soul was drawn to Larry, and he picked up the pieces afterwards. While others dismissed her as mad, he marvelled at her courage.

For Jack, Vivien would always be the girl he had first met in 1937, when he was cast as Menteith and as Malcolm's understudy in Larry's Old Vic production of *Macbeth*. His time at Oxford was cut short by his father's lack of money and he went straight into bit parts in films, followed by repertory theatre, with Larry giving him his first job. There was Vivien: she was moving like a dream and when she turned around, he was struck by her beauty. 'Good luck,' she said, as she opened the door to Larry's dressing room and flashed a bewitching smile before disappearing. His other enduring memory of her was seeing her again when he played Balthasar and understudied for Larry in *Romeo and Juliet* during the ill-fated Broadway production in 1940. But when they were together during the production, she was possessive of Larry and resented Jack's presence.

They met under happier circumstances in 1945, when Jack motored to Blackpool from his nearby RAF barracks and burnt up a month's ration of petrol. She was touring in *The Skin of Our Teeth* before its

London opening and scandalised provincial matinee-goers in her skimpy bathing suit and beauty pageant sash. 'Ee! I wish I hadn't paid my money to see this muck,'[65] a disgruntled woman said to her friend during the interval. It was the week of VE Day and spirits were high; the bunting was raised in the street outside and young boys burnt effigies of Adolf Hitler. The Germans had surrendered and peace had been restored in Europe after almost six years of war. Jack went backstage to greet Vivien and she embraced him, asking if he enjoyed the play. 'I adored it,'[66] he said, enchanted by the tiny figure standing before him, eager for his approval. As memories go, he would recall that it was 'a very enjoyable few minutes'.[67]

As far as Vivien and Jack were concerned, they each represented a link to the past. 'She despises pigeon-holing people by age, income or background. She likes spending her own money, but she doesn't know how much she has got,' a reporter wrote. 'She likes her possessions to have a meaning, a link with a place or an event or a person.'[68] He, who disliked the modern world,[69] and she, who needed someone to remember who she really was. Or maybe all she needed was someone to accept who she had become.

'You won't let them send me to the madhouse, will you?' she asked him.

'Over my dead body,' he promised. 'Absolutely *never*.'[70]

Chapter Thirteen

'The wheel is come full circle, I am here'

King Lear, William Shakespeare

❦

1964–1967

Throughout Vivien's life, some might have argued that her behaviour was impulsive; she would have described it as instinctive. She was ruled by her thoughts and feelings: emotions took precedence over hard facts and it was always that way. It had led to her magnificent achievements and failures, but she had no regrets.[1] A fatalist, she did not see the point of resisting something if it was going to happen.[2] 'We must all be students and masters of ourselves,'[3] she said.

Often, those personality traits gave way to last-minute plans, and in November 1964, she accompanied her friends Hamish and Yvonne Hamilton on a trip to India. According to Jack, he wanted to hide her passport to prevent her from going: he knew the symptoms of mania were building and pitied her travelling companions. Or was he, in his careful way, being overly cautious and overreacting? Who could blame him, given the decline of her health in recent years?

As a couple, they were experiencing a trying period. Jack was depressed and questioned their relationship, as Vivien was spending more time with Leigh, which made him feel slighted as she did not, in his words, lose control around her former husband.[4] In recognising the signs of her illness and the pattern it followed before an episode, there was a possibility that she avoided Leigh during those times. There were also differences in their respective lifestyles, which Jack came to resent, and he struggled with his pride when Vivien paid for things he could not afford, such as their two trips to Tobago in the early 1960s. His initial reaction was to turn down the holiday, but she refused to go unless he went, and so the emotional onus was placed on him.

Perhaps Jack's depression was the result of renal disease, then undiagnosed (it had killed his father), and in many cases, low moods were, and are, common before a diagnosis. From Leigh's home in Wiltshire, where Vivien spent another birthday, she wrote to Jack to assure him of her love and asked him to accompany her to India. He could not go: he had a walk-on part in *King Rat*, and regardless, if he was available, he could not afford the fare and refused to let her pay.

In Vivien's luggage were her prescriptions of Libraxin, Seconal, Serenace and Marplan[5] – hypnotics and antidepressants – and a letter from her doctor as a precautionary measure if treatment was needed while abroad. She stressed the return to India was not a 'sentimental journey';[6] however, a part of her must have been wanting to trace her roots and seek out the land of not only her birth but of her maternal ancestors. After a long flight, she arrived in Delhi, where it was sunny and clear. Once more she took to the skies, this time in a tiny aeroplane with ten seats to fly to Kathmandu and from her vantage point took in the Himalayas from the Nepalese side as the aircraft flew along the ridge of Mount Everest. Peaks of blue and white blended in with the clouds, the heavenly landscape which formed the story of her conception; her mother had gazed at the mountain range, willing its beauty to transfer to her unborn child. If the power of attraction is to be believed, she was elemental from the beginning.

Yet, Vivien did not venture to the hillside stations of Darjeeling and Ootacamund, the places of her early childhood and where her infant siblings were laid to rest. The memories conjured from the past were as intimate as Gertrude's sepia film reels, captured on her Kodak No. 2: Vivien's father, Ernest Hartley, dressed in his cavalry uniform on horseback and servants passing through doorways and verandas before the empire collapsed. Or, far more realistically, before her father's adultery and bad investments destabilised their happy home and set them on their wandering path.

Only Bombay was a familiar sight, and she visited Crawford Market, a vegetable market in a Victorian building with the sunlight streaming through its Gothic windows, illuminating her. Three Indian schoolgirls approached her at the stalls. 'Oh Miss Leigh, could I have your autograph?'[7] one asked and she casually signed her name. There, in what seemed to be the furthest point from Hollywood, Vivien's fame had eclipsed *Cinema Dekho*,[8] an exciting attraction to the children of Bombay who would rush to peep inside a box covered with a cloth as a vendor changed the slides.

Vivien stayed at the British Embassy in Nepal in a room with two beds and a view of the garden. Each morning, breakfast was brought to her in bed and she was enchanted by the waiter's name, which translated to Moon God. The Hamiltons – Hamish (known to his friends as Jamie), in particular, she had known since her days with Leigh – were aware of her mercurial nature and she bickered with them. It was not a sign of illness, as she appeared level-headed and humorous in her letters to Jack,[9] but the intense climate and culture shock which had an overwhelming effect on her sensibilities. She also felt ill from her vaccinations, which were required before travelling.

Venturing outside with the Hamiltons, she took in the sights of temples, dust roads, cows and dogs running loose, and shop owners lying down in their shops, meditating as the chaos unfolded outside. In letters to Jack, she noted her observations: the macabre beauty of the Hindu funeral pyres along the Bagmati River and phallic deities enshrined with flowers on the temples. As she was a guest at the embassy, the King of Nepal's private plane was put at her disposal and she flew to Pokhara and was taken in a carriage drawn by bullocks, at her insistence, to Phewa Lake which she likened to pale jade with Machapuchare (known as Fishtail Mountain) reflected in its waters. It disturbed her profoundly: she could not stop thinking about all she had seen. 'I want to go back there and make a film,' she said. 'An Indian film. The country, the outlook, the people captivated me.'[10]

At home, the past continued to merge with the present, when, in early 1965, Peter Finch came to visit Vivien at Tickerage Mill. Peter was in a bad way, his life had taken another tumultuous turn: his affair with the singer Shirley Bassey became public knowledge and spurred racist commentary owing to her being mixed race,[11] and his second wife petitioned for divorce, naming Bassey as the co-respondent. Soon, Peter found himself alone and, as he always did, turned to alcohol and became resentful of the path his life had taken. 'I've been in too many traps in my life! Emotional traps! Traps set by women!'[12] he announced in a restaurant, embarrassing the patrons with his candour and sobbing.

What had inspired Peter to seek out Vivien after all those years? At his lowest point and looking for comfort, he must have wondered if his feelings would be reciprocated by her. She would always be fond of him and claimed he was a *proper* man',[13] the term 'proper' being held in the highest esteem by her. However, she would not be drawn back into their co-dependent affair, born from loneliness and descending into chaos, and, ironically, she was a stable influence during his visit. In terms of her inner peace, she wanted to spend her energy wisely and surrounded herself with people who had a calming effect on her.[14]

Peter claimed to follow Buddhism but he lacked any spiritual enlightenment, instead falling back into his old patterns of drinking and womanising and leaving a trail of destruction in his wake. He wanted to retire to Italy and forget his responsibilities but instead, he would sell his possessions, except for a few sports jackets, and move to Jamaica. 'I'll be working until I drop dead,'[15] Vivien told him. Nevertheless, she continued to dream of a house in Corfu where she could paint, a hobby inspired by Sir Winston Churchill and one she enjoyed while married to Larry. 'I think I would improve there. It's all so paintable,'[16] she said of the Greek island. Her own paradise had been a dream long suspended and she was yet to make it a reality.

Although Vivien seemed to be evolving on a spiritual level, she continued to select plays that stifled her career, whether intentionally or not. How she loathed the post-war brutalism, in every aspect of her life. Given that Larry presided over the National Theatre and all of the brightest and best talent flocked to perform there, perhaps her choice was limited. Such obstacles might have crossed her mind and she wrote to Joan Plowright,[17] inviting her to come to Tickerage for lunch or dinner, so they could break the ice – which hinted at her desire for future meetings, whether private or professional – and she signed it 'Vivien Olivier'. Larry rightly sensed the meetings would intrude on his family life and feared her old feelings of possessiveness would surface. 'I like other women,' she had said in 1960, when their marriage was falling apart. 'I am not jealous of them at all except when I am in love with a man.'[18]

In the spring of 1965, Vivien appeared as Contessa Sanziani in *La Contessa*, a play inspired by Luisa, Marchesa Casati's final years in a dingy hotel room, reminiscing about her glory days as one of the world's richest women, having fallen on hard times and been forced to rummage in bins for feathers to put in her hair. Styled in a shocking orange wig and wearing alabaster makeup with eyeliner bleeding under her eyes (the real Marchesa lined her eyes with Indian ink), she played a woman of 71; artistically challenging, in its own right. Unlike in *A Streetcar Named Desire* and, to an extent, her turn in *Ship of Fools*, the explicitness and excessiveness of Casati's life (adultery, addiction, occultism) were censored by the romanticism of Paul Osborn's script and Robert Helpmann's direction. Audiences were unresponsive and the critics more so, calling it 'a quite impossible play'[19] before it closed in Manchester after a short run.

Following the closure of *La Contessa*, Vivien's disappointment was reserved for Osborn, who had adapted Maurice Druon's novel, *A Film of Memory*, a fictionalised account of Casati. Seven Arts had financed the venture, hoping to turn the play into a film but given the dire notices and unsuccessful box office, they declined.

In *The Roman Spring of Mrs Stone*, Vivien's character, Karen Stone, spoke of drifting. Drifting aimlessly from one thing to the next without any substance and falling foul of unscrupulous people. Vivien was also drifting and her sense of pragmatism allowed things to unfold without much effort on her behalf, a far cry from the woman who crossed the Atlantic and lobbied for the part of Scarlett O'Hara. 'I am happy now,' she said in the spring of 1965, with the sincerity of a person who was at peace with herself. 'I don't think life can be considered in terms of depression and elation. I just don't understand people who say they plan their careers. What do they mean by it? Planning means that the chance of opportunity, the unexpected challenge, cannot be seized. And these are the things that make life exciting.'[20]

Vivien's next play lacked the excitement she spoke of but it earned good notices and a respectable box office during its tour of North America ahead of opening on Broadway. *Ivanov*, a four-act drama written by Anton Chekhov, marked a personal milestone, as she had long admired the Russian writer and his talent for exploring humanity in all its simplistic forms. Her character, Anna Petrovna, was dying of tuberculosis, but it was a secondary part next to the play's protagonist, her husband, Nikolai Ivanov, a financially ruined government official. Sir John Gielgud directed and acted in the part of Ivanov, but he was frustrated by Jack, who had the small part of a doctor, whom he felt was not a good actor and found him 'awkward and gloomy'.[21]

During the tour, Vivien developed what everyone believed to be a cold and was suffering from a persistent cough and a rash on her face, which she thought was an allergic reaction to her quinine cure. She was still unwell when they opened at the Shubert Theatre in New York on 3 May 1966 to what Gielgud described as the worst notices of his career.[22] 'The appeal of tragedy today is a kind of inverse escapism, an appeal just as great as that of the light, frothy stuff which so many theatre people think is the only relaxation demanded by those beset by worries and uncertainties,'[23] she once said of the Greek tragedies, and she held similar feelings for Chekhov. The reception was beginning to cool and the crowds were notably absent from the evening performances, forcing the play to close a month later.

After the play's closure, Vivien, Jack and Gielgud flew to Young Island in the Caribbean, which lay approximately two minutes from the main island, Saint Vincent, set in 13 acres of tropical gardens. She appeared to be in good spirits and was 'very sweet'[24] to everyone around her, enjoying the exotic birds and swimming with the turtles and blowfish. At first, the weather was stormy with gales and rain, which made the island feel all the more remote, combined with the lack of telephones and newspapers. She and Jack stayed in a cottage with an outside shower and enjoyed the spicy food and the local band who came to play after dinner.[25] Just as the weather began to turn, ironically, for the better, Vivien's mood changed rapidly and she became hostile to Jack and Gielgud; the tell-tale signs of an incoming episode were evident from the enormous breakfasts she devoured and her repeatedly blasting her musical numbers from *Tovarich* on a record player, disturbing the peace.

Back in New York, her judgement deteriorated and she made a spectacle of herself in the Persian Room at the Plaza Hotel, named as such due to the Persian murals on the walls. Jean-Pierre Aumont was performing in a cabaret act with his wife, the Italian actress, Marisa Pavan, and introduced Vivien to the audience. 'How lovely to see you again,'[26] Vivien greeted Aumont as she bounded towards the stage and proposed they sing a duet from *Tovarich*. To everyone's embarrassment, she forgot the lyrics and attempted to dance the Charleston, which had been her showstopping piece in the musical.

Less than a month later, Vivien went to Benitses in Corfu without Jack and was often drunk and flirting with strangers at parties. Those close to her thought she was behaving foolishly and putting herself in harm's way, embodying the same impaired judgement of her character, Karen Stone. She was slipping into mania, no doubt, but the forgetfulness and apparent identity crisis might have been the result of menopause: its emotional upheaval and psychiatric symptoms were mistaken as bipolar mood swings.

At home, in London, Jack convinced her to endure a course of ECT and Gertrude was concerned about her daughter's haggard appearance and persistent cough. Somewhat restored to herself, though the cough remained, Vivien spent Christmas with Leigh in Wiltshire. As fate would have it, it would be her last.

In the summer of 1967, Vivien entered her apartment in Eaton Square and complained of feeling faint and took to her bed. Chest X-rays were taken in her bedroom and revealed a large shadow across her lung, which Jack likened to a 'great black hole'.[27] She ignored her doctor's medical advice to convalesce in a hospital and remained at home – the only doctors she liked were the ones who 'bent their laws' to suit her.[28]

There was an urgency to admit her to hospital for treatment, as her old foe tuberculosis had come back, but she refused to go. Her general defence was that she had beaten tuberculosis before and would do so again. But she had been twenty years younger and the decades of heavy smoking and abusing her health had taken their toll. As a compromise, she agreed to remain in bed for three months and to abstain from cigarettes and alcohol. She would use the time to study the script of *A Delicate Balance* but remained perplexed by Edward Albee's plot of restless suburbanites, Tobias and Agnes, and their alcoholic house guest, Claire, whose lives are upended by the arrival of their friends who are escaping an unnamed terror and, later, their daughter, whose fourth marriage had collapsed. Confused as she was by Albee's text, the opening scene of her character, Agnes, discussing the possibility of losing her mind, hit too close to home. The producers agreed to postpone the provincial tour until she recovered from tuberculosis.

In a way, Vivien must have submitted to the reality that her disease was terminal, despite her bravado in dismissing it as such. As with many who suffer a similar prognosis, her brain began to accept the inevitable and it was her loved ones who suffered the most. 'Most of all, I have learnt to say, from the bottom of my heart, that I would gladly live every moment of my life again,'[29] she had said, a decade earlier, and so in that sense, she had no regrets. Or was she in denial? At the age of 53, she was comparatively young and most people around her believed that tuberculosis was no longer fatal.

Soon, she disobeyed the doctor's orders and forgot the half-hearted promises she had made to Jack, who was in Guildford doing a play, to not smoke or receive visitors. 'I love the audience. I act because I like trying to give pleasure to people,'[30] she once said of her profession, her friends now becoming her spectators. In the old days, there was something romantic about a consumptive, particularly to those who did not see the blood-splattered handkerchiefs and only the lithe frame and pale glow of the victim.

For an hour every day, she climbed out of bed and watered her houseplants; however, her growing weakness betrayed any sign of recovery and she protested when Jack ordered her to rest. She loathed to be idle but there was nothing else she could do, except stay in her room and look out at the streetscape of Belgravia; the summer days were blistering hot, with thunderstorms at night. Further still, she continued to smoke and drink, and her bedroom was crammed with guests who brought flowers and sat on her bed, telling her news of

Larry. Jack frequently returned home to the din of guests' chatter and a haze of smoke and scolded her; when they were alone, he saw what others did not.

In a strange turn of events, Larry was also bedridden, at St Thomas' Hospital, recovering from treatment for cancer of the prostate, and her every thought was saved for him. He had told her the news before it was made public, surely, to her mind, a measure of his feelings for her. She believed that his cancer was far deadlier than her disease. On the afternoon of 7 July, he had his last treatment and looked forward to going on holiday with his wife.

As Larry's radiation treatment successfully killed his cancer, Vivien was bed-bound and growing weaker by the day. Next to her sick bed, she kept a framed photograph of Larry and the peace prayer of St Francis of Assisi:

> O divine Master, grant that I may not so much seek to be consoled as to console, to be understood as to understand, to be loved as to love. For it is in giving that we receive, it is in pardoning that we are pardoned, and it is in dying that we are born to eternal life.

She had lived all of her greatest highs and crashing lows in front of an audience, whether she wanted to or not. More times than not, the privacy she craved was seldom afforded to her. For her final act – death – she was alone.

A post-mortem declared Vivien had died from chronic pulmonary tuberculosis. On the evening of her death, she was fast asleep in bed with her Siamese cat curled up beside her. Jack returned from his engagement in Guildford and looked in on her, before going to the kitchen to heat tomato soup from a tin. He came back and found her dead on the floor, having suffered a haemorrhage and tried, but failed, to revive her with the kiss of life.

The following day, Larry discharged himself from the hospital and went to Eaton Square, where Jack left him alone with Vivien's remains. In Larry's words, he stood and 'prayed for forgiveness for all the evils that had sprung up between us'.[31]

After Vivien's death on the evening of 7 July 1967, she was cremated and her ashes were scattered in the Lake of Reveries – her pond

– at Tickerage Mill. Gertrude fretted: the water had not been blessed by a priest before the committal of Vivien's ashes. Her mother disapproved of the cremation and the watery resting place, as the Roman Catholic church dictated that ashes had to be buried. In a way, the non-conformity spoke to Vivien's sense of self. Nevertheless, it was a place she considered sacred and it had given her so much joy in the final years of her life. She loved to gaze at the water from the Oriel window, as the seasons changed and the garden succumbed to frost and came back to life in the first glimmer of spring.

When Vivien's illness was kept at bay, most days were peaceful and followed the same pattern of domestic bliss and quiet contentment of being alone in the countryside. She began her day with lemon juice and two cigarettes – 'internal cleanliness',[32] as she called it, was important to her and was a belief instilled by Gertrude, that if one's tummy worked, one would feel alright – and ventured outside to the garden in the early morning sun and picked daffodils, narcissus, forget-me-nots and tulips.[33] Absorbed in the elements, she wished for the feeling to last forever; a day, like that day, would be followed by 'another, and another, and another'.[34]

One spring day, when the whole world seemed like a garden,[35] she had rowed her wooden boat up the River Uck and leant over the side with secateurs in her hand, cutting the reeds to make a pathway, so she could pass through. It was the most perfect day: she was at peace.[36]

'I like a part full of comedy, tragedy, and not too long'

Vivien Leigh, *The Examiner*, 1950

(5 November 1913–7 July 1967)

Afterword

A Reimagining

(Based on Real Events)

The telephone rang: it was Sybil Leek, the famous trance medium and self-confessed witch. Sybil had awoken from a dream and felt agitated. At once, she had to telephone her friend and mentor, Hans Holzer, the parapsychologist. Did he know someone named Vivien? she asked. Then Sybil realised it was her friend and client, Vivien Leigh, who had come to her in the sleep realm and told her she was going on holiday. Her physical departure had to be emphasised.[1]

'I'm going to live in Corfu when I am 60,'[2] Vivien announced to the revellers in the room. Her drawing room at Tickerage Mill was filled with the usual characters, theatrical folk and old friends from her days before stardom. A great collector of people, she valued friendship above all else and could not bear to let anyone go, to lose anyone along the way even if they deserved to be lost.[3] She moved around the room, fixating on half-empty champagne glasses and ordering Jack to top them up. There were too many bottles, erroneously bought for a visit with Princess Margaret and her husband, Lord Snowdon, who had grown up at Tickerage. 'Royalty always drinks champagne,'[4] Jack advised her but she was certain the princess was a gin drinker, like herself. How right she was, she thought as she mentally tallied up the expense of the champagne. It reminded her of a time in the early 1940s when she had to return a crate of French wine because her finances were depleted after *Romeo and Juliet*. She listened to her guests' chatter and laughter, a barometer of her success as a hostess; her training was instilled by Gertrude. The guests' happiness was paramount, she must always put them first. This time, she defied her mother's instructions and did what she wanted. She had to leave.

Scents of jasmine and wild basil made Vivien forget the stuffiness of an English drawing room and the drab, grey winters spent in the countryside; the lack of sunlight surely affecting her depression. Her easel was set up, displaying an unfinished canvas of green and brown dots and crystallised blue strokes; olive groves and a seascape, her faraway view. Artistically speaking, Sir Winston Churchill's *A Study of Roses*, a gift from the statesman, was her focal point and it hung in her bedroom, always within her eyeline, giving her the courage to go on. A fellow depressive, he understood her sentiment. She was in the abandoned villa of St John of the Pigeons,[5] south of Benitses, Corfu, a fishing village thirty minutes from the town, where Larry's autograph was displayed on the wall at the Corfu Bar. But then winter came and so did the rain, endless downpours giving life to the vibrant landscape surrounding her. There was so much water; she felt as though she were drowning.

A week after Vivien's death, the medium had a message for her loved ones, even if they did not believe it. Although Jack acted for a living, he had no imagination or belief in the supernatural. He dismissed the notion of talking to the dead[6] and it was against Gertrude's Roman Catholic faith to dabble in the occult. Did Vivien believe? Throughout the years she had her palm read and her birth chart analysed. Once, she had her tarot cards read and what did they predict?[7] Perhaps the tower card was pulled, the imagery conveying a structure in flames and crumbling into the sea. Her life was nothing but tower moments, as it was called in divination circles; she was always having to rebuild. The medium saw Vivien holding a little black dog and Jack confirmed it to be genuine[8]: the dog was a black poodle named Sebastian who had lived at Tickerage and had been run over and killed a few weeks before she died.

For months after Vivien's death, Jack remained in a state of shock and slept on her sofa in Eaton Square. He was disconnected from the collective grieving process and found no closure from her Roman

Catholic funeral and committal at the crematorium – the services were too religious and impersonal for his tastes. As such, he demanded control over Vivien's memorial service at St Martin-in-the-Fields, crammed with devoted fans, the press and her former colleagues and admirers. He was pleased it had gone to his plans and remained focused on the present. Sitting off to the side, in the faraway pews, was Jill Esmond, who felt compelled to attend the memorial service of the woman who had changed the course of her life. As Jill turned around to leave, she saw Larry standing behind her, ashen-faced and bereft; she put her hand on top of his and he put his other hand on top of hers and gave it three squeezes.[9] In their hands, they held their orders of service, with 'Vivien Leigh' neatly printed in a black font, but their feelings ran deeper than the mementoes from that day. Not everything had to end beautifully for it to continue.

The medium had another message for Vivien's loved ones. Vivien's spirit was weary and surrounded by a body of water, the only thing sustaining her. She would be waiting for Larry to depart his earthly realm and when he did, she would be ready.

The spectre of Vivien would always loom over her loved ones. Her scent continued to linger in the rooms at Tickerage, months after she had died. Once, she and Jack had been motoring down to Tickerage for the weekend with their friend, Bumble Dawson, sitting in the front next to him. 'What's the smell of Pear Drops?' Bumble had asked, detecting the scent of the boiled sweets. From the back, Vivien had piped up, 'It's only me putting on Joy.'[10] There she was, putting Joy on her wrists, the most expensive perfume in the world, as her motorcar lumbered through the country roads.

It was at Tickerage where they all gathered to divide Vivien's things before selling the house for £40,000. Thieves had broken in beforehand, stealing souvenirs: a jar of her face cream; costume jewellery from her dressing table; and a few bottles of beer.[11] To her loyal fans, Gertrude, Suzanne and Jack distributed keepsakes like photographs, gloves, crystals, a paperweight and a parasol.[12] Some of her favourite items were inexpensive trinkets bought from her travels abroad, such as a pearl ring which had cost $1 in New York that she adored wearing. Jack was touched to learn Vivien had bequeathed him £6,000 and the remainder of her estate would go to Suzanne.

Leigh came to Tickerage, perhaps to support Suzanne and Gertrude in his gentle way or to blend in with the tapestry of Vivien's life. An eclectic existence, but nevertheless, they shared the same interests in antiques and gardening. Before the end of her life, she seemed to gravitate to him, marking special occasions at his home where her photograph was displayed, surprising an antiques dealer who came to evaluate his belongings. The antiques dealer wondered if Leigh was a fan of Vivien's and was astonished to learn they had been married.

The medium's messages had made a believer of Jack and the idea of Vivien existing in another dimension played on his mind. Or was it all, in his words, 'the most extraordinary coincidence'?[13] As her physical self had become an apparition on the celluloid screen, so would her energy find a way to transmit to the living.

During the gathering at Tickerage, Jack took the opportunity to tell Leigh of the medium and her messages from Vivien. There was one final message: Vivien was 'extremely displeased at having been projected through the curtain'. They both laughed. It was so typical of Vivien, who was, as Katharine Hepburn said, 'a lovely little pink cloud floating through the lives of all her friends, hovering over the setting sun'.[14]

Filmography

Ship of Fools (1965)
The Roman Spring of Mrs Stone (1961)
The Deep Blue Sea (1955)
Elephant Walk (1953. Replaced with Elizabeth Taylor)
A Streetcar Named Desire (1951)
Anna Karenina (1948)
Caesar and Cleopatra (1945)
That Hamilton Woman/Lady Hamilton (1941)
Waterloo Bridge (1940)
21 Days Together (filmed in 1937, released in 1940)
Gone with the Wind (1939)
The Sidewalks of London/St Martin's Lane (1938)
A Yank at Oxford (1938)
Storm in a Teacup (1937)
Dark Journey (1937)
Fire Over England (1937)
Gentleman's Agreement (1935)
Look Up and Laugh (1935)
Things Are Looking Up (1935)
The Village Squire (1935)

Theatre

Ivanov (1966)
La Contessa (1965)
Tovarich (1963)
The Lady of the Camellias (1961)
Look After Lulu! (1959)
Duel of Angels (1958, 1960, 1961)
South Sea Bubble (1956)
Twelfth Night (1955, 1961)
Titus Andronicus (1955, 1957)
Macbeth (1955)
The Sleeping Prince (1953)
Antony and Cleopatra (1951)
Caesar and Cleopatra (1951)
Richard III (1948, 1949)
Antigone (1949)
A Streetcar Named Desire (1949)
The Skin of Our Teeth (1945, 1946, 1948)
The Spring Party (North African tour, 1943)
The School for Scandal (1942, 1948, 1949)
The Doctor's Dilemma (1942)
Romeo and Juliet (1940)
Serena Blandish (1938)
Because We Must (1937)
Bats in the Belfry (1937)
Hamlet (1937)
A Midsummer Night's Dream (1937)
Richard II (1936)
The Happy Hypocrite (1936)
Henry VIII (1936)
The Mask of Virtue (1935)
The Green Sash (1935)

Further Reading

Aldrich, Robert. *Who's Who in Gay and Lesbian History: From Antiquity to the Mid-Twentieth Century* (Taylor & Francis, Oxfordshire, 2020)

Allen, Charles. *Plain Tales from the Raj* (Ebury Press, London, 1985)

Aumont, Jean-Pierre. *Sun and Shadow: An Autobiography* (Norton, New York, 1977)

Bawden, James, Miller, Ron. *They Made the Movies: Conversations with Great Film Makers* (University Press of Kentucky, Lexington, 2023)

Baxter, Beverley. *First Nights and Footlights* (Hutchinson, London, 1955)

Beaton, Cecil. *Memoirs of the 40s* (McGraw-Hill Book Co., New York, 1972)

Bloom, Claire. *Leaving a Doll's House* (Virago, London 1996)

Bloom, Claire. *Limelight and After* (Chivers Press, Bath, 1983)

Boland, Bridget. *At My Mother's Knee* (Bodley Head, London, 1978)

Brooks, Peter. *The Empty Space* (Simon & Schuster, London, 1996)

Bucknell, Katherine (ed.) Bachardy, Don, Isherwood, Christopher. *The Animals: Love Letters Between Christopher Isherwood and Don Bachardy* (Random House, New York, 2013)

Capua, Michelangelo. *Vivien Leigh* (McFarland, North Carolina, 2015)

Carpenter, Mary Thorn. *A Girl's Winter in India* (A.D.F. Randolph, New York, 1892)

Clark, Colin. *My Week with Marilyn* (HarperCollins, London, 2000)

Clark, Colin. *Younger Brother, Younger Son* (HarperCollins, London, 1997)

Coleman, Terry. *Olivier: The Authorised Biography* (Bloomsbury, London, 2005)

Cook, Barbara. *Then and Now: A Memoir* (HarperCollins, New York, 2016)

Cooper, Diana. *Darling Monster: The Letters of Lady Diana Cooper to her Son John Julius Norwich 1939–1952* (Chatto & Windus, London, 2014)

Cosgrave, Bronwyn. *Made For Each Other: Fashion and the Academy Awards* (Bloomsbury, London, 2010)

Cotton, Maggie. *Wrong Sex, Wrong Instrument* (Apex Publishing, Essex, 2011)

Crowley, Aleister. *The Book of Lies* (Privately published, 1912 or 1913)

Dent, Alan. *Vivien Leigh: A Bouquet* (Hamish Hamilton, London, 1968)

Diffen, Ray. *Stage Clothes* (Xlibris, Bloomington, 2011)

Douglas, Kirk. *The Ragman's Son* (Simon & Schuster, New York, 1988)

Dundy, Elaine. *Finch, Bloody Finch* (Holt, Rhinehart & Winston, New York, 1980)

Ellis, Albert (ed.), Wylie, Philip. *Sex Life of the American Woman and the Kinsey Report* (Greenberg, New York, 1954)

Emerson, Maureen. *Escape to Provence: The Story of Elisabeth Starr and Winifred Fortescue and the Making of the Colline des Anglais* (Chapter & Verse, New South Wales, 2008)

Faulkner, Trader. *Peter Finch: A Biography* (Angus & Robertson, Melbourne, 1979)

Finch, Tamara. *Dancing into the Unknown: My Life in the Ballets Russes and Beyond* (Dance Books, Hampshire, 2007)

Funke, Lewis and Boothe, John E. *Actors Talking about Acting* (Thames & Hudson, London, 1961)

Gielgud, John, Mangan, Richard (ed.). *A Life in Letters* (Arcade, New York, 2004)

Granger, Stewart. *Sparks Fly Upward* (Granada, St Albans, 1981)

Grove, Valerie. *Dear Dodie: The Life of Dodie Smith* (Chatto & Windus, London, 1996)

Halsman, Philippe. *Sight and Insight* (Doubleday, New York, 1972)

Harrison, Thomas. *Of Bridges: A Poetic and Philosophical Account* (University of Chicago Press, Chicago, 2023)

Heilpern, John. *John Osborne: A Patriot for Us* (Vintage, London, 2007)

Jose, Quintero. *If You Don't Dance They Beat You* (St Martin's Press, New York, 1988)

Kazan, Elia. *Elia Kazan: A Life* (Da Capo Press, Boston, 1988)

Keyes, Evelyn. *Scarlett O'Hara's Younger Sister* (Fawcett Cress, New York, 1978)

Kramer, Stanley. *A Mad, Mad, Mad, Mad World* (Aurum, London, 1998)

Lambert, Gavin. *On Cukor* (Capricorn Books, New York, 1972)

Levine, Suzanne Jill. *Manuel Puig and the Spider Woman: His Life and Fictions* (University of Wisconsin Press, Madison 2001)

Lisieux, St Thérèse. *The Story of a Soul* (Source Books, Trabuco Canyon, 1997)

Logan, Joshua. *Movie Stars, Real People, and Me* (Delacorte Press, New York, 1978)

Marvin, Betty. *Tales of a Hollywood Wife* (iuniverse.com, Bloomington, 2011)

Merchant, Ismail, Raw, Laurence (eds). *Merchant-Ivory Interviews* (University Press of Mississippi, Jackson, 2012)

Miles, Sarah. *Bolt from the Blue* (Orion, London, 1996)

Miles, Sarah. *Serves Me Right* (Macmillan, London, 1994)

Morley, Sheridan. *John Gielgud: The Authorised Biography* (Simon & Schuster, London, 2010)

Nicolson, Harold. *Diaries and Letters 1945–62* (Collins, London, 1968)

Niven, David. *Bring on the Empty Horses* (Putnam, New York, 1975)

O'Connor, Garry. *Darlings of the Gods* (Hodder & Stoughton, London, 1984)

Olivier, Laurence. *Confessions of an Actor* (Weidenfeld & Nicolson, London, 1982)

Olivier, Tarquin. *My Father Laurence Olivier* (Headline, London, 1992)

Pascal, Valerie. *The Disciple and his Devil* (Michael Joseph, London, 1971)

Payn, Graham and Morley, Sheridan (eds). *The Noël Coward Diaries* (Macmillan, London, 1983)

Plowright, Joan. *And That's Not All* (Weidenfeld & Nicolson, London, 2001)

Randall, John, Trow, M.J. *The Last Gentlemen of the SAS* (Random House, London, 2017)

Scott Fitzgerald, F. *The Crack-Up with Other Pieces and Stories* (Penguin, London, 1965)

Shellard, Dominic. *Kenneth Tynan: A Life* (Yale University Press, New Haven, 2003)

Tierney, Gene. *Self Portrait* (Berkley Books, New York, 1980)

Tornabene, Lyn. *Long Live the King: A Biography of Clark Gable* (W.H. Allen/Virgin Books, London, 1977)

Tynan, Kenneth. *Diaries of Kenneth Tynan* (Bloomsbury, London, 2001)

Valiente, Doreen. *ABC of Witchcraft Past and Present* (St Martin's Press, New York, 1972)

Vickers, Hugo. *Vivien Leigh* (Hamish Hamilton, London, 1988)

Walker, Alexander. *Vivien: The Life of Vivien Leigh* (Weidenfeld & Nicolson, London, 1987)

Williams, Dakin, Mead, Shepherd. *Tennessee Williams: An Intimate Biography* (Arbor House, New York, 1983)

Ziegler, Philip. *Olivier* (MacLehose Press, New York, 2013)

Notes

Chapter One

1 *The Argus*, 2/1/1953
2 Ibid.
3 Oswald Frewen recalled Vivien saying a prayer to St Thérèse of Lisieux on an aeroplane to Naples. Walker, Alexander, *Vivien: The Life of Vivien Leigh* (Weidenfeld & Nicolson, London 1987) p. 80
4 Dundy, Elaine, *Finch, Bloody Finch* (Holt, Rhinehart & Winston, New York, 1980) p. 180
5 Jack Merivale in conversation with Anne Edwards. Anne Edwards papers, 1965 – Library Special Collections, Charles E. Young Research Library
6 Faulkner, Trader, *Peter Finch: A Biography* (Angus & Robertson, Melbourne, 1979) p. 151
7 Ibid.
8 Carrol Heywood, interview. *The Sun*, 4/6/1953
9 Faulkner, *Peter Finch*, p. 153
10 Ibid., p. 159
11 Sir John Gielgud in conversation with Anne Edwards. Anne Edwards papers, 1965 – Library Special Collections, Charles E. Young Research Library
12 *The Courier Mail*, 9/2/1953. This also forms part of Vivien's mania-fuelled hallucinations, inspired by newspaper photographs of her with the snake
13 *Modern Screen*, September 1960. vivandlarry.com
14 *The Argus*, 2/1/1953
15 Cosgrave, Bronwyn, *Made For Each Other: Fashion and the Academy Awards* (Bloomsbury, London, 2010) p. 40
16 Keyes, Evelyn, *Scarlett O'Hara's Younger Sister* (Fawcett Cress, New York, 1978) p. 27
17 Dundy, *Finch*, p. 180
18 *The Beverley Times*, 25/6/1953
19 Faulkner, *Peter Finch*, p. 153
20 *The Sun*, 4/6/1953
21 Discovered by genealogist, Lisa Blosfelds
22 Jack Merivale in conversation with Anne Edwards
23 Olivier, Tarquin, *My Father, Laurence Olivier* (Headline, London, 1992) p. 226
24 Carpenter, Mary Thorn, *A Girl's Winter in India* (A.D.F. Randolph, New York, 1892) p. 60

25 Faulkner, *Peter Finch*, p. 161
26 Coleman, Terry, *Olivier: The Authorised Biography* (Bloomsbury, London, 2005) p. 252
27 *Modern Screen*, September 1960. vivandlarry.com
28 Olivier, *Confessions*, p. 153
29 Bevis Bawa's memories as printed in *The Sunday Times* (Sri Lanka), 5/8/2012
30 *Life*, 8/12/1972
31 *The Times*, 12/9/2017
32 *The Sydney Morning Herald*, 4/9/2017
33 *Ballets Russes* (documentary, Zeitgeist Films, 2005)
34 Finch, Tamara, *Dancing into The Unknown: My Life in the Ballets Russes and Beyond* (Dance Books, Hampshire, 2007) p. 142
35 Ibid., p. 143
36 Ibid., p. 149
37 *Good Housekeeping*, February 1961. Greta Ritchie Collection
38 Faulkner, *Peter Finch*, p. 193

Chapter Two

1 Olivier, Laurence, *Confessions of an Actor* (Weidenfeld & Nicolson, London, 1982), p. 156
2 As told by Barbara Packwood. O'Connor, Garry, *Darlings of the Gods* (Hodder & Stoughton, London, 1984) p. 2
3 Bevis Bawa's memories, published in *The Sunday Times* (Sri Lanka), 5/8/2012
4 Laurence Olivier interviewed by Kathleen Tynan, Part 1 of 4. Theatre Archive Project. Laurence Olivier, dubbed from tapes deposited with the Kenneth Tynan Archive to the British Library Department of Manuscripts. 4/8/1983, 16/8/1983
5 *The Sunday Times* (Sri Lanka), 5/8/2012
6 Levine, Suzanne Jill, *Manuel Puig and the Spider Woman: His Life and Fictions* (University of Wisconsin Press, Madison, 2001), p. 119
7 David Niven's memoir, *Bring on the Empty Horses* (Putnam, New York, 1975) summarised this time in Vivien's *Life*; however, he disguised her identity as 'Missie'
8 Ibid., p. 295
9 Ellis, Albert (ed.), Wylie, Philip, *Sex Life of the American Woman and the Kinsey Report* (Greenberg, New York, 1954) p. 33
10 Niven, David, *Bring on the Empty Horses* (Putnam, New York, 1975) p. 295
11 *The Sun Herald*, 22/8/1954
12 Ibid.
13 Niven, *Bring on the Empty Horses*, p. 296
14 Granger, Stewart, *Sparks Fly Upward* (Granada, St Albans, 1981) p. 292
15 Gottfried, Martin, *Nobody's Fool* (Simon & Schuster, New York, 2002) p. 193
16 Olivier, *Confessions*, p. 191

17 'She ... demanded a kiss in exchange for it. This payment having been extracted ...', Niven, *Bring on the Empty Horses*, p. 317
18 Different accounts of Vivien's escape to the swimming pool are recorded in David Niven's *Bring on the Empty Horses* and Stewart Granger's *Sparks Fly Upwards*. Vivien was often drawn to water when she was going through suicidal and/or manic spells
19 American Academy of Family Physicians, www.aafp.org/afp/990501ap/quantum.html
20 Tarquin Olivier, 'Whom you most love, the disease makes you show hatred for ...' And he [Olivier] said, 'From her behaviour, it's obvious she must love me to death.' (Documentary, *Legends: Vivien Leigh*. Carlton Television, 19/7/2000)

Chapter Three

1   *Daily Advertiser*, 21/3/1953
2   Vickers, Hugo, *Vivien Leigh* (Hamish Hamilton, London, 1988) p. 214
3   *News*, 21/3/1953
4   *Daily Mirror*, 21/3/1953
5   Finch, *Dancing into The Unknown*, p. 137
6   Ibid., p. 135
7   Ibid.
8   Dundy, *Finch*, p. 178
9   *Modern Screen*, July 1947. Vivandlarry.com
10 *The Oliviers* (Hamish Hamilton, London, 1953)
11 *Life*, 8/12/1972
12 [Recollection of Hanover Drive, before her committal] 'When she spoke to me it was in the tone of halting, dreamlike amazement that people in the theatre use for mad scenes when they can't think of anything better.' Olivier, *Confessions*, p. 188
13 Laurence Olivier, letter to Vivien Leigh, 24/6/45. Suzanne Farrington Collection. V&A Theatre and Performance Collections GB 71 THM/433/1. Coleman, *Olivier*, p. 180
14 *Modern Screen*, September 1960. Vivandlarry.com
15 'When my time came, I felt only that I had been dehumanised.' Tierney, Gene, *Self Portrait* (Berkley Books, New York, 1980) p. 211
16 *Modern Screen*, September 1960. Vivandlarry.com
17 *Life*, 8/12/1972
18 Ibid.
19 British Library record of deaths, N2-121-191. Courtesy of Shiroma Perera-Nathan
20 Allen, Charles, *Plain Tales from the Raj* (Ebury Press, London, 1985) p. 22
21 Olivier, *Confessions*, p. 157
22 Charter-genealogy.blogspot.com
23 Olivier, *Confessions*, p. 158
24 In Gene Tierney's book, *Self Portrait*, she wrote of her experiences with bipolar disorder and of her stay at the Menninger Clinic in Kansas in the 1950s, during

the same period in which Vivien was at Netherne. I used Tierney's book as a secondary source to make judgements as to how Vivien felt after receiving ECT. Tierney later became an outspoken opponent of ECT, claiming it left her with lifelong memory problems

25 Walker, *Vivien: The Life of Vivien Leigh*, pp. 37, 214
26 *Tops Magazine*, February 1955. Vivienleighlegend.com
27 Vickers, *Vivien Leigh*, p. 32
28 Oswald Frewen's diary, 10–11 April 1953. Vickers, *Vivien Leigh*, p. 215
29 Walker, *The Life*, p. 37
30 The diary of Dorothy Holman, 1932. Devon Heritage Centre, 3830M/F/35. August 1933–January 1933
31 *Philadelphia Daily News*, 31/8/1960. Rachel Nicholson Collection
32 Ibid.
33 Ibid., 30/8/1960
34 Dent, Alan, *Vivien Leigh: A Bouquet* (Hamish Hamilton, London, 1968) p. 22
35 *Everywoman*, April 1951. Vivandlarry.com
36 Olivier, *Confessions*, p. 100
37 'Insofar, she was no longer the person I had loved. I loved her that much less.' Olivier, *Confessions*, p. 195

Chapter Four
1 *The Argus*, 31/3/1953
2 *Life*, 8/12/1972
3 *Tops Magazine*, February 1955. Vivienleighlegend.com
4 Philip Ziegler, *Olivier*, (MacLehose Press, New York, 2013) p. 79
5 *Queensland Times*, 11/4/1939
6 Symbolismandmetaphor.com
7 *The Courier Mail*, 20/4/1954
8 Coleman, *Olivier*, p. 247
9 This side of Vivien's behaviour, after the manic episodes was described by Sir John Gielgud in the documentary, *Scarlett and Beyond* (Turner Pictures, 1990)
10 Hamish Hamilton diary. Vickers, *Vivien Leigh*, p. 215
11 *Barrier Miner*, 31/3/1953
12 *The Daily Telegraph*, 29/6/1948
13 23/05/1940
14 *21 Days*, screenplay by Graham Greene and Basil Dean based on *The First and the Last* (short story and play) by John Galsworthy (1920)
15 Laurence Olivier interviewed by Kathleen Tynan
16 Ibid.
17 Ibid.
18 *Daily Express*, August 1960. Vivandlarry.com
19 *Life*, 17/12/1951
20 *The New York Times*, 11/5/1951
21 Payn, Graham, Morley, Sheridan (eds), *The Noël Coward Diaries* (Macmillan, London, 1983) p. 215

22 *The Examiner*, 7/10/1950
23 Dundy, *Finch*, p. 198
24 Finch, *Dancing into The Unknown*, p. 159
25 *Daily Express*, August 1960. Vivandlarry.com
26 Ibid.
27 Ibid.
28 Coleman, *Olivier*, p. 231
29 Harrison, Thomas, *Of Bridges: A Poetic and Philosophical Account* (University of Chicago Press, Chicago, 2023) p. 54
30 *The Sun*, 23/4/1950
31 *Daily Express*, August 1960. Vivandlarry.com
32 Coleman, *Olivier*, p. 236
33 Kazan, Elia, *Elia Kazan: A Life* (Da Capo Press, Boston, 1988) p. 343
34 *The Sunday Times*, 24/9/1950. The late Julia Lockwood, actress and daughter of Margaret Lockwood, told me of an evening she spent square dancing in London and, to her surprise, seeing Vivien being hurled around the floor by a young man. She mentioned it to her mother, who was rehearsing *Night of 100 Stars*, and she asked Larry about it the following day. Julia related how Larry looked embarrassed and admitted it was true
35 Ibid.
36 Duke University's Yearbook, 1951. Duke University Archives
37 Vickers, *Vivien Leigh*, p. 200
38 Olivier, *Confessions*, p. 138
39 *Philadelphia Daily News*, 29/8/1960. Rachel Nicholson Collection

Chapter Five

1   Ziegler, Philip, *Olivier* (MacLehose, London, 2013) p. 36
2   Olivier, *Confessions*, p. 58
3   'You deserve to be kissed.' Translated by Sara Allouche
4   It was also reported that Ernest was expelled from the Bengal Club on racial grounds. Either way, he lost his membership due to his wife being of mixed race
5   Tynan, Kenneth, *Diaries of Kenneth Tynan* (Bloomsbury, London, 2001) p. 134
6   *New Idea*, 25/12/1963. Vivandlarry.com
7   Ibid.
8   Vivien Leigh Circle
9   Olivier, *Confessions*, p. 61
10 Olivier, Tarquin, *My Father*, p. 65
11 Ibid.
12 Aldrich, Robert, *Who's Who in Gay and Lesbian History from Antiquity to the Mid-Twentieth Century* (Taylor & Francis, Oxfordshire, 2020) p. 70
13 Olivier, Tarquin, *My Father*, p. 67
14 'Duet for Two Temples' article by Ian Coster, magazine unknown, dated 1946. Vivandlarry.com

Notes

15 *Modern Screen*, September 1960. Vivandlarry.com
16 'Leigh introduced that ...', Jack Merivale, letter to Anne Edwards, 6/4/1976. Anne Edwards papers, 1965 – Library Special Collections, Charles E. Young Research Library. Correspondence: Box 23
17 *Modern Screen*, September 1960. Vivandlarry.com
18 Ibid.
19 *Modern Screen*, September 1960. Vivandlarry.com
20 Vickers, *Vivien Leigh*, p. 73
21 Leigh Holman, letter to Vivien dated 3 March. *The Telegraph*, 16/9/2015
22 Ibid.
23 Coleman, *Olivier*, p. 109
24 Ibid., p. 108
25 Olivier, *Confessions*, p. 61
26 Ibid., p. 171
27 Pascal, Valerie, *The Disciple and his Devil* (Michael Joseph, London, 1971) p. 104
28 As related by Sybille Olivier. *Life*, 8/12/1972
29 Cotton, Maggie, *Wrong Sex, Wrong Instrument* (Apex Publishing, Essex, 2011) p. 69
30 Capua, Michelangelo, *Vivien Leigh: A Biography* (McFarland, North Carolina, 2015) p. 99
31 Bloom, Claire, *Leaving a Doll's House* (Virago, London, 1996) p. 95
32 Shakespeare, William, *Richard III*, Act 1, Scene 3
33 *The Daily News*, 24/3/1953
34 'I was an awful bitch on the set yesterday.' Lambert, Gavin, *On Cukor* (Capricorn Books, New York 1972) p. 149
35 *Daily Express*, August 1960. Vivandlarry.com
36 *Philadelphia Daily News*, 29/8/1960. Rachel Nicholson Collection
37 Olivier, Tarquin, *My Father*, p. 181
38 *Daily Express*, August 1960. Vivandlarry.com
39 Ibid.

Chapter Six
1 *Life*, 8/12/1972
2 Faulkner, *Peter Finch*, p. 193
3 Ibid., p. 160
4 Crowley, Aleister, *The Book of Lies* (Privately published, 1912 or 1913)
5 Finch, *Dancing into The Unknown*, p. 5
6 Dundy, *Finch*, p. 199
7 Coleman, *Olivier*, p. 140
8 *Tatler*, 8/7/2020
9 Ibid.
10 Morley, Sheridan, *John Gielgud: The Authorised Biography* (Simon & Schuster, London, 2010) p. 293
11 Jack Merivale, letter to Anne Edwards, 6/4/1976

12 Laurence Olivier interviewed by Kathleen Tynan
13 Ibid.
14 *The Sunday Express*, March 1953. Vivandlarry.com
15 Sir John Gielgud, letter to Hugh Wheeler, 26/10/55. Gielgud, John, Mangan, Richard (ed.), *A Life in Letters* (Arcade, New York, 2004) p. 188
16 Payn, Graham and Morley, Sheridan (eds), *The Noël Coward Diaries* (Da Capo Press, Massachusetts, 2000), p. 280
17 *Everywoman*, April 1951. Vivandlarry.com
18 *The Argus*, 22/1/1955
19 Dundy, *Finch*, p. 184
20 *Esquire*, February 1936
21 'From now on for the next five years, it was as if she had just lost touch with her craft.' Olivier, *Confessions*, p. 203
22 'The Oliviers', article by Alan Dent. Publication unknown, circa 1951. Rachel Nicholson Collection
23 Funke, Lewis and Boothe, John E. *Actors Talking about Acting* (Thames & Hudson, London, 1961) p. 78
24 'Leigh always called her Vivvy and that she liked' – Jack Merivale, letter to Anne Edwards, February 1976
25 Funke and Boothe, *Actors Talking*, p. 80
26 'Her face would widen … she lost her looks.' Sir John Gielgud in conversation with Anne Edwards
27 Olivier, *Confessions*, p. 202
28 Sir John Gielgud in conversation with Anne Edwards
29 Shakespeare, William, *Macbeth*. Act 5, Scene 3
30 Coleman, *Olivier*, p. 275
31 Olivier, *Confessions*, p. 204
32 *Picturegoer*, 7/12/1946
33 O'Connor, Garry, *Darlings of the Gods* (Hodder & Stoughton, London, 1984) p. 4
34 *Los Angeles Times*, 26/9/1948
35 *The Sun*, 30/12/1948
36 Thanks to Shiroma Perera-Nathan for the insight
37 Philip Ziegler, *Olivier*, (MacLehose Press, New York, 2013), p. 151
38 Olivier, *Confessions*, p. 160
39 Michael Caine, *Life*, 8/12/1972
40 Vickers, *Vivien Leigh*, p. 232
41 *La Stampa*, 18/8/1957
42 Shakespeare, William, *Macbeth*. Act 1, Scene 7
43 Olivier, Tarquin, *My Father*, p. 192
44 Payn and Morley (eds), *The Noël Coward Diaries*, p. 308
45 Dundy, *Finch*, p. 197
46 Jack Merivale supported this statement. In a letter to Anne Edwards, dated February 1976, he wrote of alcohol being the 'enemy' and of friends, who knew Vivien in the 1930s, saying that alcohol 'did not suit her'. See Anne

Edwards papers. Charles E. Young Research Library, UCLA. Correspondence: Box 23
47 Olivier, *Confessions*, p. 161
48 Ibid.
49 'Some while later a close friend said to me that I should have kicked her out, or upped and outed myself; that I should never have endured in silence such humiliation apparently for the sake of appearances.' Ibid., p. 161
50 'One disappointment was the lack of fruit on the orange trees in the garden. Sir Laurence Olivier and Vivien Leigh, the previous tenants, had eaten most of them.' Emerson, Maureen, *Escape to Provence: The Story of Elisabeth Starr and Winifred Fortescue and the Making of the Colline des Anglais* (Chapter & Verse, New South Wales, 2008) p. 221
51 'I am sending round to the theatre a record which we've always loved – it is the Chants of Auvergne, sung by Madeleine Grey – I do hope you have not already got it and that you will like it.' Vivien Leigh, letter to Katherine Cornell, 4/2/52. Greta Ritchie Collection. Otherwise, Vivien Leigh's letters to Cornell are held at the Billy Rose Theatre Division, New York Public Library
52 *Daily Express*, August 1960. Vivandlarry.com
53 Faulkner, *Peter Finch*, p. 156

Chapter Seven
1   Vivien Leigh, letter to Leigh Holman, 29/10/36. Suzanne Farrington Collection. Published in full at www.vivien-leigh.info and in Dent, Alan, *Vivien Leigh* (Hamish Hamilton, London, 1968) p. 28
2   Finch, *Dancing into The Unknown*, p. 160
3   Dundy, *Finch*, p. 207
4   Shakespeare, William, *Macbeth*. Act 5, Scene 5
5   Jack Merivale in conversation with Anne Edwards
6   John Barber, *Daily Express* [undated 1955]
7   *The Australian Women's Weekly*, 25/7/1956
8   Payn and Morley (eds), *The Noël Coward Diaries*, p. 358
9   *The Australian Women's Weekly*, 25/7/1956
10 Ibid.
11 Finch, *Dancing into The Unknown*, p. 152
12 Ibid.
13 *Modern Screen*, September 1960. Vivandlarry.com
14 Clark, Colin, *My Week with Marilyn* (HarperCollins, New York, 2000) p. 127
15 Grove, Valerie, *Dear Dodie: The Life of Dodie Smith* (Chatto & Windus, London, 1996) p. 200
16 Miles, Sarah, *Serves Me Right* (Macmillan, London, 1994) p. 16
17 *The Argus*, 25/2/1956
18 Ibid.
19 *Good Housekeeping*, February 1961. Greta Ritchie Collection
20 *The Argus*, 15/8/1956

21 Ibid.
22 'Don't be an idiot.' Letter from George Bernard Shaw to Vivien Leigh [undated]. *The Telegraph*, 16/9/2015
23 Pascal, *The Disciple and his Devil*, p. 104
24 Capua, *Vivien Leigh*, p. 91
25 In 1937, Vivien confided to her agent at the time, John Gliddon: 'What I really need is a clause in my contract giving me two or three days off when I'm filming and I feel one of these states coming on.' Walker, *Vivien: The Life of Vivien Leigh*, p. 96
26 *Everywoman*, April 1951. Vivandlarry.com
27 Trader Faulkner, interview with Kendra Bean. 'The Mystery of Suzanne Farrington.' 12/3/2015. Vivandlarry.com
28 Cooper, Diana, *Darling Monster: The Letters of Lady Diana Cooper to her Son John Julius Norwich 1939–1952* (Chatto & Windus, London, 2014) p. 245
29 Diffen, Ray, *Stage Clothes* (Xlibris, Bloomington, 2011) p. 18
30 'She failed to convince [the audience] that she was the type of married woman who would leave home in order to keep her lover.' *The Sun*, 25/1/1948
31 Beaton, Cecil, *Memoirs of the 40s* (McGraw-Hill Book Co., New York, 1972) p. 164
32 *The Daily Telegraph*, 10/10/1948
33 *Anna Karenina*, screenplay by Jean Anouilh, Guy Morgan and Julien Duvivier. London Film Productions, 1948. This particular adaptation of *Anna Karenina* is in the public domain
34 Coveney, Michael, Trader Faulkner obituary. *The Guardian*, 27/4/2021
35 Finch, *Dancing into The Unknown*, p. 144
36 Ibid., p. 152
37 *Chelsea News and General Advertiser*, 13/12/1946
38 Finch, *Dancing into The Unknown*, p. 146
39 Faulkner, *Peter Finch*, p. 161
40 *Everywoman*, April 1951. vivandlarry.com
41 Ibid.
42 *Life*, 8/12/1972
43 Funke and Boothe, *Actors Talking*, p. 86
44 *Life*, 8/12/1972

Chapter Eight

1 Brooks, Peter, *The Empty Space* (Simon & Schuster, London, 1996) p. 95
2 Clark, Colin, *Younger Brother, Younger Son* (HarperCollins, London, 1997) p. 109
3 *The Daily Telegraph*, 29/6/1948
4 'It was a disappointing surprise to see her up close, across a coffee table, for her face was an unattractive mass of tiny wrinkles, presumably from smoking.' Humphry, Derek, *Good Life, Good Death* (Carrel Books, e-book, 2017)
5 Shakespeare, William, *Hamlet*. Act 3, Scene 1
6 David Barry to author

7   *La Stampa*, 29/5/1957
8   Ibid.
9   David Barry to author
10 Morris, Sylvia, 'Slaughter in the Streets: Shakespeare's Titus Andronicus', 23.5.2013. Theshakespeareblog.com
11 Coleman, *Olivier*, p. 300
12 Ibid.
13 David Barry to author
14 Clark, *Younger Brother*, p. 115
15 *Philadelphia Daily News*, 1/9/1960. Rachel Nicholson Collection
16 *Sunday Mirror*, 27/7/1941
17 *The Daily News*, 27/2/1945
18 Ibid.
19 Ibid.
20 *News Review*, 10/2/1949. Vivandlarry.com
21 Logan, Joshua, *Movie Stars, Real People, and Me* (Delacorte Press, New York, 1978) p. 169
22 Lisieux, St Thérèse, *The Story of a Soul* (Source Books, Trabuco Canyon, 1997) p. 58
23 *The Beverley Times*, 3/10/1957
24 Olivier, Tarquin, *My Father*, p. 211
25 *Chelsea News and General Advertiser*, 12/7/1957
26 David Barry to author
27 *The Australian Women's Weekly*, 3/4/1957
28 *Belfast Telegraph*, 25/10/1957
29 Olivier, *Confessions*, p. 222
30 Olivier, Tarquin, *My Father*, p. 211
31 Shakespeare, William, *King Lear*. Act 4, Scene 6
32 *The New York Times*, 25/3/1979
33 14/07/1957
34 *The Canberra Times*, 13/7/1957
35 *Tatler*, 31/7/1957
36 *Belfast Telegraph*, 12/7/1957
37 *The Guardian*, 12/7/1957
38 'I felt extremely nervous as I got up. I still felt extremely nervous as I walked out there was such an absolute silence. It was a matter of impulse. I feel very passionately about St James's Theatre, but I went with the intention of listening to the debate. I got angrier and angrier, why don't you want to stop this theatre being destroyed?' *The Guardian*, 12/7/1957
39 Sir John Gielgud claimed he asked Sagittarius to write a poem for Vivien based on Scarlett O'Hara. Vivien recited this on her N. African tour in 1943. Sir John Gielgud in conversation with Anne Edwards
40 *The Guardian*, 12/7/1957
41 *Daily Mirror*, 1/8/1957

42 Ibid.
43 Lady Diana Cooper, letter to Jack Merivale following Vivien's death. Vickers, *Vivien Leigh*, p. 328

Chapter Nine
1 *National Advocate*, 8/7/1953
2 *The New York Times*, 25/3/1979
3 Leigh confided this to her friend, Radie Harris. Vickers, *Vivien Leigh*, p. 325
4 David Barry to author
5 *Hola*, October 1956. Greta Ritchie Collection
6 *Time*,15/11/1982
7 Ibid.
8 'She understood enough of my situation to recognise that we were both helpless.' Olivier, *Confessions*, p. 225
9 *Aberdeen Evening News*, 2/1/1958
10 *Small World*, 1958
11 Ibid.
12 Olivier, *Confessions*, p. 226
13 *La Stampa*, 18/8/1957. Author's translation
14 Ibid.
15 Ibid.
16 Ibid.
17 *La Stampa*, 30/8/1957
18 Ibid.
19 *Good Housekeeping*, February 1961. Greta Ritchie Collection
20 Baxter, Beverley, *First Nights and Footlights* (Hutchinson, London, 1955)
21 *La Stampa*, 18/2/1957. Author's translation
22 Olivier, Tarquin, *My Father*, p. 220
23 Olivier, *Confessions*, p. 223
24 07/05/1958
25 Bloom, Claire, *Limelight and After* (Chivers Press, Bath, 1983) p. 150
26 'She's super nuts, she babbles like an idiot.' Levine, *Manuel Puig and the Spider Woman*, p. 119
27 Bloom, *Leaving a Doll's House*, p. 104
28 Walker, *The Life*, p. 237
29 Vickers, *Vivien Leigh*, p. 263
30 *La Stampa*, 23/5/1958. Author's translation
31 Ibid.
32 Heilpern, John, *John Osborne: A Patriot for Us* (Vintage, London, 2007) p. 432
33 Coleman, *Olivier*, p. 306
34 'Vivien, alas, is in one of her dangerous moods', Payn and Morley (eds), *The Noël Coward Diaries* (Macmillan, London, 1983), p. 384
35 Shellard, Dominic, *Kenneth Tynan: A Life* (Yale University Press, New Haven, 2003) p. 208

36   Images appeared in *Epoca*, 19/10/1958
37   Information taken from Gertrude Hartley's diary entry, as published in *Olivier: The Authorised Biography*. Coleman, Terry, (Bloomsbury, London, 2005) p. 315
38   Olivier, *Confessions*, p. 226
39   *Philadelphia Daily News*, 30/8/1960. Rachel Nicholson Collection
40   Ibid.
41   *Everywoman* Magazine, April 1951. Rachel Nicholson Collection
42   *Photoplay*, October 1940
43   Jack Merivale in conversation with Anne Edwards
44   Merriam-Webster's definition. Also quoted as such in an interview with Vivien. *The Sun*, 19/7/1948
45   Douglas, Kirk, *The Ragman's Son* (Simon & Schuster, New York, 1988) p. 291
46   *Philadelphia Daily News*, 29/8/60. Rachel Nicholson Collection
47   Payn and Morley (eds), *The Noël Coward Diaries*, p. 392
48   Ibid.
49   Ibid.
50   Bucknell, Katherine (ed.), Bachardy, Don, Isherwood, Christopher, *The Animals: Love Letters Between Christopher Isherwood and Don Bachardy* (Random House, New York, 2013) p. 49

Chapter Ten

1   *Philadelphia Daily News*, 29/8/1960. Rachel Nicholson Collection
2   *Daily Express*, August 1960. Vivandlarry.com
3   Memories of Pieter Rogers, as told to Terry Coleman. Coleman, Terry, *Olivier: The Authorised Biography* (Bloomsbury, London, 2005) p. 508
4   Jack Merivale, letter to Anne Edwards, February 1976
5   *Daily Express*, August 1960. Vivandlarry.com
6   Jack Merivale in conversation with Anne Edwards
7   Lambert, Gavin, *On Cukor* (Capricorn Books, New York 1972) p. 148
8   Walker, *The Life*, p. 245
9   *Theatre World*, April 1949. Courtesy of the Vivien Leigh Circle
10   'I recall with tenderness the sweetness of Mary Ure in Duel of Angels', Jack Merivale, letter to Anne Edwards, 3/5/1976
11   *Theatre World*, Volume 56, 1960
12   *Daily News*, 28/5/1960
13   Vickers, *Vivien Leigh*, p. 282
14   *La Stampa*, 12/06/1960
15   Olivier, interviewed by Ed Bradley. *60 Minutes*, CBS, 1983
16   Randall, John, Trow, M.J., *The Last Gentlemen of the SAS* (Random House, London, 2017). p. 98
17   *Hollywood Dünyasi*, July 1943
18   Ibid.
19   Vickers, *Vivien Leigh*, p. 327
20   *Weekly Dispatch*, 22/5/1960
21   Boland, Bridget, *At My Mother's Knee* (Bodley Head, London, 1978) p. 57

22 Shakespeare, William, *Hamlet*, Act IV, Scene 5
23 *Woman*, 26/9/1964. Vivandlarry.com
24 Ibid.
25 'She fought to win. She fought to get Scarlett. She won Larry.' Tarquin Olivier, *Weekend*, 24/6/2000. Vivandlarry.com
26 In Sarah Miles's volumes of memoirs, Larry often claims Vivien was a 'schizophrenic manic-depressive nymphomaniac.' See *Serves Me Right*, pp. 38, 141, 144, 437
27 Vickers, *Vivien Leigh*, p. 121
28 Leigh Holman's brother Alwyn, and his niece, Benita, were killed during a German raid in 1940
29 *Life*, 20/5/1940
30 Quintero, Jose, *If You Don't Dance They Beat You* (St Martin's Press, New York, 1988) p. 277
31 *The New York Times*, 25/3/1979

Chapter Eleven
1   *Woman*, 26/9/64. Vivandlarry.com
2   *The Australian Women's Weekly*, 5/4/1961
3   *Daily Advertiser*, 16/3/1948
4   *The West Australian*, 16/3/1948
5   *The Courier Mail*, 23/8/1948
6   'I was to be responsible for her.' Jack Merivale in conversation with Anne Edwards
7   Jack Merivale, letter to Anne Edwards, [undated] February 1976
8   Jack Merivale in conversation with Anne Edwards
9   *The Australian Women's Weekly*, 15/3/1961
10 *The Age*, 3/7/1961
11 Vivien Leigh, during her radio address in Atlanta, during the *Gone with the Wind* festivities, December 1939
12 Sir John Gielgud, in conversation with Anne Edwards
13 *The Age*, 3/7/1961
14 'My first school friend as an Australian.' *The Daily News*, 15/3/1948
15 As related to Harold Nicolson in 1956. Nicolson, Harold, *Diaries and Letters 1945–62* (Collins, London, 1968) p. 297
16 Shakespeare, William, *The Tempest*, Act I, Scene II
17 *Everywoman*, April 1951. Vivandlarry.com
18 *The Courier Mail*, 10/5/1948
19 *The Age*, 20/4/1948
20 Vivien Leigh, letter to Ted Tenley, 15/7/1961. *Fan's Guide to Gone with The Wind*. Taylor Trade Publishing (E-copy pages unnumbered) 3/12/2014
21 *The Australian Women's Weekly*, 5/4/1961
22 *The Courier Mail*, 28/6/1948
23 Ibid.

24 Williams, Dakin, Mead, Shepherd, *Tennessee Williams: An Intimate Biography* (Arbor House, New York, 1983) p. 296

25 *Herald*, 3/7/1961

26 Ibid.

27 Jack Merivale in conversation with Anne Edwards

28 Ibid.

29 Ibid.

30 Ibid.

31 Ibid.

32 Jack Merivale claimed in several interviews that Vivien defined people as 'proper' meaning they were well-suited to her temperament. She called Finch a 'proper man'. The 'proper' analogy was also discussed with Anne Edwards. See Anne Edwards papers, 1965 – Library Special Collections, Charles E. Young Research Library

33 Vivien Leigh, letter to Ted Tenley, 12/7/1961. *Fan's Guide to Gone with The Wind*

34 *Tribune*, 3/7/1948

35 *The Sun*, 18/7/1948

36 *Maryborough Chronicle*, 19/7/1948

37 *The Daily News*, 17/3/1948

38 *Stuff*, 26/7/2010

39 O'Connor, *Darlings of the Gods*, p. 187

40 Miles, *Serves Me Right*, p. 38

41 Jack Merivale in conversation with Anne Edwards

42 O'Connor, *Darlings of the Gods*, p. 199

43 *Time*, 27/12/1948

44 Jack Merivale in conversation with Anne Edwards

45 Sir John Gielgud in conversation with Anne Edwards

46 Jack Merivale in conversation with Anne Edwards

47 *Caretas*, April 1962. Courtesy of the Vivien Leigh Circle

48 Miles, Sarah, *Bolt from the Blue* (Orion, London, 1996) p. 81

49 *Caretas*, April 1962. Courtesy of the Vivien Leigh Circle

50 Jack Merivale in conversation with Anne Edwards

51 Sir John Gielgud in conversation with Anne Edwards

52 English translation by Ana Claudia Paixao. Also thanks to Ana for the anecdote. 'Vivien Leigh at Sunset' by Cecília Meireles. Originally written in Portuguese. See miscelana.com/2022/05/03 cecilia-meireles-immortalized-vivien-leighs-passage-through-brazil/. Unfortunately, the copyright of Meireles's literary works is yet to be determined by the Brazilian courts, hence why the poem was not published in its entirety. The author wishes to thank Meireles's granddaughter, Fernanda Meireles, for her advice

53 Vickers, *Vivien Leigh*, p. 301

Chapter Twelve

1 'It was very sad. She appeared, at a very young age, to turn into a lovely stalk of chalk, and chipping away had begun, and you were there to see the flaking off.' – Alec Guinness. Vivandlarry.com

2 Shakespeare, William, *Henry V*, Act I, Prologue

3 Walker, *The Life*, p. 280

4 *Daily Herald*, 1/6/1935

5 *Motion Picture*, February 1940

6 Aumont, Jean-Pierre, *Sun and Shadow: An Autobiography* (Norton, New York, 1977) p. 213

7 Ibid., p. 214

8 Ibid.

9 Olivier, *Confessions*, p. 274

10 The meeting was relayed in Jose Quintero's memoir, *If You Don't Dance They Beat You*, p. 275. However, in Dame Joan Plowright's memoirs, she denies the meeting took place. 'This is pure invention.' See *And That's Not All*, p. 55

11 Jack Merivale in conversation with Anne Edwards

12 Ibid.

13 Sir John Gielgud in conversation with Anne Edwards

14 Jack Merivale in conversation with Anne Edwards

15 Sir John Gielgud in conversation with Anne Edwards

16 *Woman's Day*, 24/7/1961

17 Tornabene, Lyn, *Long Live the King: A Biography of Clark Gable* (W.H. Allen/Virgin Books, London, 1977) p. 235

18 'Voice of Broadway' column, *New York Journal–American*, 10/11/1962

19 Aumont, *Sun and Shadow*, p. 222

20 Ibid., p. 223

21 Jack Merivale, letter to Anne Edwards, 3/5/1976

22 Coleman, *Olivier*, p. 354

23 Aumont, *Sun and Shadow*, p. 226

24 Ibid.

25 Ibid., p. 232

26 29/03/1963

27 Ibid.

28 Cook, Barbara, *Then and Now: A Memoir* (HarperCollins, New York, 2016) p. 20

29 Aumont, *Sun and Shadow*, p. 233

30 Shakespeare, William, *Hamlet*, Act 4 Scene 5

31 Halsman, Philippe, *Sight and Insight* (Doubleday, New York, 1972) p. 139

32 Ibid.

33 Ibid.

34 Jack Merivale in conversation with Anne Edwards

35 Vickers, *Vivien Leigh*, p. 307

36 Jack Merivale in conversation with Anne Edwards

37 *The London Studio*, Volumes 4–5 (W.E. Rudge, London, 1932) p. 109
38 Jack Merivale in conversation with Anne Edwards
39 Valiente, Doreen, *ABC of Witchcraft Past and Present* (St Martin's Press, New York, 1973) p. 320
40 *Time*, 15/11/1982
41 Vickers, *Vivien Leigh*, p. 310
42 *Everywoman*, April 1951. Vivandlarry.com
43 Olivier, Tarquin, *My Father*, p. 250
44 'Yes! She's a very remarkable person, intellectually equipped, attractive, has hosts of friends ... and she's an absolutely fantastic mother.' *Time*, 15/11/1982
45 Jack Merivale in conversation with Anne Edwards
46 'Although she had a romantic relationship with actor Jack Merivale, who hosted many of the parties at Tickerage, pouring drinks rather like a butler, I saw very little affection between them.' *Mail on Sunday*, 12/1/2003. Vivandlarry.com
47 Jack Merivale in conversation with Anne Edwards
48 *New Idea*, 25/12/1963. Vivandlarry.com
49 Vickers, *Vivien Leigh*, p. 305
50 Dent, *Vivien Leigh* p. 67
51 'I just have the feeling there's something rather horrible going on.' Ibid.
52 Ibid.
53 'She is really labouring under the depressing fact that she is playing a supporting part for the first time, and that makes her feel she is slipping and getting old, and if she has one drink too many she gets resentful and difficult.' Gielgud, *A Life in Letters*, p. 313
54 *Time*, 15/11/1982
55 Walker, *The Life*, p. 283
56 Sir John Gielgud in conversation with Anne Edwards
57 'Leigh was a woman from whom happiness, or even contentment, always seemed to escape.' Kramer, Stanley, *A Mad, Mad, Mad, Mad World* (Aurum, London, 1998) p. 208
58 Payn and Morley (eds), *The Noël Coward Diaries*, p. 542
59 Bawden, James, Miller, Ron *They Made the Movies: Conversations with Great Filmmakers* (University Press of Kentucky, Lexington 2023) p. 146
60 Marvin, Betty, *Tales of a Hollywood Wife* (iuniverse.com, Bloomington, 2011) p. 167
61 Ibid.
62 Jack Merivale in conversation with Anne Edwards
63 Ibid.
64 Ibid.
65 Jack Merivale, letter to Anne Edwards, 6/4/1976
66 Ibid.
67 Ibid.
68 *Queen*, 10/3/1965. Vivandlarry.com

69　Sir John Gielgud in conversation with Anne Edwards
70　Jack Merivale in conversation with Anne Edwards

Chapter Thirteen

1　'I've been awfully lucky. I'm half-waiting for some blow to fall.' *News Review*, 10/2/1949. Vivandlarry.com
2　'My daughter, like myself, is a great believer in fate. If something is going to happen, it's no use trying to go against it.' Gertrude Hartley, interview, *New Idea*, 25/12/1963
3　Undated interview with Vivien Leigh. Courtesy of Michelle Beck
4　Jack Merivale in conversation with Anne Edwards
5　Vickers, *Vivien Leigh*, p. 316
6　*Queen*, 10/3/1965. Vivandlarry.com
7　Merchant, Ismail, Raw, Laurence (ed.), *Merchant-Ivory Interviews* (University Press of Mississippi, Jackson, 2012) p. 31
8　Translated to 'Cinema, look'
9　Vivien wrote to Jack Merivale, amused by how the sign for public transport was misspelt 'pubic transport'
10　*Queen*, 10/3/1965. Vivandlarry.com
11　'Another night he stood up at a dinner party and announced, "South Africa has disowned me. And why? I'm an outcast because I've had an affair with a coloured girl. They've given up on me because of my affair with Shirley Bassey."' Dundy, *Finch*, p. 280
12　Ibid.
13　'I heard her say it [proper] about Finchie.' Jack Merivale in conversation with Anne Edwards
14　'I think that at that time of her life she didn't have the time or energy anymore to be really fond of very many people.' Merchant, Ismail, Raw, Laurence (ed.), *Merchant-Ivory: Conversations* (University Press of Mississippi, Jackson, 2012) p. 30
15　Walker, *The Life*, p. 289
16　*Queen*, 10/3/1965. Vivandlarry.com
17　See Dame Joan Plowright's memoirs, *And That's Not All*, p. 122
18　*Philadelphia Daily News*, 30/8/1960. Rachel Nicholson Collection
19　*Newcastle Daily Express*
20　*Queen*, 10/3/1965. Vivandlarry.com
21　Gielgud, John, *A Life in Letters* (Arcade, New York, 2004), p. 326
22　'I don't think I ever had such bad personal notices in my life.' Ibid., p. 331
23　*Theatre World*, April 1949. Courtesy of the Vivien Leigh Circle
24　Ibid., p. 333
25　Ibid.
26　Jack Merivale in conversation with Anne Edwards
27　Ibid.
28　Ibid.

29 *Everywoman*, April 1951. Vivandlarry.com
30 *Philadelphia Daily News*, 31/8/1960. Rachel Nicholson Collection
31 Olivier, *Confessions*, p. 290
32 Jack Merivale in conversation with Anne Edwards
33 Vivien often referenced those exact flowers in letters to friends
34 'I mean, that a day like this will be followed by another, and another, and another.' Vivien Leigh to Godfrey Winn, *Woman* Magazine, 26/9/1964. Vivandlarry.com
35 'Some years ago she quoted with approbation "And the artists shall inherit the earth, and the world will be a garden."' *Queen*, 10/3/1965. Vivandlarry.com
36 Jack Merivale in conversation with Anne Edwards

Afterword: A Reimagining (Based on Real Events)

1   Holzer, Hans, *Ghosts That Aren't: True Encounters with the World Beyond* (Running Press, New York, 2012) p. 159
2   Jack Merivale in conversation with Anne Edwards
3   Ibid.
4   Ibid.
5   One Christmas Vivien Leigh came to stay and was enchanted by the abandoned villa of St John of the Pigeons, south of Benitses. She planned to buy it but sadly died shortly after her return from the island. Acorfu.com, 19/11/2023
6   'I don't believe in this thing at all.' Jack Merivale in conversation with Anne Edwards
7   Ibid.
8   Ibid.
9   Olivier, Tarquin, *My Father*, p. 255
10 Jack Merivale in conversation with Anne Edwards
11 Dirk Bogarde. Vivandlarry.com
12 See the Elvira Clara Bonet Collection, auctioned by Setdart Auction House
13 Jack Merivale in conversation with Anne Edwards
14 'A Wedding Gift from Katharine Hepburn to Vivien Leigh.' Sotheby's, 31/08/2017

Index